For the Love of *Weddings*

For the Love of *Weddings*

JENNIFER CRAFT

PALMETTO
PUBLISHING
Charleston, SC
www.PalmettoPublishing.com

Copyright © 2025 by Jennifer Craft

All rights reserved

No portion of this book may be reproduced, stored in a retrieval system, or transmitted in any form by any means–electronic, mechanical, photocopy, recording, or other–except for brief quotations in printed reviews, without prior permission of the author.

Hardcover ISBN: 9798318809583

Paperback ISBN: 9798318808265

eBook ISBN: 9798318808272

DEDICATION:

To the brides of the past, present, and future—
Your dreams have become my purpose, and your love stories
continue to inspire every beautiful detail I design.

To John—
I can't imagine this journey without you. You are my steady
anchor, the laughter in my days, and my greatest joy.

CONTENTS

Dedication: iii

Chapter 1	January 18, 2013	1
Chapter 2	Dreams Brewing	17
Chapter 3	All Things New	29
Chapter 4	From Veils to Vests	39
Chapter 5	Budgeting Bliss	50
Chapter 6	The Canvas for Your Celebration	63
Chapter 7	Ministers & Mitzvahs	101
Chapter 8	Planning on Pixels & Paper	130
Chapter 9	Lights, Camera, I Do	141
Chapter 10	Cue the Music	164
Chapter 11	Forks, Fizz and Frosting	194
Chapter 12	The Pretties	226
Chapter 13	Heart and Hustle	240
Chapter 14	The Good, The Bad & The Ugly	282
Chapter 15	When DIY goes WTF	311
Chapter 16	In the Trenches	320
Chapter 17	Reflection	351

Bonus Chapter 355
Acknowledgements 370

1

JANUARY 18, 2013

As I sit in the cold, dim church—waiting to walk down the aisle and marry my Prince Charming—the veil gently brushes my shoulder, like a quiet whisper that this is really happening. My heart begins to race, not from fear, but from the gravity of the moment. I wonder: Does every bride feel this nervous just before the long walk? The walk that marks the end of one chapter and the breathtaking beginning of another.

I would have much preferred to wait with my bridesmaids dressed in dusty winter hues, ready to fluff my train and fuel my excitement. In contrast, the church coordinator insisted I wait alone in what I can only describe as an eerie holding space. There's really no other way to put it.

The room is small, more of a glorified closet than a bridal suite, with antique furniture that creaks every time I shift. The kind of furniture that seems to sigh with stories you don't want to know. There's a haunted feel to the room—no exaggeration—and the temperature doesn't help. It's cold. Not the charming, snowy-romance kind of cold; this is the kind of cold that seeps into your skin and makes your teeth chatter. Yet here I am, in full bridal regalia, slightly shaking in a hundred-year-old chair, wondering if the ghosts approve of my dress.

John and I were engaged in the summer of 2012. When I want something—I go for it. I've always been that way. There was no drawn-out timeline or Pinterest-perfect planning year. I wanted to marry him, and I wanted it now. People probably whispered it was a shotgun wedding, but they were wrong. The only thing I was carrying was determination. I had my heart set on a winter wedding, and winter is what I got—complete with an icebox church and a flurry of emotions.

To steady my nerves, I glance down at my bouquet, wrapped in silk ribbon and layered with meaning. My "something old" is nestled inside: a delicate beaded necklace that once belonged to my great-grandmother, tucked into the ribbon like a secret blessing. My "something borrowed" glitters on my wrist—my sister Lisa's diamond bracelet, elegant and sentimental, lending me a bit of her strength and style. My "something blue" is a pair of royal blue satin heels, bold and playful. Later, I'll trade them for powder blue peep-toe shoes with a tiny vintage-inspired bow. I'm practical, after all. I knew I'd never survive the entire day in those stilettos.

Through the small window, I hear murmurs as guests settle into pews. Music hums softly through the walls. It's nearly time. Despite the cold, the nerves, and the unsettling ghost-chair in the corner, I'm ready. The door creaks open, slow and deliberate, as if the universe itself is inviting me forward. It's time.

I step to my father's left side, sliding my arm into the crook of his elbow. He stands tall and composed—a man of few words, but infinite presence. My dad has always been quietly extraordinary. Mysterious, yes. Reserved, certainly. Yet when he speaks, people listen.

He's the kind of man who raised four daughters without ever raising his voice. Through the chaos of girlhood and adolescence—prom dresses, heartbreaks, and our own growing opinions—he stayed steady. Patient. Kind.

Just as my nerves threaten to spill over, he leans close and grins. "This is your last chance to turn around." Classic Dad. His dry humor hits at exactly the right moment. I smile, then laugh—a shaky giggle that bubbles out of my chest. I'm pretty sure he tells me he loves me after that, but the moment swallows the words. Because then, the doors open.

A rush of air sweeps past me, like a whisper from the divine. The sanctuary glows in soft light. A sea of familiar faces turns toward me, smiling, watching, waiting. And just like that, emotion surges through me.

There's something profoundly humbling about seeing who shows up for you. These people didn't just mail a gift or drop a "Congrats!" on Facebook. They dressed in their finest, packed bags, booked hotels, braved airports or highways—and they showed up. Not late, not half-heartedly, but fully present. Some are family I haven't seen in years. Others are friends who stood by me through my darkest hours. A few are distant relatives I barely know—yet here they are, not just in body, but in spirit.

They've come to witness the start of this chapter, to bear sacred witness to love, to be part of something that feels larger than life. In that moment, I don't just feel seen—I feel held. Held by family, by community, by love itself.

Dad and I are only a few steps from the altar now, moving slowly down the center aisle. Every eye follows us; every heart seems to beat a little faster. As we draw closer, familiar faces come into view—our grandparents, our mothers, my sisters and brother—and a gentle warmth rises inside me.

The good news: I'm no longer freezing. The bad news? These heels are pure torture. With every step, my feet scream in protest, and I mentally kick myself for not choosing wedges—or at least sparkly sneakers. Beauty over comfort. What was I thinking?

We reach the end of the aisle, and Pastor Skipp asks the time-honored question:

"Who gives this woman to be married to this man?"

It's a simple sentence, but it lands heavy in my heart—a lifetime wrapped up in just a few words.

I hug Dad, who kisses my cheek, his quiet way of saying everything without needing many words. Then, with all the dignity and love he can summon, he turns and shakes John's hand before slipping into his pew.

Before I knew it, I'm here. Standing beside John. My hand finds his, and in that instant, everything shifts. My nerves melt away. The chill of that eerie little holding room disappears. I'm grounded again—anchored by the one person who always calms me. I'm not scared. I'm not unsure. I'm happy. Radiantly, overwhelmingly blissful.

John is twenty-five; I'm twenty-four. We're young, by most standards, but I've always felt older than my age—a little more seasoned, a little more serious. Some call me wise beyond my years; others, more playfully, call me a know-it-all. Either way, I've always known what I wanted—and in this moment, I'm exactly where I'm meant to be.

No one ever really tells you what it feels like on your wedding day. People talk about the highlights: the joy, the tears, the "best day ever." Rarely do they admit to the full range of emotions—the way it all feels surreal. How you can be nervous, grateful, proud, and deeply vulnerable all at once. Yes, people cry—but not only from fear or sadness. Sometimes, it's simply the awe of it all. The sacredness of saying yes to forever. Shouldn't two people be glowing with delight as they embark on a lifetime together? I believe they should—and I was. Not in a loud, theatrical way, but in the quiet, soul-deep kind of way. The kind of joy that anchors you and whispers: Yes, this is it. This is home.

My generation loves to say they're marrying their best friend—and for us, it's true. John isn't just my partner; he's the mirror reflecting my best self, the steady voice that quiets my chaos. He knows me—sometimes better than I know myself. From the very beginning, we made a pact: complete honesty, no secrets, no games. Just truth. Transparency. Teamwork. We didn't want a fairytale built on fantasy. We wanted a love story rooted in trust. I love us. I really do.

Hand in hand, hearts aligned, I pass my bouquet to my sister and step up to the altar with John beside me. This is the moment. We turn to face each other, smiling softly, eyes locked. Those ocean-colored eyes of his still stop me in my tracks.

It feels like a scene straight from a storybook. I'm the bride in my gown of soft white tulle, the mermaid silhouette hugging gently before flaring into a cascade of hand-sewn flowers, arranged in a delicate crescent. Tiny flecks of sparkle glint among the petals, catching the light just so. My veil—a waist-length shimmer edged in beads and rhinestones—adds the final touch of enchantment. It's elegance with a touch of whimsy.

Maybe that's why, standing here, I can't help thinking of Ariel and Prince Eric—me with my long red hair, and John with his dark locks, nearly black under the soft light of the sanctuary. A modern fairytale, unfolding not on a distant shore, but here, in the cherished space of saying "I do." This isn't just a wedding. It's the beginning of our always.

Getting married in a church was important to us—it wasn't just tradition; it was a profound grounding. Standing within those historic walls, surrounded by stained glass and silent prayers whispered over decades, we felt an undeniable closeness to The Creator. It gave our union not just weight, but reverence. This wasn't just about rings and vows—it was a covenant, witnessed not only by our loved ones, but by something greater than ourselves.

Our ceremony lasted about 40 minutes—unhurried, intentional, heartfelt. It included meaningful scripture readings, spoken with care by those we love, prayers that seemed to echo into eternity, and a unity sand ceremony that felt symbolic and tactile all at once. Grain by grain, we poured our lives into one vessel—distinct colors blending to create something new and inseparable. A simple act, yes—but rich in meaning. In that moment, we weren't just becoming husband and wife. We were building the foundation of something precious.

The Unity Sand Ceremony remains one of the most beautiful and symbolic moments of our wedding day—a quiet, visual promise of togetherness. Each grain of sand represented our individual lives, our separate paths, and as we poured them into a single vessel, we watched those lines disappear, blending seamlessly into something entirely new. That vessel, filled with soft layers of color and intention, has moved with us through every chapter since—first from our apartment to a townhouse, and now into our home. Each time, I've carefully wrapped it in bubble wrap, carried it by hand, and placed it somewhere safe. It still looks just as it did on our wedding day—

gently dusted over the years and now nestled in a glass-front cupboard, a quiet but constant reminder of the vows we made.

Speaking of vows—we chose the traditional kind. The "repeat after me" promises so many couples recite in church sanctuaries, surrounded by the echoes of spiritual tradition. On the other hand, if we could do it over again, I think we'd choose differently. Not the commitment—that part I'd choose again a thousand times—but the setting and the words. I imagine exchanging vows at the foot of a mountain or beside a rhythmic, eternal ocean. A place of natural majesty. A place formed not by human hands, but by The Creator Himself. We would speak personal vows, unpolished and heartfelt—words of love and truth that belong to no one else but us. We've always marched to the rhythm of our own drums, and that's part of why we work so well. We balance each other—faithful but free, structured but spontaneous.

When it came time for the rings, the symbolism washed over me. John's band, a sleek white gold with beveled edges, felt timeless and strong. Mine, a slender diamond band that hugs my engagement ring like a caress, sparkled with promise. Wedding bands are more than jewelry—they're circles of permanence, devotion, and resilience. Unbroken, like the love we vowed to nurture and protect.

"You may now kiss your bride!" John reaches for my waist, pulling me in with confidence and warmth. I rest my hand on his arm, steadying myself for our first kiss as husband and wife. It's sweet, it's intentional, and—let's be honest—it's perfectly appropriate for a room full of grandparents, peers, and extended family. No dramatic dip, no movie-scene moment. Just a genuine kiss, filled with meaning. Passion can wait—we've got a lifetime ahead of us for that. For now, we're keeping it classy.

The room erupts in cheers and applause, gleeful energy echoing off the church walls. Then comes the big announcement: "Presenting, for the very first time, Mr. and Mrs. Croft!"

Wait—what? John and I turn toward each other, eyes wide, eyebrows lifted in amused disbelief. *Did he just say Croft?* Yes. Yes, he did. It takes all my self-control not to burst into laughter on the spot. Croft? I suppose we could have corrected him, but in the moment, it hardly seemed to matter. We were married. Delighted, legally, spiritually united—wrong last name and all.

Looking back now, it's one of my favorite memories. Not because it was perfect, but because it wasn't. There's something so endearing about the moments that don't go according to plan. These are the things people talk about later, the details that make your wedding day yours. It's the misspoken name, the flower girl who refused to walk down the aisle, the ring bearer who nearly dropped the ring. The things that go "wrong," but somehow, make everything feel exactly right.

Weddings are meticulously planned events, and I love that—obviously. I've come to learn that the best stories live in the margins of the plan. In the surprises, the detours, the improvisations. That's where real life happens.

So, if you're a bride or groom reading this, clinging to the idea of a "flawless" day—here's a gentle nudge: let it go. Aim for beauty, meaning, and joy… but perfection? You don't need it. What you need is presence. You need connection. You need to know that when Pastor Skipp accidentally says "Croft" and your name isn't Croft, you'll look at your person and laugh together—because this is your story now. And it's already a good one.

My sister carefully placed my delicate bouquet back into my hands—a dreamy collection of pure white ranunculus, garden roses, and lisianthus, each petal a silent testament to elegance. I was on cloud nine, my smile stretching from ear to ear, a radiant mix of delight, relief, and disbelief. We did it. We were married!

As we floated hand in hand down the aisle, it felt like we were drifting on air, wrapped in a bubble of newlywed bliss. Around us, familiar faces beamed with happiness, fists pumped the air in celebration, and cheerful clapping filled the sanctuary with a soundtrack of love and support. When the sanctuary doors opened wide and sunlight streamed in, we skipped out like carefree kids, laughing and hugging as we waited for our wedding party to follow in high spirits.

Now, more than a decade into my career as a wedding planner, I see those moments through a new lens. I understand how the smallest acts of kindness and thoughtful gestures can ripple into waves of comfort and delight. Looking back, I realize how much I would have treasured having someone in my corner—a calm, reassuring presence, a coordinator who cheered me on and carried some of the weight.

I still remember that lonely moment before the ceremony, waiting alone in that cold, cramped room. As a planner now, I would never let a bride face that silence and isolation unless she truly desired solitude. I always gather parents, siblings—anyone dear—to share those precious minutes, to soak in the moment together.

We waltz back up to the altar for family photos—a process that somehow always takes longer than anyone anticipates. Honestly, why do we spend so much time on these perfectly posed, sometimes painfully formal shots? I'm pretty sure it's mostly for the older generation—the ones who want to make sure every third cousin twice removed is accounted for in a 12x18 frame.

Here's a little secret: I've never actually flipped through all those formal family photos from our wedding day. Is that weird? Maybe. On our anniversaries, John and I do crack open our wedding album and I might get a little sentimental, or binge-scroll through the entire digital gallery on the computer. But let's be real—none of those posed photos are hanging on our walls anytime soon. My advice? Don't let formal photos steal your day. Spend less time corralling Uncle Bob and Aunt Sue into perfect rows, and more time capturing those candid moments—the genuine smiles, the goofy dance moves, the unexpected laughter. Because honestly, those are the pictures you'll want to actually look at (and maybe even frame) years down the road.

After the seemingly endless family photos, John, the photographer, and I stand outside in the upper-fifties air, waiting anxiously for our transportation. I check my phone—why are we running late? Where is the car? My heart sinks as I dial the transportation company, trying to keep my voice calm but tinged with urgency.

The man on the other end calmly informs me, "Ma'am, we have your booking for Saturday, January 19th—not Friday, January 18th."

For a moment, I'm speechless. Anger and frustration start to simmer beneath my skin, but there's no time to dwell on that now. We need to get to the reception. Who do I call first? Mom.

"Hello, Miss Priss, is everything okay?" she asks, already sensing something is wrong.

"No! The driver didn't show up. Please come get us—we're still at the church," I say, trying desperately not to lose it.

"I'm on my way," she replies. My hero of the hour.

Meanwhile, my brother Chris is deep in conversation with Pastor Skipp at the reception hall, debating Taoism and religion—an oddly perfect distraction in the chaos.

Mom's silver Eclipse screeches to a halt outside the church. "Get in!" she commands. It's like we're contestants in some high-stakes game show, racing against time. John and the photographer cram into the backseat, while I collapse into the front, trying to tame what feels like a hundred yards of tulle tangled around me.

Luckily, the reception venue was less than a ten-minute drive away. As soon as we arrived, Mom skillfully maneuvered her sleek sports car into a tight spot, the engine's soft purr fading as we hurried out. We dashed through the towering wrought-iron gates, their iron bars cool beneath my fingertips, and onto the cobblestone path that crunched softly under our feet. The air was crisp and fragrant with the subtle scent of damp earth and blossoming ferns from the garden lining the walkway. The gentle splash of the nearby water fountain mingled with the rustling leaves, creating a soothing soundtrack that contrasted the whirlwind of the day.

Did we have a wedding planner? Naturally! But not just any planner—the most organized, professional, and talented planner I know. The twist? That planner was me. Now, you might think, "How on earth could she possibly manage her own wedding?" Who made sure all the vendor logistics clicked seamlessly into place? Who would direct set up, orchestrate the layout, and keep the timeline on track?

John and I were young—fresh out of our early twenties—with a budget tighter than skinny jeans. So, I got creative. I struck a deal with my former supervisor: in exchange for lending my hands and feet to floral design setups for her events, she'd step in as my wedding coordinator. Ms. Z—a powerhouse with a no-nonsense attitude and a heart of gold. Ms. Z was not only my wedding coordinator but also my florist—and she generously shared her floral talent with me at an exceptionally kind rate.

The bouquet and arrangements were stunning, exactly how I imagined them: all-white blooms with hint of sparkle that made everything look straight out of a fairy tale. I was pretty relaxed about the whole thing—my one and only rule was "keep it white, keep it sparkly, and don't mess it up." Ms. Z nailed it.

Then there was ... the transportation. Let's just say, the shuttle service did their best impression of a disappearing act. Was I irritated? Oh, totally—peeved enough to consider staging a dramatic slow clap. At the end of the day, it wasn't about flawless logistics or a perfect ride. It was about marrying my best friend, surrounded by people who loved us. I took a deep breath, shrugged off the hiccup, and danced my heart out anyway. Because, honestly? That's what weddings are really about.

Mom and Chris took their places inside the reception hall, which was transformed into a dreamscape bathed in soft blue up lighting that danced gently against the walls. The flicker of countless candles scattered across tables cast a warm, golden glow, mingling effortlessly with elegant white floral arrangements that filled the air with a delicate, fresh fragrance. The entire room felt like a scene straight out of a winter wonderland — absolute magic.

From the joyous expressions and animated conversations, it was clear our family and friends were having the time of their lives. What's not to love? There was an open bar flowing with cocktails and hors d'oeuvres trays gracefully passed through the crowd like edible treasures, and the perfect soundtrack setting the vibe for the evening. Honestly, did I just convince you *not* to elope?

Then, the moment arrived — the one we'd all been waiting for. "Give it up for our newlyweds, Mr. and Mrs. John Craft!" Thank goodness someone got it right this time! John and I slipped through a discreet side door that opened directly onto the dance floor. A surge of anticipation fluttered within me, electric and exhilarating. By this point, I'd swapped out my original heels for my second pair — dusty blue, peep-toed 3" heels that were as comfortable as they were stylish. To complete the look and combat the chill, I draped a soft, white faux fur shawl over my shoulders, adding a touch of vintage glamour and warmth to my bridal ensemble.

Stepping into the spotlight, the hum of conversation softened and the music swelled—it was time to celebrate. And oh, what a celebration it was. Hands thrown joyfully into the air, we burst through the door, swept up in the vibrant energy. John spins me in a dizzying circle, and we seal the moment with a tender kiss before gliding seamlessly into our first dance as husband and wife. In that instant, the world around us faded into a soft blur—time itself seemed to pause—and all I could see was John. My nerves melted away, replaced by a peaceful elation as we danced, our feet effortlessly gliding across the dark wood floor beneath us.

Our friends and family gathered around, some capturing the moment with glowing iPhone screens, others simply soaking in the wonder, fully immersed in the here and now. The stone walls encasing the room, the gentle wash of ambient lighting, and a grand metal chandelier scattering prismatic light above us—it was nothing short of a daydream stepping off the page.

Now, you're probably wondering what song swept us off our feet that night. Here's the kicker: neither John nor I actually remember what it was. I've since scoured every playlist, interrogated every family member, and even bribed the DJ for a clue. No luck. It's as if our first dance soundtrack was abducted by aliens or wiped clean by the chaos of the wedding day. But honestly? Does it really matter? For us, the music was just background noise to an epic moment.

If I had to pick a song today, it'd be "From This Moment" by Shania Twain—a classic, heartfelt ballad with lyrics that never get old. Because at the end of the day, it's not the song that makes the memory—it's the love, the laughter, and the fact that I somehow didn't trip on my gown. That's the real win.

The Lyrics:
From this moment, life has begun
From this moment, you are the one
Right beside you is where I belong
From this moment on
From this moment, I have been blessed
I live only for your happiness
And for your love, I'd give my last breath
From this moment on
I give my hand to you with all my heart
I can't wait to live my life with you, I can't wait to start
You and I will never be apart
My dreams came true because of you

Our favorite pastime? Partying. Full stop. John and I have always subscribed to the "life's short, order the champagne" philosophy. On our wedding day, we lived it to the absolute fullest. The dance floor was our stage, our friends the backup dancers, and yes—even my usually reserved brother emerged from the shadows like a disco ninja, busting moves that could've earned him a callback on *So You Think You Can Dance: Suburban Edition*. At one point, we were all in a circle, belting out a song from *Grease* like our lives depended on it—because nothing bonds people quite like screaming, "You're the one that I want!" at each other over a speaker system.

Let me tell you something: your wedding day flies by. Ours started with a 6:30 p.m. ceremony and wrapped up at 11:30 p.m.—five hours of pure joy (and thank the heavens, no drama). In my professional opinion, five hours is the sweet spot. Six, if your crowd has stamina. Seven? Someone's grandma is going rogue, or your flower girl is doing shots of ginger ale under the dessert table. Here's the truth they don't put in the bridal magazines: your wedding day is a beautiful, blissful, well-choreographed blur. You're shuffled from moment to moment like a high-maintenance debutante in a tiara. My advice? Try to enjoy the ride—and for the love of peonies, do not wear a watch. It'll only remind you of what you're missing while you're off smiling for the seventeenth "candid" photo.

If we could do it over again, I would absolutely hire a videographer. Some may say think that it's a toss-up category, but it shouldn't be. If you're not married, or you've never worn ten pounds of tulle while surviving on prosecco and nerves, you won't understand. The day is a dream—and not even the vivid kind. I remember flashes. John remembers that the cake was good and that he had fun. Conversations with guests? Lost to time. Adorable moments? Gone with the wind.

I do remember the cake, though (priorities). I'll never forget Kaylen—my high school gal pal and bridesmaid MVP—coaching me like a pageant mom whispering from the wings: "Smile, Jen!" And let me tell you, she was right. That soft smile makes all the difference in your photos when you're furiously trying to saw through a dense layer of fondant without looking like you're committing a pastry crime.

Now, as a wedding planner, I pass that wisdom on like a sacred torch: "Don't forget to smile!" Not because you're faking it, but because wedding photos are forever—and no one wants to look back and see themselves grimacing at a particularly uncooperative slice of cake.

As our big day came to a close, I do remember our last song—"Closing Time" by Semisonic, because obviously. Private last dances weren't a thing yet, or else I would've demanded one for dramatic effect and emotional closure. Instead, our guests lined up in two rows in the cobblestone courtyard, forming a human tunnel of love and questionable footwear. Bubbles floated in the winter air like magical wedding soap confetti.

Now, in case you were wondering: the transportation company did feel bad about completely ghosting us on the church transfer earlier that day. Consequently, they upgraded us to a white Hummer limo, which is basically the stretch SUV version of an apology bouquet. We climbed in, to-go cake and champagne in hand, and headed off into married life like the fabulous duo we are—husband and wife, partners in love and mischief.

2
DREAMS BREWING

College Years between 2008 - 2011

I was nineteen when I met John. It was December 2008—My partner-in-party-crime, Chelsea, and I had hopped off a rickety party bus somewhere between downtown optimism and bad decisions, in search of whatever came next. Naturally, that "next" turned out to be her downstairs neighbor's apartment.

Cue dramatic music and a gentle glow: John was the neighbor boy.

Let me tell you—*ta-da* is exactly the right sound effect. He opened the door, and the universe paused for a half-second to wink at me. Love at first sight? Absolutely. Or at the very least, deep interest at first beer-pong glance. The spark was instant, magnetic. One of those rare moments when you meet someone and just know. We've been together ever since.

John didn't rush into things. He courted me—yes, *courted*, like a gentleman out of a Jane Austen remix with a decent Spotify playlist—for a few weeks before we had our first kiss. He listened when I talked. We had real conversations. He didn't try to impress me with bravado or forced charm. It was simple, sincere, and deeply refreshing. The foundation of our love was built on friendship, good conversation, mutual respect—and an unhealthy number of midnight snack trips. The pivotal turning point came on the night of our sorority's Valentine's Day date party. Think: heart-shaped sunglasses, a sea of pink and red dresses, and way too many sugary cocktails. After the festivities, I found myself locked out of Chelsea's apartment—because of course I did. I rarely stayed in my own dorm. Sleepovers were my preferred way of life—like a social nomad with a hair straightener and an overnight bag.

John, ever the gentleman, had walked me up to the door like the leading man in a college rom-com. I turned to him with a giggle and a shrug: "Looks like I'm locked out... and all my stuff's up there!" I tried to appear mildly inconvenienced, but let's be honest—I was thrilled. He smiled, cool as ever. "Come on in, let's get something to eat." That night turned into one of those perfect, unexpectedly magical evenings. After raiding the fridge for snacks and fashioning makeshift pajamas—me in his oversized T-shirt and boxers (classic)—we stayed up until dawn just talking, laughing, and sharing our lives in that effortless way you only do when you're falling in love. No pressure, no pretense. Just pizza, pajama vibes, and two people who were very clearly becoming something more. Speaking of pizza—it was from Valentina's, and because fate is funny like that, it's now our annual Valentine's Day tradition. Nothing says romance like melted cheese, doughy crust and a side of nostalgia.

The next few months felt like a highlight reel of early love. One of my favorite moments? John helped Chelsea throw me a surprise 20th birthday party—princess themed, obviously. He ran sweet interference to make sure I didn't catch on, all while pretending he knew nothing. (He's lucky he's cute.) April arrived, and John casually brought up his Grandpa JB's birthday party at his aunt and uncle's house. Now, I'm not entirely sure he meant to invite me—but I invited myself, as any self-respecting almost-girlfriend would.

I tilted my head, widened my hazel eyes and asked with exaggerated innocence, "Well, if I'm going to meet your family, it'll be as your girlfriend, right?"

John shot me a look that was equal parts amused and affectionate and replied without hesitation, "Of course. How else would I introduce you?"

That was it – a moment sealed in our history—not just the official beginning of us, but the confirmation that this thing we had wasn't a phase, or a fling. It was real, rooted in something deeper than butterflies. It was the start of a life together—one pizza box, pajama night, and princess party at a time.

"When I saw you, I fell in love, and you smiled because you knew."
- Arrigo Boito, Italian poet and composer

What I didn't realize when I fell in love with John was that I wasn't just gaining a husband—I was gaining the most loyal business partner, road trip buddy, floral hauler, and shoulder to lean on. He's my reminder that real love isn't about the grand gestures (though he's nailed a few of those)—it's about showing up, again and again, with steady hands and a good sense of humor.

HOW DID I GET STARTED IN EVENT PLANNING?

Honestly, it all began with wine and a notepad. Back in college, I joined a group of like-minded, spreadsheet-loving socialites known as the Student Event Planners Association—or SEPA, for those of us who were too busy stuffing goody bags to say the full name every time. It was founded by a fellow student who, like me, had a passion for planning, aesthetics, and possibly the thrill of coordinating snack tables with military precision.

During my first semester in SEPA, the stars aligned—by which I mean I stumbled into an internship listing for a charming winery tucked away in New Braunfels. I practically skipped back to the apartment, brimming with excitement and barely able to contain myself. John—my forever hype man—was waiting, the kind of partner who doesn't just ask, "How was your meeting?" but genuinely wants the play-by-play.

"Hey, good lookin', how'd it go?" he called out as I burst through the door.

"It was amazing! Look what I signed up for!" I waved the flyer in the air like it was a golden ticket to Willy Wonka's Wine Factory. "I mean, I love wine. I love events. This feels like fate."

He laughed, that warm, steady kind of laugh that's always made me feel unstoppable.

"Go for it," he said. "Sounds like exactly the kind of experience you were meant for."

That night, like many others, we toasted to "what could be" and "future things to come." It might have been just cheap beer in a plastic cup, but in our hearts, we were already celebrating the start of something big.

After interviewing with the winery owner—a warm, whip-smart woman who looked like she could plan a wedding and run a vineyard with one hand tied behind her back—I waited anxiously for the call. When it finally came, I landed the internship. Cue confetti (and probably another celebratory toast).

The internship started off simple: I shadowed staff during lunch meetings, took notes, and practiced the ancient art of nodding enthusiastically while not always understanding what was going on. But slowly, I found my rhythm. I learned how to communicate with clients, vendors, and professionals far beyond my own age group. I sent my first few professional emails—agonizing over every exclamation point—and made myself useful around the office.

And then... came the first wedding. I was equal parts thrilled as I was terrified. To be honest, that butterflies-in-the-stomach feeling stuck with me for years after. Few things are as enchanting as a wedding day, filled with vibrant energy, eager anticipation, and the unmistakable sense that a significant and beautiful moment is taking place.

The winery hosted intimate ceremonies beneath a grove of trees, and receptions unfolded under a cozy pavilion glowing with twinkle lights and possibility. Rain was rare, but when it came, we pulled off event-planning miracles under pressure—grabbing towels to dry off chairs and herding floral arrangements indoors like elegant flamingos. My official title was "intern," but I often found myself donning multiple hats: floor manager, emotional support human, sometimes bartender when the night demanded reinforcements behind the bar. I savored every part of it.

Weddings have a way of reminding you what joy looks like—pure, messy, champagne-fueled joy. There's music, laughter, cousins reunited, grandparents telling the same stories, and people dancing like nobody's filming (though someone always is). Being in the middle of that kind of love and celebration—it's addictive, in the best possible way.

When the internship ended, I couldn't bear to walk away just yet. So, I got a job in the tasting room, where I perfected the art of describing wine like I was narrating a vineyard romance novel. My parents and future in-laws were especially supportive of this job—mostly because of the employee discount and the occasional "generous pour" when no one was watching.

Eventually, I knew it was time to move on. The winery had given me more than just experience; it gave me my footing. It taught me how to lead with heart, adapt on the fly, and that the real magic happens behind the scenes—where safety pins are currency and timelines are gospel. Looking back, that little winery in New Braunfels was the first place I truly understood what it meant to create unforgettable moments. Once you've had a taste of that—well, there's no turning back.

It was spring semester, and there I was, sitting in yet another SEPA meeting—bright-eyed, bushy-tailed, and riding high on hotel goody-bag fumes—when a new list of internship opportunities was announced. Cue the internal squeal. Among the options was something that made my Type-A heart skip a beat: wedding and event consulting. Yes, please. Where do I sign?

I applied, interviewed, and—unsurprisingly to no one, least of all me—landed the position. I dove in headfirst. We're talking hotel welcome bags, emergency kits, shadowing meetings like a clipboard-carrying maestro, and commuting every weekend from San Marcos to San Antonio, fueled by coffee and sheer ambition. I wasn't just interning—I was absorbing, soaking up every ounce of experience like a human sponge in heels. And then... plot twist.

The boutique wedding planning company I was interning with hit a crisis. One of the lead planners suddenly quit, dramatically ghosting not just the team but—gasp—the brides. I mean, who does that to a bride? These women are trusting us to be their logistics lifelines, sanity savers, and bridal bodyguards. We're their people. Their safe space. You don't just vanish mid-aisle prep. Cue drama, disarray, and the kind of team meeting that feels like the wedding-planner version of a military debriefing.

Thankfully, the company's fearless leader, Ms. Z, had one well-polished, highly experienced lead planner... and me. An eager, sleep-deprived college senior who still used a glittery planner and had a habit of saying yes to everything. It was go time.

Sink or swim. Eat or be eaten. Pick your survival metaphor—this was it. I was twenty-one, just barely of legal wine-sipping age, and suddenly I was being trusted with someone's actual wedding day. No pressure or anything, right?

My strategy: smile, nod, take furious notes, and hope no one noticed I was slightly panicked. Basically, fake it till you make it—but with better shoes and a timeline bible in hand. That year—my senior year of college—I was immersed fully into the real wedding industry. Not the vision-board version. The actual, high-stakes, things-will-go-wrong-but-you-still-have-to-smile version. And let me tell you—the struggle? Very real.

One of the biggest challenges was earning respect from clients who were significantly older than me. I was trying to convince 30-something couples that this very enthusiastic college student could, in fact, coordinate their entire wedding without losing a flower girl or setting the guestbook on fire. Not exactly a slam dunk.

Since the company was in flux, most of the major weddings went to the seasoned lead planner. I was given a modest handful of clients—enough to make me anxious but not quite enough to cry over. The owner did what she could, but looking back now, with a business owner's hindsight, I can clearly see what I would've done differently in her shoes. As a leader, it's your responsibility to care for your clients and your team—to make sure your people are trained, supported, and not quietly panicking in a corner with a folding timeline and a walkie-talkie. It's about more than just getting through the event; it's about building a team that feels empowered, even in the chaos.

Now that I manage my own business, I've absolutely had moments where I've hustled from one wedding to another, Coffee in one hand and timeline in the other, just to make sure every detail was covered. Sometimes that's what it takes, but I never forget what I learned in those early days: the value of clear communication, team support, and the power of showing up—confidently, even if you're still figuring it out as you go.

Behind every happy couple is a planner quietly making magic (and maybe silently screaming into a linen closet between grand entrances). It all started here—with one unexpected opportunity, one planner's exit, and one twenty-something girl who said, "Sure, I'll do it!" and then figured it out one wedding at a time.

THROWN TO THE WOLVES

I was sent into the field alone, which in theory shouldn't have been a problem. But in practice? Cue the stress sweat. The venue was a gorgeous art museum—beautiful, prestigious, and inconveniently still open to the public until 5:00 p.m. Meanwhile, the ceremony was scheduled to start at 6:00 p.m. Oh, and did I mention the weather had turned on us at the last minute, forcing everything indoors?

Because of course it did. With just one precious hour to flip the space, I hit the ground running.

First up: the candy bar. A trend I'm beyond thrilled has mercifully gone out of style. Sticky scoops, loose jellybeans, and tulle bows tied within an inch of their lives—it was a dental nightmare disguised as a wedding favor.

Next came the escort cards. Sounds simple, but these little devils had not been pre-sorted alphabetically—or in any order at all. They'd just been tossed into a box, as if someone lost patience halfway through the project and said, "Good luck, future you!" So, there I am: slouched over the display table, frantically sorting names while guests start arriving, and the mother of the bride is literally breathing down my neck.

"What's taking so long? Shouldn't this be done already?" she snapped; arms crossed with the precision of someone who's judged a great many brunches.

I swallowed hard, forced a smile, and replied, "Yes, ma'am. I completely understand how important this is, and I promise I'm working as quickly as possible. I'll have it ready very soon."

Internally? Screaming.

I called Ms. Z, hoping for backup, and explained the situation: guests arriving, tension rising, and one very frazzled twenty-something on the verge of crying into a bag of chocolates.

To make matters worse, I overheard the bride confiding in her bridesmaid, "That's the backup coordinator. The one we got stuck with after the other planner quit." Ouch. Still, I kept my cool. "Don't let this get to you," I told myself. "Smile and do your best."

Eventually, everything fell into place. The foyer transformed, the escort cards were sorted, guests were seated, and the candy bar—

lord help us—was fully stocked. That's when Miss Seasoned Planner finally showed up to check on me. She arrived just after the chaos had been tamed, when the worst of the storm had passed. She stuck around until the event was well underway, making sure I was okay. Which was kind... if just a touch too late.

COORDINATOR INSIGHT:
Putting out fires solo thickens your skin—whether they're emotional, logistical, or covered in chocolate-covered almonds. The wedding industry is not for the faint of heart. From that day forward, I vowed: no one goes in alone. Unless it's the tail end of the event and all that's left is the grand exit and collecting the leftover cake.

SETUP ALWAYS REQUIRES A TEAM.
You never know how many "DIY touches" a couple might show up with—bless their crafty little hearts—and how wildly unorganized it all may be. That's why, in my own business, we have systems. Clear instructions. Required alphabetization. Color-coded timelines. And enough backup plans to run a small nation. I don't send my team into battle without armor. And I certainly don't expect miracles without a second pair of hands.

LET'S GET REAL

We were all gathered around the kitchen island—coffee mugs in hand, the scent of cinnamon rolls curling through the air like a memory. The conversation was easy, familiar. Someone mentioned weekend plans, someone else laughed about a neighbor's dog. But beneath it all, I could feel it. That pause. That unspoken tension. The kind that hovers between family members who love you... but don't quite get it.

"So… wedding planning, huh?" someone finally said. Not rude. Just cautious. Curious in that way people are when they're trying to understand a path they wouldn't choose for themselves. "How many weddings would you need to do to actually make a living?"

I smiled—small, polite, trying to mask the flicker of panic. I didn't know. Not really. I hadn't run the numbers that way. I was still figuring it out as I went. But I couldn't say that.

Instead, I traced the edge of my mug and gave the best answer I had. "Well… when I started out, I charged about $1,000 per wedding. I took every client I could. Every weekend was booked—setup, teardown, timelines, unpredictable weather, tricky family dynamics. I ran on coffee and adrenaline."

I gave a soft laugh, more sheepish than confident. "Even now, at $3,000 per wedding, I'd still need 30 to 35 a year to keep things sustainable. That's nearly every weekend."

They nodded, half-impressed, half-unsure. The silence that followed wasn't judgment—it was doubt, dressed up in concern. The kind that makes people wonder if you're chasing something too fragile. Too risky.

But even in that moment, part of me knew: I wasn't just trying something—I was building something. And maybe I didn't have the math down yet. Maybe I was still guessing.

But I had a vision. I had grit. And I was willing to work for it.

One day, I'd look back at that kitchen table and think: I didn't have all the answers then. But I had enough belief to begin. One day, I'd prove it—not with speeches, but with sold-out calendars, client thank-you notes, features in glossy magazines, and my name on a book called *For the Love of Weddings*.

And I'd remember that morning. The doubt. The quiet concern. They didn't quite see it yet. But I did.

After graduating in 2011, I kept working with the boutique planning company. By then, I'd created my own systems, figured out what worked (and what didn't), and gained instincts only earned from high-stress, high-heels, high-stakes Saturdays. It was invaluable. I made connections, gathered experience, and began carving out a name in the industry. But… I was tapped out. Ramen-again broke.

My dream would have to wait. It was time for a "big-girl job"—one with health insurance and a veneer of stability. The wedding world would be there when I came back. At my core, I knew I would. For the time being, I had bills to pay—and glitter doesn't cover rent.

3
ALL THINGS NEW

The first year of marriage wasn't the fairytale I had imagined. Sure, there were moments of pure joy—laughter that echoed through tiny rooms, quiet evenings wrapped in love—but it wasn't easy. Far from it. We were living paycheck to paycheck, constantly juggling bills that seemed to multiply faster than our paychecks could keep up. Every small win felt like it was followed by a setback, and some days, the weight of "adulting" felt heavier than our wedding rings.

Even as the world spun around us, one thing never wavered: we had each other.

I can still picture the moment we moved into our first apartment, tucked away in the Medical Center. It was nothing like the dreamy space we'd once pictured during late-night talks about our future. No granite countertops. No walk-in closet. The couch was a well-loved hand-me-down from his parents, and the kitchen was so small that if I was cooking, he had to stand perfectly still by the door—unless he wanted a rogue elbow to the ribs. Still, we made it work. We laughed at how cramped it was, how our morning routines became a carefully choreographed dance, and how just opening the refrigerator required a bit of spatial strategy.

We filled that tiny space with the only currency we had then: love and intention. Wedding photos adorned the walls, a clearance-rack plant we'd named brought life to the corner, and mismatched mugs from thrift stores and garage sales filled the shelves. They weren't fancy, but they were ours. Every item carried a story, each one helping us build a life. It wasn't glamorous or easy; still, it was the beginning of everything. That was enough to keep us going. Money was tight. There were days when I'd check the bank account and feel a wave of panic. We were both working long hours, barely scraping by. John was working for a chemical company and I was working a job that drained me emotionally, but paid the bills.

Even so, my dream persisted. The one that kept me up late, sketching, planning, talking about how we were going to make it happen—someday. I felt a dream wasn't something you could just put off for another year or two, I was already 25. It had to happen now, or I feared I'd look back one day and regret it. As I sit in my cubical, feeling suffocated, I wonder why I am here? Oh, that's right, I need income, benefits, big-girl job. The joys of being a grown-up.

Nevertheless, I kept chasing my "dream" of becoming a wedding planner—because let's be honest, some dreams refuse to be ignored. I started working with a different company on the side, Lace & Logistics (L&L), and that's where I really began to tap into my inner planner and build genuine connections with brides. Getting married myself was a game-changer.

Think about it: how can you truly be a remarkable wedding planner if you've never walked in a bride's shoes? You might be able to organize events, sure, but to really understand the whirlwind—the late nights searching for the perfect dress, the endless RSVP tracking, the delicate dance of family dynamics, the bridal showers, the bridesmaid drama, and yes, the nerve-wracking task of seating divorced parents without starting World War III—you need to have lived it.

Being a bride gave me backstage access to the chaos and the joy behind the scenes, and that insight made all the difference. Suddenly, I wasn't just planning weddings—I was living them alongside my clients, with empathy, experience, and a few war stories to share. I've always strived for greatness—not just for myself, but to make a meaningful difference in people's lives, to be part of their happiest, most special moments.

The corporate grind was slowly squeezing the life out of me. There were winter days when I'd drag myself into the office before sunrise and leave long after sunset—never seeing a glimpse of daylight. That endless cycle of stress and anxiety started to take its toll. My stomach was in knots, and my spirit felt worn thin.

One evening, I came home to our little apartment just as dusk began settling through the blinds—soft streaks of gold catching dust in the air. My shoulders slumped under the weight of another long, bruising day, and the second I stepped through the door, the tears broke free. Silent at first, then hot and steady down my cheeks.

John was in the kitchen, barefoot, stirring something on the stove. He turned, and the moment he saw my face, he didn't say a word. He just crossed the room, wrapped his arms around my waist, and pulled me in. I buried my face into his chest, and he rested his chin on top of my head.

I could feel his heartbeat, slow and steady, like it was trying to remind mine how to find rhythm again.

After a long silence, he leaned back just enough to meet my eyes, wiping away one of the tears with his thumb. His voice was low and sure, almost a whisper:

"Hey... look at me. If this is making you miserable, step away. We'll figure out the rest, together."

And just like that, the knot in my chest loosened.

It wasn't a grand speech. There were no dramatic declarations or sweeping gestures. Just him. Just truth. Just love standing firm while I wavered.

For the first time in weeks—maybe longer—I felt something shift. Not everything was solved. But the idea that I didn't have to hold it all alone anymore? That I could choose a different path and someone would still walk beside me?

That felt like everything.

That night, I drafted my letter of resignation to Mr. Corporate Job. The next morning, already feeling lighter, I handed out wedding planner flyers to anyone who'd listen, telling them to call me when their big day came—or to pass it along to someone who needed a planner.

Walking into my supervisor's office, I took a steady breath and sat down. "I want to thank you for everything," I began. "This experience has shaped me in ways I'll always carry—but I've come to a crossroads. It's time I pursue what truly sets my heart on fire."

He looked up, his expression calm and kind. After a pause, he smiled. "Jennifer, you've always had something rare. I have no doubt you're going to do something remarkable."

In that moment, I knew I had made the right choice—I was finally on my path.

What is success, anyway? It's a question with as many answers as there are people in the world. For some, it's climbing the corporate ladder or building financial security. For others, it's about finding balance, nurturing relationships, or leaving a positive mark on those around them. To me, success means living in alignment with my values and passions—embracing the journey, overcoming challenges, and carving out a life that feels authentic and fulfilling. *How do you define success?*

All I knew was that I had the unwavering support of my husband, and I was ready to go all in. I picked up a few decent paychecks working with L&L, gaining invaluable wisdom and hands-on experience. Nevertheless, I found myself perfecting my own planning systems, crafting timelines uniquely tailored to my style—because I wanted to be recognized for my individuality, not just blend into someone else's brand.

One day, while sitting at the kitchen table with my sister Crystal, she asked a question that changed everything: "Why don't you start your own business?"

It was such a simple question, yet it sparked a new fire in me. Why not? I'd figured out so much on my own, had some support, but ultimately, I was learning through trial and error under someone else's name—and I sensed they were still trying to figure "it" out too. Deep down, I knew I had to create something that was truly mine.

With a leap of faith, we launched Events by Jennifer Craft—what would later become JC Events. It was terrifying. We were already navigating financial struggles, but John saw how much this meant to me and stood firmly beside me, offering every bit of support he could. Slowly but surely, things started to fall into place.

It was small steps at first—a few bookings here, a tiny breakthrough there—but those moments brought glimmers of hope that kept us moving forward. Looking back, a Day-of Coordination package was anywhere from $500 to $900, depending on how desperate we were for income at the time. I can't believe how little I charged, but when you're just starting out and hungry for experience, you're between a rock and a hard place.

Starting a business felt like diving headfirst into the deep end without a life jacket. It was the dream we'd talked about for years, but the reality was this: it wasn't just about passion—it was about survival. Every dollar mattered, and every choice felt as if it could tip us closer to success or pull us deeper into debt. Doubts crept in, yet backing down was never an option.

The first challenge arrived with something seemingly simple: ordering business cards. It sounded easy enough, but it wasn't. I spent days agonizing over the design because every detail mattered. The color scheme needed to reflect our brand's essence, the font had to be professional yet personal, and the paper needed to feel just right. Pricing became another dilemma—local printer or online vendor, quality or cost. The pressure to make it perfect was intense, since these cards were our first impression, our handshake to the world.

When the order finally arrived, excitement quickly turned to disappointment. The colors appeared muted, and the texture felt rougher than I'd imagined. Although they weren't terrible, they fell short of the polished look I had envisioned. I tucked them away, determined to hand them out at networking events while hoping no one else would notice the flaws that seemed glaring to me. Through it all, John remained my rock—my cheerleader and my realist. Although this was "my" business, every decision belonged to both of us, and I believe we understood, even then, that this was only the beginning of something much bigger.

The toughest battles were not financial but mental. Long nights were spent hunched over laptops, wrestling with tax forms, building a website, and juggling countless tasks. The grind was relentless, and it often felt as though the weight of the world rested on our shoulders. Each setback and every mistake seemed like it could be the end. However, whenever we talked about our vision and the reasons, we were pursuing this path, hope would flicker again, fueling our determination. During those first five years, John was more than just my husband—he was my assistant, my confidant, and my emotional anchor through every exciting, overwhelming, joyous, frustrating, fearful, and grateful moment. We were a team—partners in every sense.

Our early years in business were messy: imperfect cards, endless expenses, and sleepless nights. Despite everything, we kept moving forward. Starting a business isn't about having all the answers from day one; it's about learning as you go, adapting, and relentlessly chasing your dream, no matter how hard it gets. Throughout every challenge, we had each other, and that was—and still is—everything.

Looking back now, I love stumbling upon one of my old business cards. You know the ones—flimsy, glossy, printed from a Vistaprint template I thought looked so professional at the time. I remember unboxing them with excitement, thinking, "This is it. This makes me legit." Honestly, it did, in its own scrappy, determined way. Those early cards were a badge of hustle. I handed them out like gold, even if the print was slightly off-center and the font a bit... questionable. They represented something far bigger than just contact information—they embodied a dream, a beginning, and a girl chasing a big idea one wedding at a time.

Fast forward to today, and my business cards are thick, soft-touch, beautifully branded, and they feel like butter. People actually pause and say, "Whoa… these are nice cards!" I smile every time, not merely because the cards are fancy, but because they tell a story—a story of growth, grit, and the long road from paper-thin to premium. That little piece of cardstock says: I've come a long way. In business—especially this one—it's not solely about where you are today. It's about where you started, what you've learned, and the confidence you now carry in your brand, your work, and even your choice of paper stock.

Here's to the glow-up: from budget basics to bespoke elegance, from passion project to polished professional. To every wedding planner or entrepreneur holding that first humble card—keep going. Your velvet-finish moment is coming.

People often see the final product — the champagne toasts, the glimmering centerpieces, the first dance magic — and assume wedding planning is all beauty and bliss. What they don't always see? The grind behind the scenes. The years of working multiple jobs just to keep the dream afloat.

I've done it all. Anne Taylor — folding sweaters with a smile while mentally reviewing timelines. Hallmark — setting up seasonal displays while replying to vendor emails during lunch breaks. The wedding dress boutique — steaming gowns, learning silhouettes, and quietly studying what made a bride feel most beautiful. The Preschool Phase – That brief identity crisis where I thought, "Maybe I'm meant to be a teacher?" Spoiler alert: I was *very* wrong. One morning of toddler tears, snack duty, and snot on everything, and I knew—this was not my calling. God bless teachers… but I ran straight back to weddings.

That was my in-between life. The hustle. Not the glamorous "girl boss" type — the "rent is due, and I'm not giving up" type. There were months when I questioned if this dream of mine would ever become sustainable. When I was exhausted, chasing gigs and still pouring everything I had into weddings because it lit me up inside. The artistry, the people, the stories — I loved it. But loving something doesn't always mean it's easy.

Then, John and I started a family, Jameson was born — and I chose to pause. I stepped back from weddings for a while to be present with my baby and give myself the time to adjust to motherhood. That season was beautiful in a different way — slower, quieter, but full of love. Just when I was ready to return to weddings, I was fortunate enough to connect with another company that happened to be searching for a coordinator. That opportunity proved invaluable, and to this day, we remain friends and professional allies.

Once JC Events began to thrive again, the world came to a sudden halt with the arrival of COVID-19. Many businesses paused operations, while some were forced to close their doors entirely. We held on, determined to survive. Strangely enough, the pandemic became an unexpected blessing in disguise for our business. It forced us to innovate quickly, adapt to entirely new circumstances, and rethink how we served our clients. Virtual meetings replaced in-person consultations, scaled-back guest lists reshaped wedding designs, and creativity became more essential than ever.

Those challenges pushed us to grow stronger, work smarter, and ultimately emerge more resilient than before. Gone were the days of driving across town for a 30-minute consultation. Enter Zoom. Efficient, easy, and exactly what busy couples needed.

Gone were group meetings and large in-person planning sessions. We tightened up, streamlined our process, and suddenly, we were doing more in a day — not less. It wasn't easy, but it worked.

We built something stronger, more focused, and better—for both our clients and our family.

Today, when people compliment how "put together" our business seems or how smoothly a wedding day unfolds, I smile. I also remember the years of double shifts and fast-food dinners. I remember crying in a stockroom because I was exhausted, worried, and afraid of having to give up. Those struggles shaped me. They defined how I serve my clients—with empathy, gratitude, and heart. I learned that passion will carry you forward, but perseverance will keep you grounded when the world feels unsteady. Sometimes, the dream job requires side gigs, setbacks, and second winds before it becomes real. If you keep showing up—messy bun, coffee in hand, clipboard at the ready—it will all come together. And when it does, it's incredible.

Owning a business isn't just about numbers, strategy, and goals—it's an emotional journey, one that can leave you on top of the world one minute and in the depths of despair the next. It's a raw, unpredictable ride that tests your limits, pushes your resilience, and forces you to confront parts of yourself you never expected to face.

4

FROM VEILS TO VESTS

At long last, I stepped into the bridal boutique. The air felt lighter somehow—like the hush of a temple of dreams. Overhead, a crystal chandelier shimmered like a crown of stars, casting delicate flecks of light across the pristine walls. Everything gleamed in soft ivory and whispering whites, from the tufted settees to the sweeping mirrors that reflected endless dreams. And then—there they were. The gowns. Rows upon rows of tulle, lace, and satin magic. Each one seemed to float, waiting for its moment, each one a story yet to be written. I stood still, wide-eyed and smiling, letting the beauty of it all wash over me.

"Hello! We're here for a 6:00 p.m. first-time wedding dress appointment for Jennifer Dobson," I announced brightly to the front desk associate.

"Welcome! Please have a seat—we'll be with you shortly."

Walking into that bridal shop felt like stepping into a dream. The soft radiance of the lights, the delicate fabrics draped gracefully on the racks, and the quiet buzz of excitement in the air all combined to create a moment suspended in time. My heart raced with a thrilling mix of nerves and hope—would today be the day I found *the one*?

Mom and Gail, my future mother-in-law, joined me, and I caught myself imagining the bittersweet emotions they must have felt watching their children prepare to start a new chapter. Now that I'm a mother myself, the thought of my own child growing up and stepping into adulthood fills me with a strange mix of awe and nostalgia. Yet in that moment, I felt grateful to share this milestone with these two special women, knowing it was their only chance to experience it with me.

The consultant guided us through an array of gowns, each one more stunning than the last. The sheer variety was overwhelming—lace, satin, tulle—all carrying a story in their textures, each whispering of magic waiting to be discovered. With no fixed idea of what I wanted; I was eager to try on a wide selection. One by one, ten dresses came into the fitting room, each bringing new hopes and lingering doubts.

The first dress was a voluminous ball gown, perfect for my inner princess fantasies. Yet once it was on, it felt more like a costume than me—I looked like a pumpkin, big and puffy in all the wrong ways. The second was a delicate lace A-line, elegant and timeless, perhaps more suited for a spring wedding or someone a few years older; if I were choosing now, in my mid-thirties, it would have been perfect. The third was a fit-and-flare embellished with pearls and lace. I stepped onto the platform and gazed at my reflection, trying to decide if this was *the one*. Doubt crept in—it was beautiful, but not quite right.

Then came the fourth dress—a tulle mermaid gown adorned with clusters of soft tulle flowers, each accented with beaded sparkle at their centers. The moment I stepped into it, something shifted.

When you find a dress that makes your heart skip a beat, you know. The world seems to pause. In that instant, I saw myself—radiant, confident, ready for the next chapter. No tears fell, but laughter came forth as I twirled and wiggled, caught in a wave of pure joy.

The consultant added a waist-length veil with a beaded edge that perfectly complemented the gown. "Jen, is this your dress?" she asked.

"Yes!" I squealed, grinning from ear to ear.

It wasn't the dramatic, tear-filled moment I'd imagined. Instead, it was a light, bubbly thrill—the kind of excitement that tells you you're getting closer to making a dream real. It wasn't perfect in the way I'd expected, but it was perfect for me.

Later, as I called Dad and Bonus Mom, Charlotte, to share the news, it sank in: this was the last dress I'd wear as Jennifer Dobson. Luckily, Houston had the same boutique where I could bring my sisters and Charlotte to share in the experience. While there, Crystal and Lisa tried on bridesmaid dresses and we checked another big item off the list.

With a semi-short engagement, I was in full checklist mode. Looking back, I would have chosen bridesmaid dresses in midnight blue chiffon, champagne, or even black—something less matchy-matchy and more timeless. I love today's style much more—mix-and-match dresses that reflect each bridesmaid's personality and body type. It's a small change that makes a huge difference in comfort, confidence, and style. Allowing your bridesmaids to choose dresses that make them feel beautiful is a gift—for them, and for the bride.

THE PERFECT FIT

When it comes to shopping for your wedding dress, timing is everything—start about nine to twelve months before your big day to allow for ordering, alterations, and any unexpected delays, but avoid rushing into a decision too early, as your style preferences may evolve. Do your homework beforehand by exploring bridal magazines, websites, and inspiration boards to get a clear sense of what you love, and bring those visuals with you to your appointments to help guide the consultants. Setting a realistic budget upfront is crucial, so you can include not only the dress itself but also alterations, accessories, and undergarments.

Keep an open mind as you try on a variety of silhouettes—even those you might not have considered—because sometimes the dress that surprises you is the one that truly fits your personality and body. Bring along just a few trusted friends or family members whose opinions you value and who will offer positive support; too many voices can make the experience overwhelming. Remember to think about comfort as much as style—you'll be wearing your dress for many hours, so sit, walk, and dance in it to see how it feels beyond the mirror.

Also, consider your wedding venue and theme, making sure the gown suits the atmosphere and season, whether that's a grand ballroom or an intimate beach setting. Alterations are part of the journey, so plan ahead to work with a skilled seamstress who can tailor the dress to flatter you perfectly. Above all, trust your instincts—when you find a dress that makes you feel **luminous, empowered, and truly happy,** you'll know it's the one. Most importantly, savor the experience; dress shopping is a cherished moment in your wedding journey, so enjoy every step as you prepare to walk down the aisle in the dress of your dreams.

THE FINISHING TOUCH

Choosing the perfect veil or headpiece is an essential part of completing your bridal look—it's the crown that complements your dress and reflects your personal style. Here's how to find the right one: First, consider the style of your wedding dress. A delicate lace veil pairs beautifully with a vintage or romantic gown, while a sleek satin dress might call for a minimalist, modern headpiece or a simple veil. Length matters too: a cathedral veil creates drama and elegance, perfect for formal ceremonies, whereas a birdcage veil or a short blusher can add a playful, retro touch for a more casual or vintage vibe.

Next, think about your hairstyle. If you're planning an updo, a tiara, comb, or jeweled headband can add sparkle without overwhelming your look. For loose curls or half-up styles, a floral crown or delicate pins might feel more natural and whimsical. Also, consider comfort—choose something secure but lightweight, so you can enjoy your day without fuss.

Lastly, try on different options with your dress and hairstyle well before the wedding. Once in a while, the simplest pieces surprise you with how much they elevate the entire look, and sometimes a bold statement piece becomes your signature. Remember, your veil or headpiece should make you feel confident, beautiful, and truly yourself on your special day.

SQUAD GOALS

Everyone has different body shapes, preferences, and personal styles, and when they have the freedom to select a dress they truly love and feel good in, it boosts their self-esteem. A confident bridesmaid is sure to bring positive energy to the wedding day. When bridesmaids are free to choose their own styles (as long as they stay within certain guidelines like color or fabric), it takes the pressure off the bride to make a decision that everyone will love.

Instead of worrying about what dress to pick for each individual, the bride can focus on other aspects of planning, like flowers, decor, and personal touches for the wedding. Bridal party photos often reflect the personalities of the individuals within it, and letting your bridesmaids choose their own styles can create a visually pleasing contrast. The overall aesthetic can look more natural and cohesive, rather than staged. Plus, these photos will age better because the dresses won't look as "trendy" or out of date as a uniform style might in the years to come.

Bridesmaids often cover the cost of their dresses themselves, and giving them the freedom to pick their own style allows for greater budget flexibility. They can choose a dress that fits within their personal price range while still adhering to the wedding's color scheme and theme. This ensures that no one feels financially burdened by the dress, making the experience more enjoyable for everyone involved.

When bridesmaids have the freedom to choose their own dress, they're more likely to feel engaged in the wedding process. It's an opportunity for them to express themselves, and they'll be happier knowing that their comfort and style matter. This increased engagement can lead to stronger bonds and an even more positive, supportive attitude on the big day.

DRESSED TO IMPRESS

Helping parents and the groom's party find the perfect wedding attire is just as important as the bridal gown—it's about creating a cohesive look that complements the overall wedding style and honors the special roles these men play on the big day. When working with the groom and groomsmen, the goal is to strike a balance between classic elegance and personal comfort. Start by understanding the wedding's color palette and formality. Are you leaning toward a black-tie affair with tuxedos, or a more relaxed garden wedding with lighter suits or even coordinated separates? This foundation helps narrow down options and ensures everyone feels confident and looks their best.

Coordinating colors among the groom, groomsmen, and parents requires thoughtful planning. While the groom's outfit should stand out in a subtle yet distinctive way—perhaps a different tie, boutonniere, or even a unique jacket—there should still be harmony with the groomsmen's looks. Using varying shades of the same color or mixing textures can add visual interest without feeling mismatched. For parents, comfort and style go hand in hand. Their outfits should complement the wedding's vibe but also reflect their personal tastes. Coordinating with the wedding colors through accessories—like ties, scarves, or pocket squares—is an easy way to tie everything together without requiring a full uniform look.

Remember, communication is key. Encourage the groom and parents to try on multiple options, think about fabric choices that work with the season, and consider tailoring for the perfect fit. Sometimes, subtle details like cufflinks, suspenders, or custom shoes can add personality and polish to the look. Ultimately, the goal is to create a unified aesthetic that honors tradition but feels fresh and authentic, helping everyone feel confident as they stand by the couple on such a meaningful day.

TINY TRENDS

When it comes to the littlest members of your wedding party, dressing your flower girl and ring bearer is about balancing cuteness with comfort and coordinating their looks seamlessly with the overall wedding theme. These tiny stars bring a special charm to your day, so their outfits should feel just as thoughtful as everyone else's.

Start by considering the colors and styles already chosen for the wedding palette. Flower girls often wear dresses that complement the bridesmaids' gowns, whether it's matching fabric, color accents, or similar styles with a playful twist. Soft pastels, delicate hues of white, ivory, and even subtle hints of your wedding colors can tie their look into the bigger picture beautifully. Comfort is key—choose breathable fabrics and designs that allow little ones to move freely and enjoy their roles with ease.

For ring bearers, coordinating with the groomsmen is usually the way to go. Mini tuxedos or suits that echo the men's attire help create a polished, cohesive look. However, there's room for creativity: consider adding fun accessories like bow ties, suspenders, or even colorful socks that echo your wedding colors and inject a bit of personality. Keep in mind the ages and comfort of the boys, making sure their outfits aren't too heavy or complicated. Don't forget about the practical side—plan for quick changes or backups, especially for younger kids who might get messy or tired throughout the day. With thoughtful planning, the littlest members of your wedding party will not only look **charming** but feel **confident,** making their moments down the aisle as memorable as yours.

THROUGH THE LOOKING GLASS

Over the years, I've had the joy of accompanying many brides on one of the most emotional parts of their wedding journey—finding the dress. It's always a privilege, yet one moment stands out vividly in my heart.

Her name was Anna. She didn't have any family nearby, and when it came time to search for her wedding gown, I became her person—her planner, her cheerleader, and her honorary sister. We walked into the boutique together, both buzzing with anticipation. For her, it was a blend of nerves and excitement. For me, it was the quiet responsibility of holding space for someone who deserved to feel completely seen and celebrated.

When Anna stepped out of the fitting room for the first time, she stood before the mirror in a soft ivory gown. Her fingers traced the fabric as her eyes scanned every angle with uncertainty. Like many brides I've known, she wasn't merely seeing the dress—she was seeing herself, imperfections and all.

"My hips look weird in this," she murmured, tugging gently at the sides. "I don't know… maybe I'm just not built for this style."

I stepped beside her, catching her reflection as I said, "Anna, we all have parts of ourselves we critique. That doesn't mean they aren't beautiful. You are beautiful. Let's find a dress that feels like you."

Several dresses later, she slipped into a vintage-inspired beaded gown that shimmered subtly, hugged her curves perfectly, and exuded an old-soul elegance that matched her spirit. She turned to face the mirror and paused. This time, there was no tugging or adjusting— only a small smile spreading across her face and a calmness settling into her shoulders.

"This is it," she whispered.

It truly was.

Standing there in that moment, just the two of us, felt like more than a professional duty. It was friendship, sisterhood, and one of those quiet life snapshots I'll always hold close. Helping Anna find her dress was never solely about fashion or fit. It was about helping her see herself the way we all did: radiant, worthy, and ready to walk into her next chapter. Moments like those are why I am a wedding planner. It's not merely about planning weddings. It's about walking beside someone during one of the most vulnerable, beautiful, and unforgettable seasons of their life.

TOO MANY OPINIONS, ONE BEAUTIFUL BRIDE

Wedding dress shopping is meant to be magical—a moment when a bride sees herself stepping into a lifelong dream. At times, however, too many voices in the room can drown out the one that matters most: hers.

Brigit was one of the kindest, most gentle-spirited brides I've ever worked with. From our first meeting, she radiated grace and sweetness. When she invited me to join her at her bridal appointment, I felt thrilled. Nothing could have prepared me, though, for the entourage—a well-meaning group of family and friends, each armed with loud opinions. The first dress appeared, and before Brigit could speak, comments started flying:

"Too poofy."
"Too plain."
"Too much lace."
"That belt is weird."

It felt like watching a live episode of *Say Yes to the Dress: Unfiltered Family Edition*. Poor Brigit stood there, smiling softly, though I could see it in her eyes—she was shrinking under the weight of their words. I held my tongue for as long as I could. Seeing her slip back into the fitting room looking visibly deflated, I quietly followed.

She looked up at me, fighting back tears, and my only instinct was to protect her from the noise.

"Brigit," I said, kneeling beside her. "You look stunning in all these gowns. Truly. Yet what you think is what matters. Which dress are you drawn to?"

Her hand reached for the A-line lace gown with beaded accents on the bodice. "This one," she whispered. "It feels like me, but they all said it's too plain."

"Let's try something," I said with a smile. "Put it back on—this time with a veil and a pearl belt. Let's see you in it, the full vision."

Before she stepped out again, I returned to her entourage and did what any good planner-bestie does: played mediator. "The dress Brigit about to come out in—she loves it. I'm kindly asking that this isn't treated like a game show. Please hold your opinions and let her feel it. She's feeling overwhelmed, and I know we all want this to become a happy memory."

The room fell silent in response. Her mother immediately stood and hurried to the fitting room. She hugged Brigit tightly, apologized for the chaos, and urged the rest of the group to follow her lead. When Brigit stepped out in that gown—soft lace, the perfect belt, and a delicate veil catching the light—no critiques echoed through the room. Only tears remained. Happy, heartfelt tears. Hers. Her mother's. Mine.

She said yes to the dress with her voice strong and her smile wide. In that moment, I felt reminded once again that my role isn't solely about planning a wedding. It's also about helping brides find their voice when they need it most.

5

BUDGETING BLISS

At 22 years old, fresh out of college, I had very little concept of what "real life" actually cost. Rent, groceries, insurance—sure, I knew those things existed. But a wedding? That was a whole other financial universe I was about to enter, and let's just say, I wasn't exactly prepared.

Dad and Charlotte generously gifted me a "wedding budget," and while I was truly grateful, I immediately fell into the trap that ensnares so many brides. I looked at the number, compared it to my Pinterest dreams, and decided it wasn't enough. My arguments included inflation, the claim that times had changed since my sisters' weddings, and the insistence that I would "need" more.

Looking back, I cringe and wish I had simply said thank you, tucked that gift into savings, and eloped barefoot in the Virgin Islands. The little princess inside me—the one who planned color palettes for every season back in middle school—still wanted the grand, fairytale experience. The gown. The cake. The flowers.

Fortunately, I had already begun building relationships in the wedding industry before getting engaged. Vendor friends, a solid reputation, and growing confidence were all in my corner. The day after John proposed, I shifted into full throttle—emails, phone calls, vendor meetings. Within two months, every major vendor was booked. Planning felt like muscle memory, as if this was precisely what I was meant to do.

Even with connections and favors, weddings proved expensive. The true cost of each detail became clear as expenses rapidly accumulated. Dad, ever the wise man, sent wedding funds and encouraged me to open a dedicated wedding checking account. "It'll help you learn how to budget," he said. He was right. I tracked every expense, deposit, and invoice meticulously.

Although I called in a few favors and secured some savings, the experience humbled me. The speed with which costs snowball took me entirely by surprise—from postage for invitations to last-minute décor fixes. I managed most of the planning on my own and kept others at a distance. Only one flower meeting included Mom, who graciously covered that category, while I handled everything else independently—not out of pride, but from a deep desire to prove to myself that I could succeed.

Now, with over a decade of experience in wedding planning, I no longer dance around conversations about money. I approach them directly, guided by compassion and clarity. Budget discussions aren't merely about numbers. They encompass expectations, priorities, boundaries, and open communication. Success lies in finding the balance between what is meaningful and what is manageable.

The persistent question, "How much should we spend?" confronts every couple. Tension often arises, particularly when family contributions come into play. My advice remains consistent: seek clarity early. Tackle uncomfortable conversations sooner rather than later. Know precisely who is paying for what. Above all, remember that regardless of budget size, the true value of a wedding is never measured by the price tag. It's measured by the memories created and the love that's celebrated.

UNDERSTAND YOUR PRIORITIES

As a planner, I always ask my couples during our initial consultation: *What are your top three priorities?* This question helps me gather crucial insights at the very beginning of the planning process and allows me to identify where to focus first—the areas where they're most willing to splurge. More often than not, the categories couples value most are the venue, photography, food, music, and flowers.

From a bride's perspective, it's helpful to step back and reflect on what parts of the wedding are most important to you. For some, it's securing a breathtaking venue; for others, it might be an exquisite meal or hiring a dream photographer. Identifying what will bring you the most joy on your wedding day allows you to focus your budget on what truly matters. With those priorities clear, it becomes easier to see where you can scale back without sacrificing the experience.

BUDGET LIKE A BOSS

As a planner, honesty is everything. One of the greatest gifts you can give your clients is clarity. Many couples enter the wedding planning process with little to no understanding of what things actually cost. That's not their fault—it's unfamiliar territory. The best approach is to educate them. Break down the numbers. Create a detailed budget spreadsheet and present it from day one.

When a couple comes to you with a $30,000 budget but has their hearts set on a $15,000 venue, it's immediately clear the math doesn't add up. Deliver the news gently yet directly: they'll either need to increase their overall budget or choose a different venue.

Our role is to guide, not merely plan. Starting with their top three priorities and building from there is crucial. Price out vendors by category, compare costs, and help clients understand where their money will stretch best.

For brides and grooms, once you've pinpointed what truly matters—whether it's the venue, photography, florals, or food—sit down with your partner and, if applicable, any family members contributing financially. Establish a realistic budget. Be honest with yourselves and with each other.

Review your finances and determine what you can comfortably afford without tapping into emergency savings or going into debt. It's easy to get swept up in the magic and momentum of planning. Yet it's important to remember: your wedding is one day; your marriage is for life. A beautiful celebration doesn't have to cost a fortune. The best weddings reflect your love, not your wallet.

As a planner, one of the first—and most crucial—conversations you must have with your couple involves understanding where the wedding funds are coming from. It's essential never to assume that the bride's parents will cover the entire celebration; for many families today, those traditions no longer hold true. In reality, wedding budgets often become a patchwork of contributions: the couple themselves, both sets of parents, and occasionally grandparents or other relatives who wish to help in their own way.

Gaining clarity on who is contributing—and how much—is vital for establishing a realistic budget and preventing misunderstandings or tension down the line. Some contributors may choose to cover specific elements, such as the rehearsal dinner, the gown, or the bar, while others might prefer to offer a set monetary gift. Regardless of the arrangement, it's your responsibility as the planner to ask thoughtful questions, gather the complete picture, and guide the couple in managing expectations with both grace and transparency.

This financial clarity not only informs vendor choices and planning decisions but also provides the couple with peace of mind and a clear understanding of what's achievable. While money can be an emotional topic, addressing it early and honestly lays the groundwork for a smoother, more joyful planning journey. Although budgeting for a wedding can initially feel daunting, approaching it with a clear plan and well-defined priorities transforms it into a manageable—and even empowering—process.

PRACTICAL, STEP-BY-STEP GUIDE ON HOW TO BUDGET FOR A WEDDING:

DETERMINE YOUR TOTAL BUDGET

Start with the big number:

How much can you contribute?

Are any family members offering to help?

Be honest and realistic—avoid starting your marriage in debt

Tip: Consider setting a slightly smaller number than your max, so you have a buffer.

LIST YOUR PRIORITIES AS A COUPLE

What matters most to you?

Examples: The venue, live music or DJ, a designer dress, great food, high quality photographs, showstopper cake, stunning florals, custom dancefloor

Choose your **top 3 priorities**, and allocate more of your budget to those.

BREAK DOWN YOUR BUDGET BY CATEGORY

Here's a rough starting point for a traditional wedding. Adjust based on your priorities.

Venue, Catering & Rentals: 40–50%
Often the biggest chunk of your budget. Includes venue fee, food, beverages, tables, chairs, linens, dishware

Photography & Videography: 10–12%
Professional photo/video services, and includes albums, edited films, engagement sessions if desired

Attire: 7–10%
Wedding dress, suit/tux, accessories, shoes, alterations

Music & Entertainment: 8–10%
DJ or live band, ceremony or cocktail-hour musicians

Flowers & Décor: 8–10%
Personal flowers (bouquets, boutonnieres).
Ceremony décor, reception centerpieces, rental décor items

Planner/Coordinator: 5–10%
Full-service planning, partial planning, or day-of coordination

Stationery: 2–3%
Save-the-dates, invitations, programs, menus, signage

Transportation: 2–3%

Limo, party bus, shuttle services for guests

Cake/Desserts: 2–3%
Wedding cake, dessert table, late-night treats

Favors & Gifts: 1–2%
Guest favors, gifts for bridal party or family

Beauty & Personal Care: 1–2%
Hair, makeup, grooming, trial sessions

Miscellaneous / Cushion: 5–10%
Tips, taxes, service charges, unexpected costs, overtime fees

TRACK EVERY EXPENSE

- Use a spreadsheet, wedding budget app, or planner-provided template.
- Include: Estimated vs. actual costs
- Deposits and due dates
- Paid in full? Highlight it!
- Advice: Don't forget to include taxes, service fees, and gratuities.

PLAN FOR HIDDEN & UNEXPECTED COSTS – THEY ADD UP!

- Alterations
- Beauty trials
- Overtime charges
- Postage for invites
- Vendor gratuities

- Weather backup plans (like heaters, portable AC units or tent rentals)
- Set aside 5–10% of your budget for surprises.

BE CREATIVE TO SAVE

- Host on a weekday or Sunday
- Choose a non-peak season
- Re-purpose florals from ceremony at the reception
- Trim your guest list—this is the biggest money-saver of all
- Hire a DJ instead of a band, or go local for vendors

Stay Grounded in What Really Matters: At the end of the day, it's about celebrating love, not impressing anyone. A thoughtful, intentional wedding will always feel more meaningful—no matter the budget.

THREW IN THE TOWEL

It's a post-COVID world, and most couples are still adjusting to planning weddings on limited funds. As a result, I continued to see more intimate gatherings and careful budgeting. This particular couple started out as an absolute joy to work with. The bride found me, and we clicked right away—I thought it was a match made in heaven. That was true until the groom entered the picture. For reasons I'll never fully understand, he took an instant dislike to me. Any vendor I recommended was, in his view, either questionable or simply not good enough. Despite my efforts to remain professional, the working relationship grew increasingly strained.

Financially, they were barely able to afford the wedding. Then, out of nowhere, they decided to buy a new car, a new house, and who knows what else. It was perplexing. Then, one fortunate day, I received a phone call from the groom letting me know they had decided to elope instead. I was beyond thrilled!

PLANNER INSIGHT: Don't force the fit—if it's not right, it's okay to let a client go. Working with someone you don't genuinely connect with can drain the joy from the process. And in a season that's meant to be filled with warmth and excitement, both you and your clients deserve to feel the magic.

WEDDING WISDOM: If your wedding budget is under $20,000, consider the beauty of an intimate elopement. A destination celebration with your closest loved ones might offer more happiness, less stress—and a built-in vacation to remember.

DEBTS AND DREAMS

Another post-COVID wedding, another story of expectations colliding with reality—and falling short of both. The couple had envisioned a grand affair in the Texas Hill Country: 150 guests, an elegant outdoor venue, and all the trimmings. Yet, as we all know, the post-pandemic world had other plans.

After postponing once, twice, and ultimately a third time, we abandoned the original dream and pivoted to something more realistic: a smaller, centrally located venue that suited their new guest count of 50. The venue was lovely, though it lacked the sprawling hilltop views they had initially imagined. Even the season changed. It wasn't merely a scaled-down version of the original plan—it became an entirely different wedding.

As a planner, my role is to advocate for my clients. I reached out to vendors to request date changes without penalty. Some, like the DJ, were incredibly accommodating and moved the date without hesitation—multiple times. Others, understandably, were less flexible. As a fellow business owner, I couldn't fault them.

Despite these challenges, I remained committed to protecting the couple's interests. I suggested they downgrade their package with me from full-service planning to day-of coordination to reduce costs. Although it was clear they were financially overwhelmed, they insisted on maintaining full-service planning. I continued with my usual level of dedication—designing budget-friendly solutions, coordinating vendors, and offering guidance—but the stress steadily mounted.

Soon, payment issues began to surface. Calls from vendors started coming in: payments declined, charges disputed. Suddenly, I found myself not only as a planner but also acting as a debt collector, a therapist, and a crisis manager. I was spending more time negotiating with vendors and resolving unpaid balances than actually planning the wedding itself.

Eventually, I had to establish boundaries. I issued an ultimatum: payment in full, or I would step away. They paid—barely—and I pressed on, determined to see it through. We made thoughtful cutbacks, eliminating the mariachi band and simplifying the centerpieces with candles and strategic pops of color. I advised canceling the photo booth and the oversized floral installation—both costly and unnecessary—but the bride was emotionally attached to them. As I suspected, those elements sat nearly untouched all evening, serving as a visual reminder of misplaced budget priorities.

On the wedding day, I didn't exhale until the couple made it down the aisle. During the reception, my heart sank as I surveyed the room. Fewer than 25 guests had shown up. Perhaps people had lost faith after so many date changes. Perhaps deeper tensions simmered beneath the surface—family debt, unresolved dynamics. The true reason will likely remain unknown. What is certain is that I showed up, executed every detail, and gave them the best version of the day I could deliver.

A week later, the venue manager called me. "Did you get paid in full?" she asked.

"Yes, I always collect no later than 30 days out," I replied confidently.

She sighed. "We gave them an extension. They still owe us 50 percent. Their card won't go through."

I shook my head, hardly surprised. It's a hard lesson in this business: no matter how kind your heart or how well-intentioned your clients may seem; wedding vendors must protect themselves. Always collect payment before the wedding. Generosity doesn't pay your bills.

PLANNER INSIGHT: If a client can't pay, let them go. It's that simple. Holding onto a client who is financially unprepared will only drain your energy and, trust me, add gray hairs faster than time ever could. As planners, we reserve dates well in advance, and from the moment we're booked, the work begins—emails, meetings, timelines, vendor outreach, and countless hours that accumulate long before the wedding day ever arrives. Your time is valuable, and your policies should reflect that.

Always require full payment no later than 30 days before the event. No exceptions. All payments should be non-refundable, and this must be clearly outlined in your contract. Protect your business, protect your peace, and remember: you're not just a planner—you're a professional running a business. You can't pour from an empty cup, especially when your client is draining it dry.

WEDDING WISDOM: If you truly can't afford a wedding right now, it's perfectly okay not to have one—at least, not in the traditional sense. There's no rule stating that love must come with a price tag or that starting your marriage in debt is a rite of passage. In reality, all you need to get married is a marriage license, two rings, and someone to officiate. Everything else is optional.

There is absolutely no shame in choosing a courthouse ceremony or a backyard celebration with close family and friends. Some of the most meaningful weddings I've witnessed have taken place in simple settings, filled with heartfelt words and genuine love. If you have a dream wedding in mind but the finances just aren't there, consider waiting. Save intentionally and plan an incredible anniversary celebration a year or two down the line. You'll have more clarity, more resources, and perhaps an even deeper appreciation for what you're able to create together.

Remember: your wedding is the beginning of a marriage—not a one-day event that defines your relationship. Spend wisely, love deeply, and never feel pressured to go into debt for a single moment.

Dreaming of a beautiful wedding doesn't require a limitless budget. In fact, some of the most heartfelt, memorable celebrations happen when couples get creative, resourceful, and intentional with every dollar they spend. If you're planning your special day on a modest budget, know this: your dreams are entirely valid, and your love story deserves to be celebrated with joy, not stress.

Who doesn't want all the magic—the romance, the laughter, the unforgettable moments—without sacrificing financial peace of mind? Whether you're trimming the guest list, limiting the bar, simplifying the menu or finding affordable venues and vendors who are local, there's a beautiful wedding waiting for you.

6

THE CANVAS FOR YOUR CELEBRATION

Imagine this: you're newly engaged, a sparkling ring on your finger, your perfect partner by your side, and a flood of cheerful congratulations pouring in from friends and family. Life feels like a fairytale. Then comes the inevitable question: *Where are you getting married?* Suddenly, you're struck by a thrilling—and overwhelming—realization: you can get married anywhere. And I mean *anywhere*.

Some couples opt for simplicity—a courthouse ceremony, a marriage license, and a celebratory dinner at their favorite restaurant. Mission accomplished; marriage secured. Others go full fantasy mode, hosting an opulent event worthy of a glossy bridal magazine: champagne towers, string quartets, elaborate ceiling installations, and a six-tier cake. You'll often find this level of spectacle in a grand hotel ballroom, a modern museum, or a sleek venue designed to impress.

These venues frequently start at **$15,000 and up just for the rental fee,** depending on the city, date, and package inclusions. In major metropolitan areas like New York, San Francisco, or Chicago, rental fees alone can range from $15,000 to well over $30,000 for high-end spaces. Exclusivity indeed carries a price tag.

Then there's everyone in between—the vast majority of couples seeking something elegant and beautiful, yet also practical. They're searching for a charming venue with personality, some flexibility, and essential amenities included. This could be a modern event space with sleek architecture, a historic barn adorned with vintage décor, or a picturesque vineyard offering weekend rentals and romantic sunset ceremonies. For these types of venues, **current rental fees (2025) typically range from around $7,000 to $14,000,** depending on location and what's included. Still gorgeous. Still dreamy. Just not requiring you to sell a kidney.

Here's the truth: the "perfect" wedding venue depends on more than just your vision board dreams. It comes down to your budget, personal style, accessibility needs, guest count, getting-ready suites, proximity to hotels, parking, access times, and about 27 other small but important details. That's the true wonder of it all: a thoughtfully selected venue becomes a canvas that captures your unique love story.

Are you outdoorsy, earthy, and love a mountain breeze? Hello, scenic ranch venue with Hill Country views.

Prefer a sleek and stylish flair? Bring on the art gallery or downtown rooftop.

Swoon for hometown charm and timeless romance? Find the historic estate with a garden straight out of a classic literary romance.

Your venue sets the stage. Literally.

Think of it this way: if I receive an invitation printed on cotton paper with gold foil and silk ribbon, and then arrive at a barn with folding chairs and Mason jars… I'm confused, and probably overdressed.

If your venue radiates elegance, your wedding design—from paper goods to table settings—should echo that motif. On the other hand, if you're marrying under an oak tree in boots and lace, your guests likely aren't expecting filet mignon and Baccarat crystal. (And that's perfectly okay!)

Allow me to share a candid perspective: this is a wedding venue—not your forever home. I've seen brides tour over a dozen venues, paralyzed by indecision. The hesitation makes sense; you want to make the right choice. Unless your plan involves hopping between venues like a pub crawl in stilettos—which I wouldn't advise—there's no need to tour 15 or more places.

A savvy bride starts by researching and focusing on her preferred style, budget, and key priorities.

Spend a bit of time on pre-wedding research if you can. Before hiring a planner, think through your vision—or at least what you know you *don't* want.

Rustic barn or luxury ballroom?

Coastal views or urban skyline?

A large guest list or a cozy micro-wedding?

Indoor or outdoor?

You don't need all the answers immediately, but having even a rough idea of your desired setting will streamline the search considerably. Touring a dozen venues only to discover you never wanted a vineyard wedding in the first-place wastes valuable time.

Talk it out with your fiancé. Discuss the look, feel, and budget for your day.

Do a casual search. Scroll through venues online, browse social media and take note of styles that catch your eye. Narrow it down to three to five venues. Once you identify what appeals to you, focus your tours on a handful of places aligned with your style and budget.

Ask about restrictions early. Details like end times, alcohol policies, vendor requirements, and even candle rules can become deal-breakers.

When you bring in a wedding planner, the process becomes far more efficient. We help you review contracts, identify red flags, and assess logistics—because nobody wants to trek half a mile to the restroom in heels. The art of venue shopping lies in balancing vision with practicality, and when those two align, that's when the magic truly happens.

Contracts deserve attention. The pandemic taught us many lessons, including the importance of solid cancellation policies and ironclad clauses. Venues now tend to have detailed rules covering everything from candle usage and guest capacity to noise ordinances. Reading the fine print before falling in love with the Instagram photos is crucial.

During COVID, venues elevated their game with virtual tours and improved communication—a small silver lining in an otherwise challenging season. These days, you can narrow your list from your laptop while lounging in sweatpants. Efficiency like that is always worth celebrating. Your venue is where the magic begins. It's the place where you'll say "I do," dance under the stars (or chandeliers), and celebrate alongside your favorite people. Choose a venue that feels right—not just because it's beautiful, but because it fits you, your partner, and the type of experience you want to share with your guests. The biggest or fanciest venue isn't necessary. What matters is finding the one that makes you think, *"Yes. This is our place."*

In many ways, selecting a wedding venue is like choosing the setting for a movie—*your* movie. The venue sets the tone, the mood, and the entire vibe for your day. Consider it the backdrop to all your most cherished moments: your walk down the aisle, your first dance, your friends belting "Sweet Caroline" – Neil Diamond. It truly matters, and choosing the right venue can feel like a full-time job all its own.

PLANNER INSIGHT: Avoid overwhelming your bride with a buffet of venue options. Presenting three to five carefully curated locations is more than enough for a thoughtful decision. Once you've narrowed down the top contenders, encourage your couple to create a vision board inspired by those venues—it's a brilliant way to bring their dream to life and keep everyone focused. Trust your expertise; you know their vision, budget, and the local market inside and out. Lead your couple confidently toward the venue that makes the most sense and checks the majority of their "must-have" boxes. This focused approach not only streamlines the process but also builds trust and excitement along the way.

VENUE EXPECTATIONS VS. REALITY

Over the years, I've heard just about every dream, demand, and dilemma when it comes to choosing a wedding venue. It's one of the most important decisions a couple will make—it sets the tone, reflects their style, and often swallows a significant chunk of the budget. Yet sometimes, dreams and logistics don't quite see eye to eye.

Here are a few of my favorite quirky client moments that perfectly capture the dance between expectations and reality:

"I want the perfect venue! It must have a huge dance floor, floor-to-ceiling windows with breathtaking views, and a modern glam setting."

This usually comes from a bride with a tight budget and a guest count pushing 200. I gently explain, *"You can absolutely have a breathtaking venue, but with your current numbers, something's got to give. Reduce the guest list, and we can make the venue magic happen. Fewer guests, bigger wow factor."*

"We want onsite lodging for everyone—it's important since all our guests are from out of town. We're thinking something casual and fun, maybe a weekend getaway escape… but definitely not the Hill Country or a downtown hotel."

This one's always a puzzle. They crave convenience, ambiance, and exclusivity but dislike the two main categories Texas venues usually fall into. My go-to response? *"Sounds like you need a resort. Stay and play, all in one place. That way your guests can kick back, enjoy themselves, and you'll still get that all-weekend experience—minus the endless shuttles."*

"We want everything outdoors! We love nature, hiking, and the open air. We're thinking September for our Texas fall wedding—it'll be beautiful."

Cue the internal sigh. As much as I adore an outdoor wedding, I always have to bring couples back to reality when it comes to the Texas climate. *"You do realize that September is still summer here, right? Full sun, sweat-down-your-back, 95 degrees with humidity. Fall doesn't truly arrive until late October, and even then, it can surprise you. I love your outdoor vision—we just need to plan smart with shade, hydration, and a solid backup plan."*

The venue hunt brims with excitement, but it also demands clear priorities, honest conversations, and a healthy dose of realism. As a planner, my job isn't merely to book the pretty space—it's to guide couples through the maze of logistics and help align their dreams with real-world possibilities.

REAL WEDDING DIARIES

I want to share a collection of weddings that hold a special place in my heart—each one infused with the flavor and soul of San Antonio. While it may not be the first city that comes to mind for a destination wedding, San Antonio often surprises people with its charm, culture, and character. For many couples, it's more than just a beautiful backdrop—it's a place filled with meaning, memories, and a sense of home.

Sometimes it's sentimental, rooted in family ties, or simply the perfect midpoint between guests traveling from both coasts. No matter the reason, San Antonio's vibrant charm makes it an irresistible choice for tying the knot. And if you're getting married here, we believe you should go all out, offering guests an experience as colorful and lively as the city itself. From a welcome dinner aboard a river barge featuring upscale Mexican cuisine under the stars, to elegant events immersed in art and culture, San Antonio offers countless ways to celebrate in style.

One of my favorite venues for such celebrations is the McNay Art Museum—a local gem and Texas treasure. For those unfamiliar, the McNay is the first modern art museum in Texas and a stunning blend of history, architecture, and artistic beauty. The museum's story is as captivating as its collection. Ohio-born heiress Marion Koogler first came to San Antonio in 1918 after marrying Sergeant Don Denton McNay, who was stationed in Laredo. Tragically, Don passed away later that year during the Spanish flu pandemic. In 1926, Marion returned to San Antonio, remarried prominent ophthalmologist Donald T. Atkinson, and began collecting art, starting with Diego Rivera's *Delfina Flores*.

In 1927, the Atkinsons commissioned architects Atlee and Robert Ayres to design a 24-room Spanish Colonial-Revival mansion, which became the heart of the McNay. Marion's passion for art continued to grow, and by the time of her passing in 1950, she had amassed a collection of over 700 works, which she bequeathed along with her home, surrounding 25 acres of land, and an endowment to establish the museum.

The McNay opened in 1954 and has since expanded to include over 23,000 works spanning medieval art to modern American pieces, including the renowned Tobin Collection of Theatre Arts. The museum's architecture and galleries provide a stunning backdrop for weddings, with spaces like the intimate Octagon Room, serene courtyard, and grand Leeper Auditorium transforming any event into something unforgettable.

A SPRING FLING FIESTA AT THE MCNAY ART MUSEUM

Elizabeth and Michael's spring wedding at the McNay was one I'll always remember. Their color palette was a dreamy mix of pastels—soft pinks, sunny yellows, and delicate blues. The floral designs turned the museum into a romantic garden oasis. A highlight was Elizabeth and Michael's portraits on the museum's iconic Talavera-tiled staircase, a vibrant Southwestern detail that added beautiful color and cultural significance to their photos.

During cocktail hour, guests mingled in the enclosed garden, sipping margaritas while a lively mariachi band played. The tranquil setting, complete with a koi fish pond and historic fountain, felt like stepping back in time. Guests also enjoyed private access to the museum's galleries—a unique treat before moving into the

Octagon Room, where the seating chart, an indoor bar, and more artwork awaited.

Dinner and dancing took place in the Leeper Auditorium, adorned with spring blooms, while papel picado banners hung overhead in the dining space, catching the elegant lighting and adding a perfect touch of San Antonio flair. It was a night filled with laughter, dancing, and pure joy—a wedding that embraced the city's artistic beauty and cultural richness. the McNay Art Museum isn't just a venue—it's a canvas that helps couples create unforgettable memories. Elizabeth and Michael's spring fling fiesta proved that when you blend love, art, and a touch of San Antonio magic, the result is pure perfection.

A SOFTLY LIT LOVE STORY AT THE MCNAY

Some weddings shimmer not with grandeur, but with grace. Ashley and Thomas's celebration was one of those quietly dazzling evenings—full of intentional softness, delicate romance, and a color palette that felt like a whisper of spring: sage green, soft peach, pale blue, and creamy whites, with just enough warm gold to glow.

The couple exchanged vows offsite in a private ceremony, but by the time guests arrived to the McNay, the celebration was in full swing. The art galleries offered a slow, thoughtful beginning—guests strolled through the curated halls, admiring masterworks, enjoying the serene courtyard, and admiring the koi fish swimming in the sunlit fountain. It was especially sweet to see children pointing and counting aloud, giggling with each flash of orange and gold.

As guests made their way into the Octagon Room, they paused for selfies in sleek and modern welcome mirror—a trend that, in my opinion, is here to stay. Between sips of craft cocktails and bites of elegant hors d'oeuvres, everyone mingled beneath the soft glow of the candlelight. The room shimmered with soft gold and silver mercury glass vases—each filled with delicate florals that seemed to dance atop their stems: peach ranunculus, garden roses, sprigs of blue delphinium, and fluttery bits of blush astilbe.

When it was time to transition into the Leeper Auditorium for dinner, guests took their seats at long, linen-draped tables adorned with layered textures and flickering candlelight. Then came the cue: *"Don't Stop Me Now"* by Queen burst through the speakers, and the wedding party made their grand, joy-filled entrance. Energy was high. Smiles were contagious. And when Ashley and Thomas walked in as newly minted Mr. and Mrs., the whole room lit up.

They moved seamlessly into their first dance—graceful, sweet, and completely present with each other. The soft pastels of their color palette wrapped the evening in warmth, and there was a kind of peaceful merriment that settled over the room like a sigh of contentment.

After dinner and heartfelt toasts, we snuck in a group photo with all of the guests—one of my favorite moments, a literal snapshot of love and community. From there, the party kicked up: music, dancing, laughter echoing through the room. Ashley and Thomas ended the night beneath a tunnel of waving ribbon wands, surrounded by family, friends, and the hum of cheer. A perfect ending to a perfectly romantic evening—proof that some of the most unforgettable weddings are the ones that whisper instead of shout.

A TROPICAL ESCAPE IN THE ART MUSEUM

There are weddings that feel like art—and then there are weddings that happen *in* an art museum and still manage to steal the show.

Susan and Jaime's celebration at the McNay Art Museum was exactly that: part gallery soirée, part tropical daydream, and 100% unforgettable.

From the moment guests stepped onto the grounds, the setting transported them. Lush greenery framed every view, palm leaves swayed in the breeze, and bursts of Birds of Paradise in fiery oranges and golden tones made it feel more like a Caribbean escape than a museum in the heart of San Antonio. But this wasn't just vacation—it was elegance with purpose, designed down to the last detail.

The floral story was bold yet refined. Towering palms anchored the courtyard, while luxe low arrangements in gleaming gold vases dotted each cocktail table. Tropical textures mingled with modern minimalism, and even the breeze played along, rustling the leaves like nature's own string quartet.

The ceremony took place beneath the historic arches of the courtyard, framed by greenery vines and kissed by golden hour light. A live guitarist strummed "I Do (Cherish You)" as Susan made her entrance—poised, radiant, and confident—winding gracefully around the fountain and down the aisle to meet Jaime, who waited with awe and love written all over his face. Cocktail hour began with a literal pop: Susan and Jaime kicked things off with a dramatic champagne tower pour, bubbles cascading down coupe glasses like liquid gold.

As the sun dipped behind the museum walls and dinner was announced, guests flowed into Leeper Auditorium. Inside, tables shimmered with soft linens, gold flatware, and centerpieces that echoed the vibrancy of the courtyard—a harmonious blend of tropical romance and refined style. Maracas were placed at each setting, a playful touch that tied it all together with festive flair.

The newlyweds made their grand entrance hand-in-hand behind a full mariachi band playing Selena's "Bidi Bidi Bom Bom"—a joyful, high-energy moment that brought the room to life. With dinner, laughter, music, and heartfelt toasts, the evening unfolded like a celebration meant for the pages of a storybook.

When it came time to say goodnight, Susan and Jaime bid farewell through a tunnel of joyful guests, shaking maracas in celebration. The sound was electric, echoing through the courtyard as the couple danced their way into forever. Some weddings you remember for the details. Others, for the energy. This one? You *felt* it—heart and soul.

ANOTHER FAVORITE OF MINE IS HOTEL EMMA.

Originally a Brewery established in 1883, the building that is now Hotel Emma began its life as the Pearl Brewery, founded in 1883 as the J.B. Behloradsky Brewery. It was soon acquired and expanded by Otto Koehler, a German immigrant and savvy businessman. Under his leadership, it grew into one of the largest breweries in Texas by the early 20th century.

The hotel's name pays tribute to Emma Koehler, Otto's wife. After Otto's sudden and scandalous death in 1914 (he was reportedly shot by one of his mistresses, who also happened to be a nurse hired by Emma), Emma took over management of the brewery—a rare move for a woman at the time. She steered it successfully through Prohibition, diversifying the business by producing near beer, soda, and dry goods. Her leadership preserved jobs and sustained the company until the repeal of Prohibition.

The Pearl Brewery operated until 2001, when it closed its doors. In the early 2000s, the site was purchased by Silver Ventures, who began transforming it into the vibrant **Pearl District** you see today—filled with shops, restaurants, and cultural spaces.

Hotel Emma officially opened in **2015**, transforming the old brewhouse into a 146-room hotel. The design brilliantly preserves much of the industrial character—original fermenting tanks, vintage machinery, and brickwork remain intact—blended with warm, eclectic luxury and literary flair (yes, the hotel has its own library).

A VIOLET-TINGED FAIRYTALE AT HOTEL EMMA

Some weddings are simply stylish. Others are heartfelt. And then—every once in a while—you get one that feels like a movie. That was Michelle and Eduardo's wedding at Hotel Emma: a June celebration bursting with personality, purple petals, and pure joy.

Guests arrived to the historic hotel's shaded courtyard greeted by two things San Antonio summer calls for—signature cocktails and custom fan programs. The signature drink? An homage to their beloved dog, whose name adorned the cocktail menu and charmed every guest.

As friends and family took their seats beneath towering beams, bistro lights and the soft hum of ceiling fans, Michelle made her entrance—radiant in the golden-hour light, with her gown catching the breeze just right. She met Eduardo in front of the ivy cascaded bricked fountain surrounded by the Hotel Emma's rustic-meets-industrial charm. Vows were exchanged, tears were dabbed, and when they sealed it with a kiss, the string trio struck up, serenading the couple as they recessed down the aisle.

But this wasn't the kind of wedding where the energy peaked at "I do." After the ceremony, the courtyard transformed into a festive cocktail hour. The mariachi band played, weaving through clusters of mingling guests sipping more signature drinks and nibbling gourmet bites. Laughter echoed beneath twinkle lights, and kids (and grown-ups) couldn't resist the iconic library backdrop for a selfie or two.

As the music shifted and dinner was announced, the mariachi band led the newlyweds into the main reception space like royalty. Inside, the room was aglow. Lavender, plum, and violet blooms cascaded across long tables, tucked between glowing candlelight and elegant place settings. The floral story was lush and romantic—purple ranunculus, roses, and hydrangea dancing beside mercury glass votives and delicate floating candles. Every corner shimmered with intention.

Michelle and Eduardo's first dance played out like a scene from a classic romance. Glasses clinked, toasts were shared, and then came the sweet surprises: an ice cream sundae bar and late-night taco station that had guests swooning all over again. As the night came to a close, ribbon wands were passed out and guests lined up to cheer on the couple's grand exit. With streamers fluttering and cheers filling the night air, Michelle and Eduardo dashed off into forever—hand in hand, hearts full, and love glowing brighter than ever.

A SYMPHONY IN WHITE BREWING

Some weddings feel like poetry. Gabrielle and Abraham's wedding at Hotel Emma? It was a full symphony—elegant, timeless, and composed with the kind of grace that lingers in your memory.

From the moment guests arrived, they were swept into a world of refined beauty. The scene was set in the heart of San Antonio's most iconic hotel, where history meets luxury. But that evening, it was transformed—draped in white blooms, glowing candlelight, and the sounds of live music echoing through every corridor.

Gabrielle, radiant in a gown that felt both classic and couture, walked down the aisle to the soft notes of a string trio. The ceremony was held in the courtyard, where lush white florals bloomed in every direction—clouds of hydrangea, roses, and orchids spilling over urns and climbing up the altar arch. It was as if the whole garden had been dipped in moonlight.

Cocktail hour followed, with the trio continuing to play as guests sipped signature drinks and explored the charm of Hotel Emma's industrial elegance. Inside, The Elephant Cellar was nothing short of breathtaking. Tables were dressed in soft, ivory linens. Glass and gold candlesticks flickered between full, cascading arrangements of white blooms. The effect was serene, sophisticated, and utterly enchanting.

And then—those tanks. The original orange fermenting tanks stood proudly against the soft backdrop, becoming an unexpected design feature. Instead of hiding them, we celebrated them. Lit to glow with warmth, their bold hue popped beautifully amid the monochromatic palette, adding just the right touch of character and history to the evening.

As dinner began, the mariachi band entered, serenading guests between courses. The energy was vibrant yet graceful—a perfect pairing to the refined meal and champagne toasts. Gabrielle and Abraham stole soft glances across the candlelit table, the kind of love you don't need words to understand. But this celebration wasn't slowing down. After dinner, a full band took the stage and brought the party to life. Guests filled the dance floor, champagne glasses in hand, the joyful rhythm pulsing through the room. Every note, every detail, every carefully chosen element told a story of elegance, love, and music.

Gabrielle and Abraham's day was more than just beautiful—it was intentional, layered with personality, and composed like a favorite song. One you want to play again and again. And that's exactly how it felt.

WHEN IT RAINS, IT POURS… CRAFT BEER AND CHARM

It was 2017, and Hurricane Harvey had just made its stormy debut. While San Antonio was mostly spared the brunt of it, the corridor between here and Austin turned into a wet mess of flooded roads, last-minute changes, and one massive headache for a wedding planner.

The wedding was set at none other than Hotel Emma, San Antonio's historic brewery-turned-boutique hotel. With exposed brick walls, cast-iron beams, and chandeliers that dripped old-world glamour, the place oozed charm. It was the kind of venue where even the air feels curated—equal parts luxe, history, and just a hint of mesquite smoke from the Pearl.

Megan and John—true craft beer enthusiasts—had chosen a bold and vibrant palette of amber orange, marigold, forest green, and deep red. The florals were wild, earthy, and unforgettable, featuring real beer hops intertwined with orange ranunculus and golden roses. Their ceremony arch? A living IPA dream, filling the room with that crisp, citrusy hop aroma.

Then the calls started rolling in.

First up: hair and makeup.

"I'm not comfortable driving in this weather," she said.

Translation: "I'm out."

My response (sweet but steel):

"I totally understand, but since you're not rendering services, we'll need that deposit returned."

Cue radio silence.

Behind the scenes, I was going full MacGyver—scrambling to find a replacement artist on short notice. And bless the hair gods, I did. She showed up the next morning with hot tools blazing and a no-nonsense attitude that could part clouds. (The original stylist? Never heard from again.)

No time to breathe. The band was next.

Stranded in Austin. "We can't make it."

Oh no, no. Not today.

I calmly—okay, firmly—explained that this wasn't just another Saturday gig.

"This bride is chill, but her father has exactly one wedding wish: live music. He doesn't care about signature drinks or sweetheart tables. He wants you. How do we make this happen?" A long pause. Then: "We'll figure it out."

And they did. Hours later, they rolled in, soaked but triumphant. Dripping instruments, damp suits, and relieved faces. A minor miracle.

Now here's where Hotel Emma comes in like a hero in a vintage suit.

We were originally set for a charming courtyard ceremony, hops arch and all. But the weather had other plans. Without hesitation, Hotel Emma's staff jumped into action. They helped us pivot indoors to one of their exquisite private rooms, complete with exposed brick, vaulted ceilings, and just enough moody lighting to make it feel romantic rather than reactive.

They flipped the space with us, placed extra candles, adjusted the layout, and made sure guests stayed dry, comfortable, and none the wiser. The staff was calm, collaborative, and somehow made it all feel effortless. That's the Emma magic.

And the result? Pure ambiance. Candles glowed. The florals came alive against the brick. The whole place smelled faintly of hops and victory. The band played their hearts out. The food? Chef's kiss. Guests were raving about the aesthetic, the cocktails, the vibe.

And the father of the bride? Absolutely beaming. He found me before he left, pulled me aside, handed me a folded bill with a generous "thank you," and said: "You saved this day."

But the truth is, *we* saved it—me, the amazing vendor team, and the ever-gracious, ever-adaptable Hotel Emma. Because sometimes, wedding planning isn't about perfect weather or flawless timelines. It's about rolling with the storm, trusting your team, and finding beauty where you least expect it—even in the glow of hurricane-day candlelight beside a bouquet of beer hops.

LOVE IN THE TIME OF BLACKOUTS

Ah, electricity—one of those little luxuries you don't think much about… until it vanishes. Twice. Let's rewind to a beautiful summer evening wedding. The weather was warm with a slight breeze. The setting was a lovely chapel ceremony space attached to a country-style venue with an indoor reception hall. The couple? Utterly smitten with each other. The power? Well… let's talk about that.

The ceremony began right on time. Guests were seated, the DJ was softly playing instrumental music, and the bride was moments away from walking down the aisle. I was actually a guest at on this happy day, John's cousin was getting married! There we are smiling and soaking in the joy—when suddenly, silence. The music cut out mid-song, and there was a collective "huh?" from the guests. Yep—the power was out. One minute we were serenading the bride in; the next, it was dead air and confused glances. Luckily, Aunt Joan had the brilliant idea of everyone humming "Here Comes the Bride." Imagine the bride gliding down the aisle as her family and friends are supporting her in this moment.

We were determined to keep the celebration going despite the blackout. Lauren and Jason exchanged vows in a beautifully raw, unplugged moment that somehow felt even more romantic than we could have planned. Crisis mostly averted. But wait—the real fun was yet to come.

Fast forward to dinner, we get our food and visiting with family, when all of a sudden, the power blows again. Time to pivot. I grab Lauren and Jason; we cut the cake and move into toasts.

Now the reception was in full swing; guests were dancing, the DJ was crushing it, lights were flashing. And just as the beat dropped during the Cupid Shuffle... darkness. Complete blackout. Music gone. Dance floor frozen. One guy actually yelled, "What the hell?!"

Turns out, the venue's aging electrical system wasn't quite prepared for the record-breaking heat wave, the DJ's full setup, and a sea of twinkling lights all drawing power at once. Boom—transformer blew. Darkness fell like a curtain mid-scene.

Guests instinctively pulled out their phones, sweeping flashlight beams across the room like we were suddenly starring in a haunted house tour. The bar, bless them, stayed open. The DJ was sweating bullets, frantically checking cables and equipment while trying not to panic.

Meanwhile, I was sprinting through the venue in heels, channeling my inner power-line technician—a role I was wildly underqualified for. I hunted down the manager, reset breakers, and issued stern warnings to the kitchen not to plug in *anything else.*

After about fifteen suspenseful minutes, the power surged back to life. The music returned, the lights twinkled, and the crowd let out a collective cheer. We resumed the evening—slightly glistening, mildly rattled, but fully committed to the celebration. We laughed about it later, joking that their marriage began with an electrifying start—literally.

Cautionary Takeaway: Always ask your venue—especially older or rural ones—about its electrical capabilities. Can it support a DJ and catering simultaneously? Is there enough power for up lighting or a photo booth? And if there's no backup generator, make sure you know what your Plan B is. You don't want your first dance performed under flashlight mode.

THE BATHROOM COORDINATOR

Every wedding planner has crossed paths with this character: the in-house coordinator who insists, "Don't worry, I'll handle all of that on the wedding day!" But what she really means is, "I'll pop in to check the toilet paper situation and then vanish like a ghost at sunrise."

I remember this particular wedding vividly. A kindhearted bride brought me onboard for partial planning. She had already booked a charming venue that "included a day-of coordinator." She told me, "Jen, they said the coordinator will be handling things—so I think we're covered!"

I had a feeling this "coordinator" was going to be more of a light monitor meets bathroom patrol—and I wasn't wrong. Wedding day arrives. Everything is running smoothly on my end. I'm cueing vendors, wrangling groomsmen (a.k.a. adult toddlers in tuxedos), setting tables, fixing boutonnières. Meanwhile, the elusive in-house "coordinator" has been spotted...she gave me a tight smile when I arrived, pointed vaguely at a closet, and said, "Light dimmers and supplies are in there. I'll be around if you need me." Spoiler alert: she was not around.

As I'm juggling my own responsibilities along with the dozen tasks, she claimed she'd handle—linen placement, climate control, lighting cues—I can't help but notice something hilarious. The only times she reappears are to check the bathrooms, slipping in and out like a stealth operative. No joke—I catch glimpses of her darting into the women's room, armed with a 12-pack of Charmin, as if she's on a covert mission.

I started joking with the photographer: "Have you seen our phantom in-house coordinator?"

He goes, "You mean the one with the plunger?"

At one point, a groomsman actually asked me who that lady was because he thought she might be a janitor. I said, "Oh no, that's your 'venue coordinator.' But don't worry—I've got your timeline. She's got the toilet paper."

The event ended beautifully—because I was there. I stayed until the end, packed up the décor, hugged the family, and made sure every vendor was squared away. Meanwhile, the "coordinator" vanished again, probably off to fluff the hand towels.

BRIDAL BRILLIANCE When a venue offers an "included coordinator," ask what that actually means. Is she managing your timeline? Communicating with vendors? Or just refilling soap dispensers? There's no shame in bathroom checks—they are important! But let's not confuse facilities management with wedding coordination. There's a difference—and you deserve to know it.

THE DIY VENUE THAT THINKS YOU WORK THERE

There's a special place in my memory for venues that look stunning but sneak in a little surprise clause that basically says, "Oh, and by the way... you're also the moving crew."

You know the ones. The rental fee might be five, six, even seven thousand dollars, yet somehow that doesn't include the setup of the tables and chairs they provide. You're paying thousands just to use the space, but they expect your mom, your fiancé, your bridesmaids, or your wedding coordinator (hi, me!) to show up in sneakers and break a sweat hauling 60-pound banquet tables across the room.

I've arrived at these venues fully prepared to do what I was hired to do—plan and coordinate the event—only to find a warehouse of stacked chairs and an empty floor staring back at me. And suddenly, I'm part wedding coordinator, part professional furniture mover.

"Can't the venue staff handle this?" you ask. Apparently not. That'll be extra.

So, let me get this straight: you've built this gorgeous property, marketed it like a luxury wedding dream, and charge thousands just for people to walk through the door... but you can't hire three people at $20 an hour to handle setup and teardown?

No one wants to see family members in fancy outfits and dress shoes dragging folding chairs through a field—that's not the wedding vibe we're going for. I've watched groomsmen sweating through their rehearsal outfits, trying to make sense of a table chart. I've seen myself, dressed in all black, moving tables with one hand and texting a florist with the other, wondering if I should've just gone into accounting. It's not just frustrating—it's absurd.

HITCH-FREE HINT: Always ask your venue, "Who is responsible for setting up and breaking down tables and chairs?" If the answer is "you," either budget for a crew to help or keep shopping. Your wedding day should start with champagne toasts—not manual labor.

And venues? If you're reading this—for the love of all things beautiful and balanced—please include set up in the package. Your couples (and planners) will thank you.

ALL OUTDOOR EVENTS: A LOVE LETTER TO SHADE AND SANITY

Sure, I enjoy being outside too—on a breezy spring morning with zero bugs, 72° temps, and an iced coffee in hand. But planning an all-outdoor wedding in the Texas heat? In the middle of summer? With no backup plan? Hard pass.

Here's my professional advice: No. Just… no. Why would you do that to your family, your friends, or frankly, your sweat glands? Listen, just because you love hiking, camping, or hugging trees doesn't mean your grandma wants to watch your vows while being eaten alive by mosquitoes. Not everyone is built for the outdoors—especially not in full glam. And bless those poor guests—the ones who show up to your rustic ranch venue dressed to the nines, only to be met with uneven gravel, fire ants, and zero shade. I've watched women's stilettos sink into the grass like quicksand. I've seen grown men in three-piece suits melting into puddles before the cocktail hour even starts.

The only ones who seem truly happy at these events are the cows nearby and the one guy who showed up in boots and a fishing hat "because he knew better." Don't get me wrong—I love an outdoor moment. A short, sweet ceremony beneath grand oak trees? Gorgeous. A garden cocktail hour at golden light? Yes, please. But there needs to be a plan: shade, hydration, air circulation, and ideally, an indoor backup.

Therefore, if you're dead set on that "all-outdoor experience," do your guests a favor: keep the ceremony short, provide lots of fans, spray for bugs, rent the tent. And for heaven's sake—don't schedule it at 3 p.m. in August. Because your guests came to celebrate your love, not survive a wilderness challenge.

THE DREAMY YET PRACTICAL OUTDOOR WEDDING PLAN

Let's talk about outdoor weddings—the dream of golden sunsets, gentle breezes, and magical "I do's" under the open sky. But here's the thing: Texas heat and unexpected rainclouds have no respect for your vision board. Here's your guide to keeping your nature-inspired soirée gorgeous *and* guest-friendly.

First, if you're planning a ceremony outside, do yourself (and your guests) a favor and keep it breezy—literally. Aim for a start time after 6:00 PM, especially in late spring or summer, when the sun's a little lower and the temps are dropping. Pick a shady spot under mature trees, a pergola, or a custom-built arch. No trees? No problem. Rent a chic canopy or sail shades.

And skip metal chairs unless you want your guests sizzling like fajitas—opt for wooden chairs or cross-backs with light cushions instead. Consider cute umbrellas for chairs or pass out handheld parasols. It's all about comfort, darling. Think cold towels, pretty paper fans, and hydration stations. Don't forget the bugs—hide citronella torches in your décor or slip chic little bug-spray towelettes into welcome bags. No one wants mosquito bites as wedding favors.

Next up: cocktail hour. Picture garden-style lounging under umbrellas with soft seating and perhaps misting fans—yes, they exist and they're glorious. Keep the bar shaded, offer passed drinks, and have high-top tables so guests aren't wandering like lost cattle in search of shelter. And please, serve iced beverages. Cucumber water, frozen sangria pops—anything to avoid sweaty, cranky guests.

Now, the reception. Best case scenario? Move the party indoors once the sun goes down and the AC can save everyone's makeup. Still determined to stay outdoors? Rent a high-end tent—think sailcloth or clear-top depending on your vibe. Just make sure it comes with fans or portable AC units, solid flooring (so heels don't sink into the grass), and proper lighting. Bistro lights, chandeliers, up lighting—it all makes a huge difference in turning a tent into a twinkling wonderland.

Design-wise, keep your aesthetic cohesive. If you're aiming for elegant-rustic, blend natural textures like wood and rattan with refined details—draped fabrics, metallic accents, flickering candles. Stick to neutral tones plus one pop of color, like dusty blue, sage, or rose. Classy and timeless.

Finally—the all-important contingency plan, aka your sanity saver. Have a crystal-clear Plan B in writing. Know exactly where everything will move if rain crashes the party (or if the heat index dares to hit triple digits). Make sure you're clear on how quickly the flip happens, who's handling it, and what your vendor contracts say about emergencies. Because while outdoor weddings are magical, they're even better when you've got a solid backup plan in your pocket. So go ahead—chase that outdoor wedding dream. Just do it smart. Your guests, your hair, and your sanity will thank you.

GOLDEN RULES FOR OUTDOOR EVENTS

If you wouldn't personally attend your own event in a particular kind of weather, don't force your guests to either. Comfort equals fun, plain and simple. Happy guests linger longer, dance harder, and don't mutter complaints under their breath. Yes, you can absolutely have Pinterest-pretty without sacrificing practicality—and here's how.

First off, remember that Mother Nature doesn't care about your timeline. She's got her own plans, and they rarely involve sticking to your weather app. Always have a Plan B that's just as beautiful as your Plan A. Hope for sun, but be prepared for a downpour worthy of a drama series finale. Permits and power might sound boring, but they're non-negotiable. Want music, booze, and tents? Great—make sure you're legally allowed to have them. And for the love of everything floral, confirm there's enough power for your DJ, catering team, and twinkly lights. Generators might not be glamorous, but in a field, they're your BFFs.

Let's talk wind. Wind is not a vibe. It's the silent saboteur of lightweight décor, escort cards, and elaborate veils. Skip flimsy signage, use weighted bases, clothespins, or even command strips to secure your stuff. Unless you want your vows punctuated by a rogue table number cartwheeling across the lawn, plan accordingly.

Speaking of plans—sunset is not a lighting plan. It might be dreamy for photos, but once it's gone, you'll need actual lights—for pictures, for dancing, and for grandma trying to find the bathroom. Think bistro lights, lanterns, chandeliers in tents, or heck, all of the above.

Shoes matter more than you think. Grass, gravel, and sand are not heel-friendly. Give guests a heads-up on the terrain so they're not sacrificing their Manolo Blanhniks to the lawn gods. Offer heel protectors, flip-flop baskets, or even gentle encouragement that sneakers are totally chic.

Another critical point: always feed the vendors and fight the bugs. Vendors need shelter and meals, especially when they're busting their tails to make your day perfect. And don't underestimate mosquitoes or ants. Citronella candles and diffusers are nice, but bug bombs and barrier sprays are next-level lifesavers.

Don't assume the venue or property has what you need. Check whether they offer restrooms (and consider renting luxury portable ones if not), trash services, lighting, parking staff, and water access for your caterer or florist. Those details can make or break your day.

Hydration stations aren't just trendy—they're essential. Guests will turn cranky fast without water, especially during summer events. Keep things classy (and refreshing) with infused waters, lemonades, or even cute signature mocktails.

And here's a little-known secret: music doesn't always carry well outdoors. Wind messes with sound, and nobody wants to strain to hear your vows or miss the DJ's killer set. Make sure your sound crew has the right gear for open-air audio and that microphones are on standby for the ceremony. Finally, comfort equals classy. A bit of thoughtful planning—fans in summer, blankets in winter, shade, clear signage—goes a long way. Because at the end of the day, your guests won't remember every floral detail, but they'll absolutely remember how they felt.

TALES FROM THE TENT

A SOUTH TEXAS RANCH TALE

It was mid-September in South Texas, about an hour and a half from the coast—a prime time for hurricane season, but who checks the calendar? We pulled up to a private ranch that looked like it was straight out of a history book. Tall trees lined the gravel driveway, which crunched under our tires like an old-fashioned welcome. The house itself dated back to the mid-1800s, a patchwork of structures added over decades, filled with antique furniture and artwork that practically screamed haunted. I'm convinced those ghosts weren't thrilled about an outdoor wedding disturbing their peace.

Our "vendor break room" was an old servant's kitchen with a noisy screen door that sang with every open and close—the kind of door that transports you back to simpler times: squeak, slam, rattle. The humid South Texas air felt thick enough to swim through. Humidity was off the charts, and honestly, there was no real backup plan beyond "hope it doesn't rain."

A tent and dance floor were ready for the band and party, but dinner tables were spread out in the open beneath grand oak trees. The ceremony was set there too, surrounded by nature's beauty—and plenty of bugs. Giant ants, the size of small dogs and seemingly pumped up on steroids, were feasting on any exposed skin, including my poor, defenseless feet. By the end of the night, I had at least fifty bites—and that's just what I noticed.

Setup went smoothly, the décor looked picture-perfect, vendors were handling their tasks, and the wedding party was ready for the first look. The moment was classic: a slight breeze, tears, smiles—

pure magic. I hovered at a respectful distance, careful not to ruin the vibe. Then, crack!

A lightning bolt struck nearby, sharp and electric enough to make my skin tingle. I gave the photographer a polite signal to pause and get everyone inside. Rain began falling—just a drizzle at first—but enough to derail the pre-ceremony cocktail plans. Guests were supposed to enjoy an open bar outdoors; instead, they huddled under any cover they could find, trying to dodge both raindrops and bugs.

Despite the downpour, the ceremony carried on beautifully. Chairs were wiped down, smiles stayed bright, and vows were exchanged with trees whispering softly in the background.

The toasts arrived next. The videographer's light became a beacon for every bug within a five-mile radius. The white linen at the wedding party table quickly turned into a scene from Bugged Out: The Wedding Edition. Bridesmaids started panicking, yelling at me to fix it. *Fix it?* Unless I had a bug-swatting superhero cape hidden away, my options were limited. We switched off the light, grabbed rags, and did our best to clear the critters without spraying chemicals near the food. I probably lost a few "cool points" in that moment, but survival mode took over.

Eventually, the band hit the stage, and the dance floor sprang to life. Guests forgot about rain and bugs as they danced the night away under the big tent. I'm officially over ranch weddings in September. Beautiful? Certainly. Bug-infested, unpredictable, and sweaty? Also, yes. Every wedding has its stories—and this one was truly unforgettable.

THE RAIN-SOAKED MICRO WEDDING

It was supposed to be an intimate tented wedding—fewer than 75 guests, a gorgeous backyard, and the sweetest couple. Cue the romantic movie trailer music…The skies were overcast, yet spirits were high. The plan was tight, the décor was flawless, and the tent stood proudly like a white castle.

Just as the music cued for the ceremony to begin, the drizzle began. And no, not the poetic kind—it was just enough to dampen the chairs and cause a collective guest shuffle under the tent. Radios weren't working – because of course they weren't. I call my assistant, "Carissa, I'm on my way down with the bride in the golf cart. Get everyone in their seats—rain or not. It's happening."

We rolled with it. The ceremony was short and sweet; we snapped photos in under 15 minutes and pushed up the timeline. Boom! Cocktail hour, dinner, and even the cake-cutting were underway earlier than planned. But the party gods had other plans. Just as we opened the dance floor, the drizzle turned into a downpour. The once-gentle patter became thunderous applause from the sky. Water started creeping into the tent. We hung tarps around the DJ setup like I was protecting the crown jewels, but Mother Nature just laughed. The DJ gave me the look—you know the one.

Within minutes, the couple said, "Let's move the party into the house." Which sounds simple—until 50 guests try to shimmy into a living room that was never designed for it. Vendors were excused and made a run for it (literally), and I swear I heard a raccoon cheering us on as we escaped just before the roads flooded.

WE FORGOT A BATHROOM

It's one thing to forget extra napkins. It's quite another to forget toilets. Yes, it happened.

The client assumed the charming country house they rented would have enough bathrooms for 150 guests. Spoiler alert: it absolutely did not. The water pressure was pitiful, and the septic tank was older than the bride's vintage lace dress inspiration—and far less pretty.

By mid-cocktail hour, the line to the single working bathroom snaked through the hallway like a theme park ride. Guests shifted from foot to foot, politely pretending they weren't in gastrointestinal distress, while glancing around like meerkats hoping to spot another restroom.

Meanwhile, outside, it was pitch black. Guests were wielding their phone flashlights like torches, trying not to twist an ankle on gravel paths that felt longer and darker with each trip. Inside the tent, the lighting was warm and romantic. Outside? It was the abyss.

By the time I realized just how dire the bathroom situation had become, it was too late. A panicked call to a portable toilet company set a hero in motion—a lone driver who arrived two hours later, rolling in with a 4-stall sparkling clean portable restroom (with AC blasting). Bless that man.

But the damage was done. Rumor had it the groom's uncle disappeared behind the barn "to find a tree." A bridesmaid confessed she'd considered hopping into an SUV and driving to the nearest gas station. And one poor guest announced that if she missed the cake cutting, "so be it, my bladder takes priority."

Outdoor weddings require portable restrooms. Nice ones. With good lighting, actual handwashing stations, and preferably the faint scent of vanilla instead of that infamous chemical blue.

Also—bring lighting, and power, and backup everything. Because if you don't plan for it, your guests will… and trust me, it's not the kind of adventure anyone wants to remember.

WINTER WEDDINGS & WEATHER WARNINGS

It was February—arguably the coldest month in Texas—and someone, somewhere, decided it would be a brilliant idea to host a tent wedding. In a field. In the dead of winter.

To anyone considering the same, I have a revolutionary suggestion: rent a venue. With walls. And heat. But maybe I'm the fool for saying yes. The bride came to me in a panic, "I thought I could do it myself… but I need help!"

I hesitated. Conditions were… less than ideal: DIY décor, questionable rental logistics, catering mysteries, and the entire event set under a tent on a patch of dirt in the kind of cold that makes your face ache just stepping outside. But my heart got the best of me, and I said yes.

We were granted access to start setup the day before. The property manager assured us the tent was staked and secure, the sides would be down, and everything would be fine.

Until 7:00 AM on wedding day. The best man called me, voice trembling, "The tent site is a disaster." He texted a photo. Shattered glass. Tent collapsed. Total chaos.

Cue damage-control mode.

My assistant, Mikaela, and I raced to the scene. It looked like a tornado had thrown a tea party and stormed out halfway through.

Cold wind howled across the field, cutting through layers of jackets as if we were wearing tissue paper. Our breath came out in clouds. Fingers went numb within minutes. We started triaging: sweeping up shards of glass, salvaging rentals, wringing out soaked linens stiff from the cold.

A replacement tent crew arrived—thank goodness—but it was just four guys battling winds that could have doubled as slapstick comedy props. I nearly jumped in myself just to keep things moving. Between the staffing crew, tent crew and my team – it just wasn't enough. Weather conditions slowed us down tremendously.

The ceremony was scheduled for 4:00 PM. At 4:00 PM, we were still dragging heaters and tables into place, our cheeks stinging like sharp little needles pricking your skin. It was twenty degrees and gusty—the kind of bitter cold that makes your eyes water and your brain question every life choice. I had to make the call no planner ever wants to make: "We can't start on time."

Worst of all, I had to tell my bride.

It broke my heart to call her. I couldn't control the weather or the delays, but I still felt the weight of it all. Yet she was calm, understanding—graceful, even. She trusted me, and that meant everything.

By 5:00 PM, the ceremony finally began. The heaters buzzed and glowed like tiny beacons of hope. Guests huddled close, wrapped in coats, scarves, and sheer determination. And despite everything—the chaos, the cold, the impromptu fixes—the couple said "I do," and the tent glowed with laughter and love.

People left the party a bit early, bundled up in blankets and shuffling like penguins, but not before dancing, toasting, and finding warmth in each other. Later, the bride told me she couldn't believe how beautifully everything turned out—and how I managed to handle it all like a pro. She even wondered how on earth I do this for a living. Would I do it again? Let's just say… maybe in the spring.

PLANNING POINTERS: Tents are gorgeous, but they're not foolproof. Always account for weather, insects, electricity, lighting, portable AC or heating systems, and restroom access. If you're not hiring a seasoned planner for a tented event, at least consult one. These setups involve way more logistics than your typical venue.

THE PERFECT VENUE?

If I could craft the perfect wedding venue from all the pieces I've loved and experienced, it would be a seamless blend of nature's charm and sophisticated elegance—a space that feels both timeless and effortlessly inviting. The ideal wedding venue, in my mind, is one that harmoniously blends the comfort and luxury of an indoor setting with the beauty and freedom of the outdoors—a place where you're completely protected from the elements yet never feel confined.

Imagine a venue designed with a spectacular glass-walled room set right in the heart of a lush grove of trees. Floor-to-ceiling windows surround you on all sides, dissolving the boundary between inside and out. Sunlight filters through the leaves, casting dappled patterns across sleek white floors, while a soft breeze rustles the branches just beyond the glass. It's a sanctuary that feels both intimate and expansive, offering panoramic views of nature's beauty without sacrificing modern comforts like climate control and perfect acoustics. And the best part? Step through any set of glass doors, and you're instantly outside, free to wander into a serene courtyard, a hidden garden, or a winding forest path.

Whether couples want to host their ceremony under the open sky, enjoy cocktails surrounded by blooming flowers, or simply give guests a breath of fresh air between dances, this kind of venue offers endless possibilities—all while ensuring that rain, wind, or summer heat never threatens the celebration. It's a harmonious balance of practicality and enchantment—the perfect backdrop for a day as unforgettable as a wedding.

DREAMS & DANCE FLOOR WISHES

Closing my eyes, I can still vividly picture the day John and I toured our wedding venue—then known as Southwest School of Art (SSA). Searching for the perfect place to say "I do" is a whirlwind for any bride. What do you see? For me, it's hope, dreams, and a sprinkle of wonder.

It was a June afternoon in 2012. John pulled into the SSA parking lot in his sleek black Acura. I remember feeling relieved—it was free parking, a true downtown luxury. I wore a navy summer dress dotted with white polka dots, paired with burlap wedge heels and bright hot pink earrings. John looked effortlessly stylish in khaki shorts, tan Sperry loafers and a crisp white short-sleeve button-down. I always like to coordinate our looks for special days—just in case a moment calls for photos. "You'll thank me one day," I teased, knowing my love for selfies and capturing memories is legendary.

Hand in hand, we strolled across the lot. I glanced at John, catching the playful sparkle in his eyes—I'm pretty sure he already knew I'd set my heart on this place long before we arrived. We reached a stately iron gate that opened into a tranquil enclosed garden. A gentle fountain murmured nearby; its pool scattered with lazy fish.

Ferns and trees framed the space perfectly—not too dense, but lush enough to feel like a secret oasis.

I turned to him and asked, "Are you ready?"

He leaned in and said, "As long as you're smiling, I'm all in. Let's check it out."

As a bride, I can't speak for all grooms, but I've noticed many men live by the silent motto: "Yes, honey," "Whatever you want, dear," and "Happy wife, happy life." Honestly, I'm all for it.

If John's willing to let me have my princess moment, I'm embracing it wholeheartedly.

We drifted through the courtyard, past a small hallway leading to the restrooms, and into the stone plaza—the venue's heart. If I could go back, I'd do it all in one location. SSA offered several ceremony locations: a cozy nook with a canopy of trees, clusters of towering trees, and a charming white gazebo.

I sometimes wish we'd chosen the gazebo with a 4:00 pm ceremony, followed by cocktails, dinner, toasts, and dancing until 10:00 pm. That would've made everything flow beautifully. But there's no sense dwelling on what-ifs.

"Hello! You must be Jennifer and John!" The venue manager's voice snapped us back to the moment. Frank was a middle-aged man with decades of experience etched into his features. Slightly balding and wearing frameless glasses, he sported plaid button-down and black trousers. He knew this venue inside and out, sharing anecdotes and helpful tips as he guided us through our tour. We started at the guest entrance and ended in what they called the chapel—though for us, it would become our reception space.

John took my hand and twirled me on the dance floor. "Can you imagine dancing here after we're married?" I asked, breathless with joy.

He grinned, wrapping an arm around my waist. "Picture this: our first dance ends, and I steal a kiss right here."

I squealed and squeezed his hands. "I'd love that!"

"Frank, let's take care of the paperwork," John said with a smile and calm certainty.

We left SSA that day with a huge checkmark on our wedding to-do list—and, even more importantly, hearts soaring, knowing we were one step closer to our dream day.

History

The roots of the Southwest School of Art trace back to 1851, when the Ursuline nuns established the Ursuline Academy on a 10-acre campus near downtown San Antonio. This institution served as a Catholic convent and boarding school for girls, featuring a Gothic Revival chapel and a series of academic and residential buildings designed by François Giraud and French mason Jules Poinard. The campus was listed in the National Register of Historic Places in 1969.

In 1965, the Ursuline Academy vacated the property, and in 1971, the Southwest Craft Center purchased the campus at the invitation of the San Antonio Conservation Society. This acquisition marked the beginning of the institution's transformation into an art school. Under the leadership of President Paula Owen, who began her tenure in 1996, the institution expanded its offerings beyond traditional community classes.

In 1998, the name was changed to the Southwest School of Art and Craft, reflecting its broader mission. Throughout its history, the Southwest School of Art has played a pivotal role in fostering artistic talent and enriching the cultural landscape of San Antonio. Its commitment to high-quality arts education continues through its integration with UTSA, ensuring the legacy of the institution endures in the heart of the city.

ar
7

MINISTERS & MITZVAHS

When was the last time you attended a religious wedding ceremony? For me, these moments are some of the most profound—and occasionally theatrical—experiences in wedding planning. Over the years, I've had the privilege of witnessing countless ceremonies led by all kinds of religious figures: priests, church coordinators, pastors, ministers, rabbis—you name it. Each one brings their own unique traditions, style, and heart to the sacred day. Every ceremony has its own rhythm, customs, and expectations, and understanding those nuances is essential for any planner—or any couple—about to walk down the aisle.

SERMONS & SMILES

In my journey as a wedding planner, I've learned that no two religious leaders approach a wedding ceremony quite the same way. Titles, roles, and traditions vary—sometimes subtly, sometimes dramatically. That's why I'm sharing the insights I've gathered, so you can dive into ceremony planning with confidence and respect, armed with knowledge instead of uncertainty.

Take Christian ceremonies, for example. I've worked closely with many pastors and ministers over the years. People often use those titles interchangeably, but they're not exactly the same. Here's the scoop: all pastors are ministers, but not all ministers are pastors. A pastor typically leads a local congregation, providing spiritual care, preaching, teaching, counseling, and generally shepherding the flock. A minister, meanwhile, is a broader term that covers anyone serving in a religious leadership or spiritual role. Ministers may preach, teach, administer sacraments, or offer pastoral care—but they might not oversee a specific congregation the way a pastor does.

In my experience, pastors and ministers are some of the most pleasant people you'll ever work with. They're warm, respectful, and often happy to share a bit of small talk—or even a laugh—while waiting for the family to arrive for rehearsal or the big day. A fun bonus: many of them have that delightful Southern hospitality that makes everything feel just a little cozier.

Of course, occasionally a friend or family member steps in as officiant, and that's when things can get... interesting. Suddenly, I'm coaching them through ceremony etiquette, sharing templates, or even helping write the service to keep things on track. It's all part of the adventure.

Most Christian weddings include familiar elements, but the overall length and style of the ceremony really depend on which traditions—and how many personal touches—the couple decides to include.

Whether you're drawn to a traditional church wedding, a contemporary spiritual ceremony, or a beautiful interfaith blend, understanding the "holy ground" you're standing on can only deepen your experience—and add even more meaning to your special day.

Processional: Grandparents, Parents, Wedding Party, Bride + Father (traditionally)

Welcome & Opening Prayer: The pastor welcomes guests and opens with prayer.

Scripture Readings: Focused on love, faith, and unity.

Message or Homily: Short sermon or talk about the meaning of marriage in a Christian context.

Exchange of Vows: Traditional or personalized

Exchange of Rings: A symbol of eternal love and commitment.

Unity Ritual *(optional):* Unity candle, sand or cross ceremony

Pronouncement of Marriage: The pastor declares the couple husband and wife.

The Kiss (cue the officiant side stepping before this moment)

Recessional: The couple exits joyfully, usually to music and applause!

Marriage License Signing: Often done during or right after the ceremony.

THE CASE OF THE MISSING MINISTER

It was the day after Thanksgiving—a crisp, beautiful afternoon at a stunning Hill Country venue. The air buzzed with a mix of excitement and nerves as everyone prepared for the ceremony. The officiant was a minister and a longtime family friend of at least a decade—a middle-aged gentleman with a solid reputation. We'd connected over the phone, confirmed all the details via email, and, being the over-communicator that I am, I even sent him a text the day before. He replied, so I felt confident everything was in place.

Fast forward to thirty minutes before the ceremony—and there was still no sign of the minister. The question echoed in every direction: "Jennifer, where's the officiant?" I frantically called him, but he didn't answer. The tension in the room was palpable. The family, both confused and anxious, started calling and texting their "friend." As the clock ticked down, I offered to reach out to other officiants I knew, but before I could, another family friend stepped in and contacted someone he knew who might be available.

An hour behind schedule, just as anxiety was peaking, we finally saw them—rushing into the chapel side by side: the original minister and the backup officiant. Shock and frustration were written all over everyone's faces, but we kept calm and carried on. It turned out the minister had simply misread the start time—a costly mistake in the world of weddings. I was seething beneath the surface but forced myself to focus, quickly getting him mic'd and in position. Thankfully, the ceremony ended up being short and sweet. We even caught the last rays of a breathtaking sunset for the bride and groom's portraits, salvaging a bit of magic from the day.

FIRST TIME JITTERS

There's a special kind of charm when a close friend offers to officiate your wedding. It's personal, heartfelt, and incredibly meaningful — after all, it's someone who knows and loves you. But let's be honest: friends don't always come with professional officiating experience, and that's okay! You can't expect them to nail every moment like a seasoned pro.

I visited with one such friend-officiant a few times before the big day. It was his very first wedding ceremony, and let's just say, the nerves were real. I coached him during rehearsal, offering gentle tips and encouragement. By the end, he seemed far more confident than during our initial phone call. I even sent him a custom script the couple had crafted to help keep him on track.

Of course, that didn't stop a few comedic moments from unfolding. Once the bride returned to her spot at the altar, he completely forgot to say, "You may be seated." So, there we were — my assistant and I — standing at the back, subtly motioning and smiling like flight attendants trying to wordlessly convey, "Everyone, please take your seats!" It was hilarious, lighthearted, and honestly, perfectly human.

You know that classic moment, "You may now kiss the bride"? Well, our friend forgot to step aside for the big moment. And there he stood, practically photobombing the couple's first kiss, peeking right between the bride and groom! Cue the adorable, slightly awkward photo that's sure to become a cherished family memory for years to come. This whole experience reminded me that while professionals bring polish and precision, sometimes those imperfect, genuine moments are what make a wedding truly memorable. If you're thinking of having a friend officiate, just be prepared to coach them, share a few laughs, and embrace the wonderfully unpredictable magic of the day.

MAZEL TOV MOMENTS

A Rabbi is a Jewish religious leader, teacher, or scholar who is trained in Jewish law, tradition, and sacred texts. The word *rabbi* comes from the Hebrew term *ravi*, meaning "my teacher" or "my master." It reflects the rabbi's role as a guide and educator in matters of Jewish faith and practice.

Orthodox Judaism adheres strictly to traditional Jewish law and practices, emphasizing continuity with the past. Conservative Judaism balances respect for tradition with a willingness to adapt Jewish law and customs to the modern world. Reform Judaism is the most liberal, encouraging personal autonomy in religious observance and embracing modern values and societal changes.

My experience with rabbis has been mostly positive and enriching. I still remember my very first solo wedding coordination gig—an elegant affair at a stunning museum. The ceremony was a Conservative Jewish wedding, a tradition I knew little about at the time. Naturally, I dove into research to prepare, but no amount of reading could fully equip me for the real-life whirlwind that unfolded.

One of the most memorable moments came just minutes before the ceremony was set to begin. I was tasked with ensuring the wine for the Kiddush blessing was ready. Simple enough, right? Except in my frantic rush through the museum's catering setup, I realized we had wine—but no corkscrew. The clock was ticking, guests were starting to take their seats, and there I was, scrambling to locate a corkscrew in a place that was definitely not a home kitchen. It was a classic "panic and problem-solve on the fly" scenario, leaving my heart pounding and adrenaline surging. Eventually, I found one—thank goodness—and the wine was opened just in time for the blessing.

That experience taught me so much about the nuances and rituals of a Jewish wedding—from the significance of the wine and the breaking of the glass to the beautiful blessings and traditions that shape the day. It was an eye-opening crash course in cultural sensitivity and quick thinking, reminding me that beyond timelines and logistics, every wedding embodies deep meaning and unique customs.

Since then, working with rabbis has been a wonderful part of my planning journey—filled with respect, warmth, and the joy of witnessing traditions passed down through generations. Each ceremony is a chance to learn, appreciate, and celebrate something truly special. A Jewish wedding is rich with meaningful traditions that symbolize love, commitment, and the joining of two families.

Before the wedding, the couple signs a legal and religious document called the **ketubah**. This marriage contract traditionally outlines the husband's responsibilities toward his wife, including financial and emotional support. While its legal weight varies depending on civil law and denomination, the ketubah remains a significant and formal part of the wedding, often beautifully designed and displayed.

The **chuppah** is a canopy under which the couple stands during the wedding ceremony. It symbolizes the new home they are building together and the shelter and protection they will offer one another. A chuppah typically stands on four poles and is open on all sides, representing hospitality and openness to community and family.

During the ceremony, the couple or the officiant recites blessings, including the **Sheva Brachot** (Seven Blessings). These blessings express joy, gratitude, and hopes for a joyful, fruitful marriage.

Depending on tradition, the blessings might be recited by the rabbi, family members, or friends, sometimes shared among honored guests.

The groom places a ring on the bride's finger, and in many modern ceremonies, the bride also places a ring on the groom's finger. Traditionally, the groom's ring is plain, without gemstones or breaks in the band, symbolizing an unbroken and eternal bond.

At the end of the ceremony, the groom—or sometimes both partners—breaks a glass by stepping on it. This tradition has several interpretations: it commemorates the destruction of the Temple in Jerusalem, serves as a reminder of sorrow even in joyful moments, and symbolizes the fragile nature of life and relationships. Afterward, guests shout "**Mazel Tov!**" meaning "Congratulations" or "Good luck!"

Following the ceremony, the couple spends a few moments alone in a private room, known as **yichud**. This special time allows them to reflect on their new status as a married couple and enjoy a brief moment of privacy after the public celebration. The festivities then continue with a meal and dancing. A popular tradition is the **hora**, where guests lift the couple on chairs and dance in energetic circles around them, symbolizing communal support and collective joy.

The **Sheva Brachot** (Seven Blessings) are not only recited during the wedding ceremony but may also be repeated during festive meals throughout the seven days following the wedding, reflecting ongoing bliss and celebration of the couple's new life together.

The Groom's Aliyah: In some communities, the groom is called to the Torah for an aliyah (the honor of reciting blessings over the Torah reading). This may happen on the Shabbat before the wedding or at another service surrounding the event.

Badeken (Bride's Veiling): Some couples observe the tradition of the groom lowering a veil over the bride's face before the ceremony begins. This symbolizes modesty and the groom's commitment to care for and protect his bride.

If you haven't previously interacted with someone from the Orthodox Jewish community, especially Orthodox men, there are a few customs that might be new to you. One important point to understand: it's customary for Orthodox men to refrain from physical contact, including handshakes, with women who are not immediate family. This practice arises from religious principles surrounding modesty and respect, serving as a way to maintain personal boundaries in accordance with Jewish law. While it may feel unfamiliar at first, it's not intended to be rude or dismissive—it's simply a deeply rooted expression of faith.

As a planner, I've learned to navigate these moments with sensitivity and respect. A warm smile and a thoughtful verbal greeting go a long way, and honoring each person's beliefs contributes to the beauty of a truly inclusive celebration.

ORTHODOX TRADITIONS & TRIAL BY FIRE

Fast forward a few years from my first Jewish wedding, and I found myself coordinating a beautiful Orthodox Jewish wedding in 2015. This time, I was extra excited—I knew a bit more, had a few more weddings under my belt, and was eager to soak up the richness of Orthodox tradition up close. And let me tell you, it was an incredible experience. The customs, the symbolism, the reverence—it was deeply moving to witness a ceremony so steeped in history and meaning.

Of course, my humility as a planner was kept firmly in check.

As I greeted the Rabbi—a dignified, older gentleman—I instinctively extended my hand. Rookie move. He glanced at my outstretched hand, then met my eyes with an expression somewhere between polite surprise and gentle disapproval. Without uttering a word, he simply shook his head and tucked his hands behind his back. I froze for a split second, silently facepalming, then quickly pivoted.

Trying to regain my footing, I offered, "Shall we confirm the essentials together?" attempting to smooth things over.

The Rabbi raised a knowing eyebrow and calmly began rattling off the essentials with ritual precision: "Challah, kosher white wine, kiddush cups, the glass…"

I nodded along like an eager bobblehead, pretending I wasn't mildly spiraling inside, and jogged—gracefully, or so I hoped—back to the chuppah to check every item. Kiddush cup? Check. The glass for the breaking ceremony? Check. White wine? Check… or so I thought. I suddenly realized the bottle was still sealed tight. Cue me racing off to hunt down a corkscrew, heart pounding.

Meanwhile, guests were already seated, watching me as if I were the opening act before the main event. I could practically feel their eyes burning into the back of my head.

Then came the whispers:

"Who is this coordinator?"

"Oh, the wine is sealed?"

"She doesn't know what she's doing…"

Each comment felt like a tiny paper cut to my professional pride. But there was no time to wallow—I had a wedding to run. Naturally, I straightened my shoulders, took a deep breath, and carried on with gathering the family, lining up the processional, and prepping the ceremony start, as if I hadn't just endured an emotional roller coaster.

It's a memory I hold onto not with bitterness, but as a powerful lesson. In the years since, I've had the joy of coordinating many more Jewish weddings—often beautifully blended with other faiths, or more spiritual than strictly religious. Each one teaches me something new. That 2015 wedding taught me about grace under pressure, cultural sensitivity, and the quiet power of humility. And now? I never show up to a Jewish wedding—Orthodox or otherwise—without a solid checklist, corkscrew, a respectful smile, and a genuine appreciation for every tradition, even the ones that keep me on my toes.

WHEN A RABBI AND A PASTOR WALK INTO A CHURCH

One of the most memorable ceremonies I've ever had the honor of coordinating was a beautifully blended interfaith wedding between a Jewish bride and a Christian groom. Both were deeply rooted in their faiths and wanted their wedding day to reflect each of their traditions equally, harmoniously, and meaningfully. What unfolded was one of the most touching and intentional ceremonies I've witnessed.

This wasn't your typical 20-minute vow exchange. It was a rich celebration, artfully weaving together Christian and Jewish customs—Scripture readings, blessings, prayers, and symbolic rituals from both faiths—all as their families looked on with pride and emotion.

The officiants, each representing one side of the couple's heritage, were true stars of the day. The Rabbi, a Reform leader with a warm presence and a wonderful sense of humor, balanced reverence with levity, putting everyone at ease with his gentle tone and thoughtful insights. The Pastor was equally gracious and heartfelt, delivering sincere words with calm composure. There was genuine mutual respect between them as they passed the mic, seamlessly guiding the couple through their sacred traditions.

This was no plug-and-play ceremony. Everything was customized for the couple, down to the minute. A string trio and pianist provided the soundtrack, so timing was critical. The music had to flow perfectly with transitions, leaving no room for guesswork. That's why the rehearsal was absolutely essential. With so many moving parts—two officiants, multiple readers, musical cues, and unique rituals—precision was key.

At rehearsal, we walked through every detail. From the placement of the chuppah to the pouring of the wine, nothing was left to chance. When the wedding day arrived, all the preparation paid off. The ceremony unfolded beautifully. The air was rich with emotion, respect, delight—and a perfect dash of humor. The blending of traditions wasn't merely symbolic; it was deeply heartfelt and intentional. You could feel the love radiating not only between the couple but in how their families embraced each other's traditions with open hearts. It reminded me that love doesn't live in just one tradition, language, or way of celebrating—it thrives in those extraordinary moments when people come together to honor and respect one another's stories.

MASS & MATRIMONY

A Catholic priest is an ordained minister in the Roman Catholic Church who's received the sacrament of Holy Orders. He's the one who celebrates Mass, hears confessions, performs baptisms, marriages, and funerals, and offers spiritual guidance to his community. You'll often see him preaching or teaching the faith, whether in a church, school, or even as a chaplain somewhere special. While "priest" describes his official role, most people simply call him "Father." It's a respectful, affectionate title that reflects his role as a spiritual guide and caretaker for his parish.

As a wedding planner based in San Antonio, Texas—just a few hours from the southern border—I've come to deeply appreciate the richness and cultural significance of Catholic traditions woven into many of the weddings I help coordinate. With more than 120 Catholic churches in the San Antonio area alone as of 2025, it's no surprise that Catholic ceremonies remain a meaningful and popular choice for so many couples.

I hold immense respect for all faiths and believe every person has the right to worship in the way that feels true to them. My job as a planner isn't to judge—it's to support my couples and help them navigate the unique intricacies of their chosen path to the altar. That said, Catholic weddings, particularly within large dioceses, come with their own set of personalities and processes that any planner should be prepared for.

Let's talk about one notorious aspect: the elusive parish office. Some Catholic churches operate in what I jokingly call "ghost mode." Emails go unanswered, voicemails vanish into the ether, and the entire communication process can feel like chasing shadows. Occasionally, I finally reach someone—a kind assistant or administrator—who assures me everything is in place with the calm confidence of someone who's done this a thousand times. While I appreciate that reassurance, what they often don't provide is equally important: names, on-site contacts, or any clear point of accountability.

"We have you scheduled for a Friday rehearsal at 4:00 p.m., and your ceremony is Saturday at 3:00 p.m. Doors open at 2:00 p.m., and you must be completely cleared out by 4:00 p.m. for Mass," I'm told.

"Great," I reply. "And who will be there to help coordinate—someone I can meet ahead of time?"

The answer: "Oh, that's usually the janitor. He'll unlock the doors and turn on the lights. The priest arrives about 30 minutes before the ceremony. Someone will set the altar."

"Someone."

It's enough to make any planner's eye twitch. In these cases, you're operating almost entirely on blind faith—and while that might be spiritually appropriate, it doesn't always translate into logistical peace of mind. That's why I strongly encourage every Catholic bride to hire a professional planner or at least a day-of coordinator. Not only for emotional support but for practical guidance—especially during the rehearsal, where planners often end up leading the charge in the absence of official church personnel.

If you're unfamiliar with Catholic wedding practices—like the Rite of Marriage within a Mass versus outside of one, the placement of the unity candle, or the significance of the offertory—it's essential to do your homework. Understanding these elements allows you to serve your couple with confidence and grace, even when no one else seems to be "on duty."

Because at the end of the day, the sacrament will happen. The vows will be exchanged. And if all else fails, your clipboard, calm demeanor, and ability to roll with the punches will ensure the bride walks down that aisle feeling supported, seen, and ready to say "I do."

Couples preparing for a Catholic wedding are typically expected to fulfill several requirements beforehand. They'll attend marriage preparation sessions (often called "Pre-Cana"), guided by a priest or deacon, to discuss topics like faith, communication, and family planning. In some parishes, the upcoming marriage is even announced publicly during Mass for several weeks, inviting both blessings and any potential objections. Couples are also often encouraged to go to confession before the wedding to enter into marriage in a state of grace.

Structure of a Nuptial Mass
A Catholic wedding ceremony, known as a Nuptial Mass when it includes the Eucharist, follows a beautiful and meaningful structure. It begins with the **Procession**, which is similar to other weddings but can vary depending on cultural traditions. For instance, in some cultures, both parents walk the bride down the aisle.

Next comes the **Liturgy of the Word**, featuring readings from the Bible, a Responsorial Psalm, and a Gospel reading, all chosen to reflect the sacredness of marriage. Following this, the **Homily** is delivered by the priest, offering a sermon focused on the significance of marriage and the couple's journey ahead.

During the **Exchange of Vows**, the couple declares their intent and recites their vows in front of the priest and gathered guests. This is followed by the **Blessing and Exchange of Rings**, where the rings are blessed and exchanged as symbols of eternal love and fidelity. The **Prayer of the Faithful** includes prayers offered for the couple, their families, and the world.

If the couple has chosen to include a full Mass, the ceremony continues with the **Liturgy of the Eucharist**, where Communion is offered—though traditionally, only Catholics may receive it.

After Communion comes the **Nuptial Blessing**, a special prayer asking for unity, fidelity, and fruitfulness in the couple's marriage. Finally, the ceremony concludes with the **Sign of Peace**, Communion (if included), and the **Final Blessing and Recessional**, as the newlyweds exit to begin their life together.

Several meaningful traditions may be incorporated into a Catholic wedding. The **Unity Candle**, though optional, symbolizes the joining of two lives into one. In Hispanic and Filipino weddings, the **Veil and Cord Ceremony** is common, where a veil is draped over the couple, and a cord or lasso is placed in a figure-eight around them, representing unity and eternity.

Another tradition is the **Arras**, where the groom presents the bride with 13 coins as a symbol of his commitment to support their household and to share blessings. Many couples also include a moment of **Marian Devotion**, offering flowers to a statue of the Virgin Mary and asking for her blessing on their marriage.

To be married in a Catholic ceremony, there are a few essential requirements. At least one person in the couple must be Catholic, and the wedding must take place in a Catholic church unless a special dispensation is granted. Additionally, both individuals must be free to marry—meaning neither is previously married without having received an annulment.

FAITH, FORMALITIES & A FEW CURVEBALLS

It was a sweltering summer afternoon in downtown—the kind of day when the pavement radiates heat, and the air vibrates with a slow, heavy stillness. I'd arrived early, determined to beat the traffic, secure a parking spot, and steal a moment to breathe before the Catholic wedding rehearsal began. Just a week prior, I'd spoken with Maria, the church's office assistant, who had assured me, *"You're all set for the 4:00 p.m. rehearsal. Everything will be ready for you."*

Armed with that confidence and my trusty file, I approached the grand, historic church, its stone façade glowing gold in the late-afternoon sun. I reached for the ornate iron handle—and found it locked. Hmm. *Maybe just this door?* I hustled to the side entrance. Also locked. Every door I tried was bolted shut.

Panic didn't come crashing in all at once; it started as a whisper in the back of my mind, then quickly swelled into a mental scream. I rummaged through my bag with slightly trembling hands, found my phone, and dialed the only number I had for the church office. Straight to voicemail. Desperate, I scanned the bulletin board taped to the glass entryway—gift shop number? No answer. Maintenance? Still no answer. I fired off a polite but urgent email to Maria:

Dear Church Office,

I'm here for the 4:00 p.m. wedding rehearsal that was confirmed by phone. Unfortunately, the church is locked and no one seems to be answering the contact numbers listed. Can someone please assist?

Warm regards,

Jennifer Craft

I hit send and whispered a silent prayer—equal parts desperation and irony.

Just then, the bride's family began arriving. I greeted them warmly, keeping my professional smile steady even as my stomach twisted in knots. "Oh, they usually open the doors right at the scheduled time," I said lightly, trying to smooth over the awkwardness with small talk and calm reassurance.

Then—click. A lock turned, and the heavy doors creaked open. Relief washed over me like a cool breeze on that blistering day. A young man appeared, possibly the priest's assistant—perhaps an altar server or sacristan. He didn't offer any explanation, just gave a curt nod, flipped on the lights, and gestured for us to come inside.

We filed into the pews, expecting a cool sanctuary. Instead, the heat hit us like a wall. The A/C clearly hadn't been switched on in time, and guests fanned themselves desperately with ceremony programs. The mother of the bride leaned over to whisper furiously to her sister, then shot me a look sharp enough to curl ribbons.

The rehearsal itself was over in a flash—blink, and you'd miss it. The church staff member—whose name I never managed to catch—rushed through the run-through with vague directions and vanished as quickly as he'd appeared. Before he left, I managed to corner him—right in front of the family—to confirm that the A/C would indeed be on for the wedding. *"Yes, yes. It'll be nice and cool tomorrow. No worries,"* he promised.

Thankfully, he kept his word. The wedding day arrived, and everything was seamless. The doors were open, the lights glowed, the musicians played beautifully, and the priest was exactly where he needed to be. The sanctuary was blessedly cool, and the bride and groom were radiant. Guests beamed at me with gratitude rather than concern.

THE ONE WITH FATHER DARK CLOUD

It was a bitterly cold February afternoon—the kind of chill that cuts through your coat and stings your fingertips. As I reached for the towering, castle-like arched chapel doors, a gust of wind whipped behind me, flinging them open so forcefully they slammed against the stone wall with a thunderous BANG. Heads turned. Conversations stopped mid-sentence.

"Oops," I thought. Well done, Jen. Way to make an entrance.

I flashed a smile, quickly smoothed my coat, and scanned the room. Familiar faces came into view—ah, there was the mother of the bride. I made a beeline for her.

"Helen, hello! So great to see you—happy rehearsal day! How's everyone feeling?"

"Oh, just splendid," she replied warmly. "Margaret is on cloud nine and can't wait to see you!"

As I mingled with the family and wedding party, I felt a shift in the air. A presence—unmistakably cold—approached.

"You must be Jennifer," he said flatly.

I extended my hand. "Yes, and you must be Father—"

"Here are the rules," he interrupted. "I don't need you to do anything except line up the wedding party ten minutes before the ceremony. When the bell rings, we begin. I walk out first, then the wedding party follows. That's it."

I blinked. "Understood. Just to clarify—what about the parents and grandparents? I have them processing first."

"I don't care about them," he replied without missing a beat. "If you want them to walk, they can do so before the bell rings."

Charming.

To everyone else, he wore a polite smile and played the part of a gracious officiant. But to me and my assistant, it was crystal clear—he didn't want an outsider anywhere near his sacred domain. The territorial vibe radiated off him like incense on Easter Sunday.

Come wedding day, though, everything went off without a hitch. Two can play that game, after all. I decided to counter his icy demeanor with extra warmth and professionalism—sugar-sweet smiles, gracious compliments, and a voice as smooth as velvet. Passive-aggressive? Maybe. Effective? Absolutely.

Now, let's talk about the unsung heroes—or sometimes the villains—of Catholic weddings: the Church Coordinators. Or, as I affectionately call them, "The Church Ladies." From one planner to another, here's what you need to know. These women—well-intentioned, devout, and sometimes delightfully quirky—come in all varieties. And oh, how those varieties matter.

THE CHURCH LADY SPECTRUM

The Non-Existent: You know her. Or rather, you don't—because she's never there. Emails go unanswered, voicemails are left in limbo, and if you're lucky, you might get a vague verbal confirmation from someone's cousin's secretary that the church is booked. No name. No point of contact. No phone number. You're left relying on faith—and not just the spiritual kind. Doors may or may not open. Lights may or may not turn on. This is my least favorite type because, as planners, we thrive on details, and this leaves us completely in the dark—literally and figuratively.

The Friendly Neighborhood: Bless her. She's as sweet as can be, maybe a little forgetful, probably volunteers part-time—but she welcomes you with open arms and lets you do your job. She's cheerful, warm, and genuinely happy to be there. Doors open early. You're free to fetch your bride, line up the family, and help everyone feel calm and cared for. This, friends, is our favorite type of church lady. Keep her in your prayers—and in your contacts list.

The Controlling: And then there's the enforcer. She rules the church with an iron clipboard and isn't afraid to remind you that you're in her house. You might be told—plainly—that your services aren't needed. If you insist on being there, you're permitted only to line up the wedding party—nothing more. Start five minutes late, and you'll feel her wrath. But you smile, nod, and press on—because the bride needs peace, not power struggles.

WHEN THE DRESS RIPPED AND TIME SLIPPED

It's a bustling Saturday afternoon, and I'm downtown co-coordinating a ceremony at a historic Catholic church—partnered, of course, with one of our more… shall we say, particular church coordinators. You know the type: she's got the rulebook memorized, and a stopwatch practically ticking in her head.

With twenty minutes until ceremony start time, I glance toward the groom's waiting room in the back right corner of the sanctuary. All the guys—groom, groomsmen, and close family—are present and accounted for. I exhale, just a little.

I smile, walk over, and greet everyone warmly, expertly pinning boutonnieres and handing out wrist corsages like a seasoned florist in heels. Things are moving smoothly on the gentlemen's side. But as I step outside to check for the ladies… nothing. No bridal party in sight. The clock is ticking.

I pull out my phone and call the maid of honor, keeping my voice light and stress-free.

"Hi! Hope you're all doing great! Quick check-in—any idea when you'll be here? Our sweet church coordinator's keeping a close eye on the clock, as always!"

There's a pause, then a slightly frazzled voice responds, "Yes, yes—we're coming! But Jana's dress ripped as we were leaving the hotel. We're stitching it up right now!"

"Oh no! Okay—thanks for letting me know," I say, forcing a cheerful tone while gripping my clipboard a little tighter. "Just so you know, I have a full sewing kit here if you need it when you arrive. I'll be waiting out front. Keep the bride calm—we'll handle it."

Ten minutes before start time, the black SUV finally pulls up. Jana and her girls pile out, breathless but beaming. I greet them with open arms and a smile that says, *We're fine. Everything's fine.*

"Okay, ladies, let's head to the back and get lined up!" I say enthusiastically. But instead of falling into place, they insisted on putting their bags in the bridal suite and making a quick restroom run. I offered to take their bags, but they shooed me off, determined to freshen up first.

Looking back, I probably should've staged a polite intervention—snatched those bags, promised them they looked fabulous, and hustled everyone into place. But in the moment? I chose peace over a bridal mutiny. I chose to protect the bride's energy and keep her happy, calm, and centered. Rushing her just didn't feel right—so I didn't.

We started the ceremony ten minutes late, but everyone was seated, the music played, and the couple said "I do" well before the start of Mass. From where I stood, it was mission accomplished: they made it down the aisle, the guests were delighted, and the sacred moment came together beautifully.

But… the church coordinator didn't quite see it that way.

The following week, I received a pointed email expressing disappointment in our tardiness and my "lack of adherence" to church timing protocol. Ouch. I read it, digested it, and—truthfully—laughed a little. In the end, what mattered most was that my couple was beaming, the guests stayed happily oblivious, and love filled every corner of the room.

As planners, we meticulously craft wedding day itineraries and share them in advance—rehearsals, welcome dinners, ceremony details, photo sessions—all documented and distributed. Still, we can't force clients to enforce them. I do my best: I send reminders, create schedules, and give pop quizzes at rehearsal to ensure everyone knows where they need to be the next day.

If there's one thing I've learned, it's this: weddings aren't only about timelines and tradition. They're about people—and we're all just doing our best to walk the aisle together. Every Catholic wedding is a beautiful blend of tradition, devotion, and family. But behind the scenes, it's a delicate dance between protocol and personalities. And sometimes, dodging dark clouds simply requires a little sunshine—and a whole lot of finesse.

SARIS & SACRED FIRE

In a Hindu wedding, the ceremony is typically led by a **pandit**, or Hindu priest, who guides the couple through the sacred rituals and recites Sanskrit mantras that invoke blessings for their marriage. The pandit plays a crucial role in explaining the significance of each tradition, from the lighting of the holy fire to the seven steps the couple takes together around it. While "pandit" is the most common term, you might also hear titles like **pujari** or **acharya**, depending on regional customs or the officiant's level of religious training. Whether simple or elaborate, the ceremony is deeply spiritual, with the pandit ensuring that each ritual is performed correctly to honor both tradition and divine blessings.

Hindu weddings are full of vibrant and meaningful traditions that unfold across several days, each one adding its own layer of joy and symbolism to the celebration. It all often begins with the **Roka** or **Rokna** ceremony, which is essentially the engagement. This is when the families formally announce the union, exchange gifts, and offer blessings, officially sealing the match.

Next comes the **Haldi ceremony**, usually held separately for the bride and groom a day or two before the wedding. Here, family members apply a turmeric paste to the couple's skin, believed to purify them and give their skin a beautiful glow. Then there's the **Mehendi ceremony**, a lively gathering where the bride's hands and feet are adorned with intricate henna designs. This event is filled with singing, dancing, and plenty of festive food.

Another highlight is the **Sangeet**, a joyful evening of music and dance performances where friends and family come together to celebrate the merging of two families. Before the main wedding day, many families also perform a **Ganesh Puja** or **Graha Shanti** ceremony, offering prayers to Lord Ganesha to remove obstacles and bless the upcoming nuptials.

On the wedding day itself, the festivities kick off with the **Baraat**, the groom's grand procession. He might arrive on a horse, elephant, or even a car, surrounded by dancing friends and family. Upon arrival, the bride's family greets him warmly, often with a **milni**, an exchange of garlands and greetings.

During the ceremony, the bride and groom exchange floral garlands in the **Jaimala** or **Varmala**, symbolizing mutual acceptance and respect. The heart of the wedding takes place under a beautifully decorated canopy called the **mandap**.

HERE, SIGNIFICANT RITUALS UNFOLD:

Kanyadaan, where the bride's parents formally give their daughter to the groom.

Mangalpheras or **Saptapadi**: the couple takes seven sacred steps around the holy fire, each step representing a vow for their new life together.

Havan, where offerings are made into the sacred fire to sanctify the marriage.

Sindoor Daan: the groom applies vermillion powder (sindoor) in the bride's hair parting.

Mangalsutra, a sacred necklace tied around the bride's neck as a symbol of marriage.

And sometimes, there's even an exchange of rings, though this is optional in certain communities.

Together, these customs create a wedding that's not just a union of two people, but a beautiful tapestry of family, culture, and timeless traditions.

After the ceremony, the emotional **Vidaai** marks the bride's farewell from her parental home. It is a deeply symbolic moment of transition as she steps into a new chapter with her husband and his family. Upon arriving at her new home, the bride is welcomed in the **Griha Pravesh** ceremony, where she may gently kick a pot of rice and step into a tray of vermillion-tinted water, symbolizing prosperity and her auspicious arrival.

A **wedding reception** typically follows, hosted by the groom's family as a grand celebration of the newlyweds, often complete with a formal dinner, dancing, and toasts.

Depending on the region, additional rituals may be observed. In Punjabi weddings, for instance, you might find the **Chooda and Kalire** ceremony where the bride is adorned with red bangles and gold or silver trinkets for good fortune. A **Satyanarayan Katha** may also be held—a prayer service asking for continued blessings and joy. In recent years, many couples have embraced interfaith or intercultural elements, adapting these beautiful traditions in meaningful and personalized ways.

SACRED STEPS, SHARED HEARTS

It was all about Holly and Ashwin—a couple whose story feels like a love song that kept playing in the background until they finally heard it. They'd known each other most of their lives, mainly as friends, but somewhere along the way, life gently turned that friendship into love. And oh, did it blossom! It was as if they were made for one another, two souls perfectly in sync.

I've met many amazing couples over the years, but Holly and Ashwin truly left an imprint on my heart. Their energy radiated positivity and kindness, wrapping everyone around them in a sense of warmth and joy. And it wasn't just them—it was her whole family. I'd been blessed enough to plan her sister Hannah's wedding a few years before, and Hannah and Pierce were also one-of-a-kind, heart-warming souls who made you believe in love and the beauty of simply living. The way these families love each other, and love life, is genuinely awe-inspiring.

This is why my only experience with an Indian wedding ceremony so far remains etched in my memory. It was for a beautiful and intimate Hindu celebration, honoring Ashwin's heritage in a thoughtful, condensed format. Though Holly is Christian, they chose to hold a traditional Hindu ceremony on the first wedding day, with Christian elements woven into the second day's celebration. It was a perfect reflection of two worlds coming together, a testament to how love bridges every distance.

What unfolded was a 45-minute spiritual experience, vibrant and moving, filled with color and meaning. The guest list was just right—around 60 close family and friends—creating a cozy, inviting atmosphere. The colors chosen for the day were exquisite: deep reds, shimmering golds, soft peach, and crisp white that wove through every detail, from lush florals and draping fabrics to the couple's stunning attire.

One of the most unforgettable moments came with Ashwin's entrance. Surrounded by his friends and wedding party, he paraded into the ceremony to the lively sounds of live instruments. It was an explosion of music and joy, setting a festive tone from the very start. The energy was utterly contagious, sweeping everyone into the celebration.

Though I wasn't deeply familiar with Hindu ceremonies at the time, I found the rituals beautifully rich with symbolism, even in their abbreviated form. The ceremony still carried the essence of tradition—honoring the sacred bond of marriage, the significance of family, and the spiritual joining of two souls. Holly and Ashwin sat under a beautifully adorned mandap, Ashwin beaming with pride and joy, and Holly glowing with quiet grace. Her family, though new to these customs, was filled with genuine curiosity and openhearted joy, embracing every moment with respect and wonder.

One of my favorite memories from the day came just after the ceremony. We invited guests to form a soft aisle and handed them handfuls of rose petals in every imaginable shade. As Holly and Ashwin made their recessional walk, they were showered in a cascade of petals—cheers echoing around them, the petals floating through the air like confetti caught in a gentle breeze. It was spontaneous, vibrant, and so deeply sweet—a perfect reflection of their love story.

That day taught me something I'll always carry with me: even a shortened version of a deeply traditional ceremony can hold tremendous meaning. With thoughtful intention and respect, it becomes more than just a wedding—it's a celebration of love, heritage, family, and the merging of two worlds. I walked away from Holly and Ashwin's ceremony feeling humbled and incredibly grateful to witness such a sincere, joyful expression of culture and love. To this day, it remains one of the most soul-filling experiences I've had the privilege to coordinate.

PLANNER INSIGHT: Always greet every interaction with a warm smile and a flexible, professional attitude. Whether you're collaborating with church ladies, priests, rabbis, pastors, or any other officiants, a dose of kindness and a bucketful of patience can work wonders in keeping things running smoothly. And remember—show up prepared. Keep a detailed order of ceremony in your bag of tricks so you're crystal clear on what's happening when.

Will there be a unity table?
Is wine or bread involved?
How long is the ceremony slated to run?

These nuggets of info are gold when coordinating with caterers and bartenders to keep the day flowing seamlessly. Communication is your secret weapon, especially with musicians. Whether it's discreet radios, subtle hand signals, or well-timed eyebrow raises, ensure the music cues hit right on target with the ceremony's rhythm.

Your mission as a planner is simple but mighty: keep the family, the wedding party, and—most importantly—the couple calm, happy, and blissfully unaware of any behind-the-scenes chaos. And, of course, get them down that aisle and married without a hitch!

BRIDAL BRILLIANCE: If your package doesn't already include day-of coordination at the ceremony venue, think about adding it. Trust me—there's nothing quite like having a seasoned planner or coordinator by your side during those quiet, butterflies-in-the-stomach moments before the walk down the aisle.

Having someone there to share a laugh, soothe your jitters, and gently steer the day back on track if things go sideways is priceless. Open, honest communication with your planner about every single ceremony detail is essential. The more your planner knows, the more magic they can work—and the smoother, happier, and more joy-filled your day will be. After all, the goal is to let you savor every second of your "I dos" and focus on the only thing that truly matters: the start of your beautiful new chapter together.

8

PLANNING ON PIXELS & PAPER

My wedding dress had finally found me—a moment that felt both thrilling and surreal. The church and reception venue were secured, and suddenly, the wedding felt undeniably real. The dream was no longer just a fantasy; it was taking shape right before my eyes.

Naturally, the next question was: what comes after that? Wedding experts love to preach about their tried-and-true timelines, each task marching along in perfect order like a well-rehearsed bridal party. Me? I barreled ahead like a runaway bouquet toss.

In the whirlwind of excitement and pressure, I transformed into a relentless box-checker, tackling every task with almost comedic urgency. Did I truly savor the experience? Maybe a little—but mostly, I was tangled in the chaos of trying to do everything flawlessly and fast. By day, I sat in my tiny office cubicle, diligently handling grown-up responsibilities. The moment I was alone, though, my brain switched to Wedding Channel mode, plotting, organizing, and obsessing over every little detail. It was a dizzying blur of vision boards, color swatches, and enough spreadsheets to terrify a CPA. Looking back, I can admit the process was far from the calm, blissful journey I'd imagined—unless you count spontaneous crying fits over napkin folds as blissful.

This chapter is about moving beyond the checklist. It's about leaning into the rhythm of planning, leaving room for genuine joy, and transforming those meticulous plans into real-life moments that are as beautiful—and sometimes as hilariously unexpected—as the love story behind them.

Date ✔ Church ✔ Reception venue ✔ Dress & veil ✔

Let's start with the most important thing: **why.** Before you dive headfirst into colors, flowers, or deciding whether Aunt May sits near the dance floor, take a breath and remember what this day is truly about: celebrating love, unity, and your story. Keeping that perspective makes everything feel a lot more meaningful—and a whole lot less like you're starring in your own personal reality show.

Shift your focus to **setting realistic timelines.** Avoid the last-minute chaos by pacing yourself. Make a simple checklist, spread out the tasks, and tackle the big-ticket items first—think venue, dress, and vendors. Trust me, you don't want to cram it all into one frantic week unless you enjoy living dangerously.

Delegate, delegate, delegate. Repeat after me: "I do not have to do everything myself." Hand off tasks to your partner, bridal party, family, friends, or better yet bring in a professional planner. Give them clear instructions and let them shine. It's a whole lot more fun when you're not single-handedly hauling the entire wedding like a bedazzled pack mule.

Make it fun! Turn vendor meetings into date nights. Sip wine while stuffing invitations. Create a playlist for planning sessions.

Celebrate the mini victories—because finding the perfect napkin color is worthy of a toast.

Don't forget to **capture the moments before the wedding.** Take selfies at cake tastings. Record your face when you find "the dress." Snap videos of you debating linen colors. These behind-the-scenes bits often become your most cherished memories.

And please, **stay flexible.** Things will absolutely go off-script. The cake might show up late. The flower girl might refuse to walk (or worse, decide to freestyle her own interpretive dance). Laugh it off instead of stressing out—it'll keep you in the joyful zone.

Remember to **create space for mental breaks.** You're allowed to have wedding-free weekends. Take breaks. Go see a movie. Protect your peace. The wedding will still be there when you return, refreshed and ready.

Focus on **your style, not just what's trendy.** Pinterest and TikTok are wonderful—but also overwhelming. Choose what feels right for *you two*, not just what looks fabulous in a viral video.

Here's a sweet one: **write little love notes.** To your partner. To your future self. To your bridesmaids. Even to your grandma. It'll keep your heart rooted in gratitude and romance—and that's what this whole wedding thing is really about.

Finally, **celebrate everything.** Booked a DJ? Celebrate. Found the perfect shoes? Celebrate. Managed to complete the seating chart without flipping a table? Pop some champagne, friend—you've earned it.

PIXELS

Next up on my wedding planning adventure was building our wedding website. Now, let me set the scene: this was back before today's sleek, trendy platforms were the norm. Zola, Minted, and all those ultra-chic options weren't exactly mainstream yet, so we went with The Knot because it was simple and easy to navigate. The process was pretty straightforward: pick a theme, upload some photos, fill in all the crucial details, add a registry page, toss in a song request form, accommodations, and directions—and voila, website complete. We kept it basic but effective, and honestly, it got the job done.

Now, people often ask me, **"What should I include on my wedding website?"** Oh, I *love* this question because wedding websites can either be a lifesaver or a rabbit hole of endless extras. The key is to focus on the essentials that keep your guests informed and excited—without making you want to throw your laptop out the window.

So, here's my take on the must-haves, plus a few fun extras if you're feeling fancy:

First things first, **date and time.** Yes, it's obvious, but you'd be surprised how often people forget to list the actual day of the week. Save your guests from frantic calendar-checking by writing something like, "Saturday, October 4th, 2025, at 4:30 PM."

Next, **locations.** Include the ceremony and reception addresses—and please, for the love of Google, link those maps. Also, add any parking info or shuttle details if Aunt May is likely to panic about city traffic.

RSVP details are a biggie. Online RSVPs are the way to go (no one wants to chase paper cards anymore). Make sure you include the RSVP deadline and meal choices if guests have options—because nobody wants to play "Guess What's on My Plate" in formalwear.

Then, there's the **dress code.** Be clear and specific— "semi-formal," "beachy cocktail," or "black tie optional." Also mention things like outdoor terrain or expected temperatures if you don't want your guests sinking into grass or shivering through dinner.

Don't forget **travel and accommodations.** Share hotel blocks with booking links and deadlines, a range of nearby options for different budgets, the closest airport, and any transportation details that might keep out-of-towners from getting lost in the great unknown.

Add a **short and sweet love story.** Keep it breezy—how you met, the engagement story, a few fun facts. A paragraph or two max—no one wants a novel here.

And of course, **registry info.** Include links to your registry (or registries). If you're opting for honeymoon funds or requesting "no gifts," just say it kindly and graciously.

Honeymoon Fund Example: "As we begin our journey together, we're planning a honeymoon to create memories that will last a lifetime. In lieu of traditional gifts, we invite you to help us make this dream come true."

No Gifts Example: "We are so grateful for your love and support. We kindly request no gifts as your presence is the greatest gift of all."

Donations to Charity Example: "Your presence is the greatest gift of all. In lieu of other gifts, we kindly invite you to support [Charity Name], a cause close to our hearts."

Now, if you're in the mood to go big, here are some **nice-to-have extras**:

Wedding Party Bios. Quick intros to your bridesmaids and groomsmen (bonus points for humor).

Weekend Schedule. Handy for events beyond the ceremony, like welcome parties or brunch.

FAQs. Think: "Can I bring a plus-one?" "Is this kid-friendly?" "Are sequins encouraged?"

Photo Gallery. Engagement pics or favorite memories of you two being adorable.

Song Requests. Let guests submit their must-dance-to songs—because there's always that cousin who insists on The Wobble.

Stick to the fundamentals, let your personalities shine, and don't forget—this is about clarity for your guests, not extra stress for you.

PAPER

Woo-hoo! You've accomplished a major milestone. Now that you've gathered the essential details for your guests, it's time to share some "literature" that points your friends and family to your wedding website.

Remember, save-the-dates don't need to be elaborate—they just need to be clear and concise. Their purpose is simply to give guests enough information to mark their calendars for your big day, without diving into all the fine details that will come later with the formal invitation.

SAVE THE DATE 101: THE MUST-KNOWS

Your Names: First names are enough (unless you're super formal).

The Wedding Date: Make it clear and easy to read (Month, Day, Year)

Location (City + State or Destination): You don't need the exact venue yet, just where guests are heading. Example: Napa Valley, California or Houston, Texas

Formal Invitation to Follow: A simple line so people know more info is coming. Example: Formal invitation to follow or Details to come

Wedding Website: Especially useful for destination weddings or if you want to share hotel info early. Keep the URL simple and short or opt for a QR code.

When to send Save-the-Dates:
   6-8 months before (domestic)
   8-12 months before (destination)

When it comes to save-the-dates, there are a few optional add-ons you might consider, like including a favorite engagement photo or a cute graphic, sharing your wedding hashtag if you have one, or showcasing your wedding logo or monogram for a personal touch. However, there are also some details you should leave out at this stage. Avoid including RSVP information, registry details, or the exact timeline and venue address—those specifics will come later with your formal invitations.

If you'd like to include a professional engagement photo on your save-the-date, it's wise to adjust your planning timeline so that you book your photographer around the same time you shop for your dress. Photo turnaround times can vary depending on the studio, with editing often taking anywhere from two to six weeks.

INVITATION ETIQUETTE

When it comes to your wedding invitations, the details you include—and the tone you set—play a significant role in giving your guests a preview of what to expect on your big day. Invitations aren't just a notice; they're the first impression of your celebration.

Who's Hosting: Traditionally, this is where you acknowledge who is inviting guests—parents, the couple, or both.

The Names: Your full names, spelled exactly how you want them presented. The Bride's name is always listed first.

The Date & Time: Clear and precise; spell out the day, date, month, and year.

The Venue: Name and full address, plus any details like whether it's indoors or outdoors.

Reception Info: Whether it's immediately following the ceremony or at a different location.

RSVP Details: How and when you want guests to respond—include a deadline and preferred method (mail, online, etc.).

Dress Code: Optional, but helpful if you have something specific in mind (formal, cocktail, casual, cultural attire).

Your invitations should totally reflect the vibe of your wedding.

Throwing a black-tie affair? Go classic with fancy fonts, formal wording, and phrases like "request the honor of your presence."

Planning a laid-back beach bash? Feel free to get playful and creative with the design and wording—flip-flops optional.

There's no one-size-fits-all rule here. Your invitations should feel like *you* as a couple, whether that's ultra-elegant, modern minimalist, delightfully whimsical, or somewhere in between. The goal is simple: keep things clear and friendly, get your guests excited, and make sure they know exactly where to show up—and when.

A little planning goes a long way. Give yourself plenty of time for editing and shipping when ordering your paper goods like save-the-dates and invitations. If your wedding date is sneaking up faster than you'd like, digital save-the-dates can be a lifesaver. They land in inboxes instantly and save you from sprinting to the post office in a panic.

For printed invites, start early to allow time for proofing, printing, and mailing. The last thing you want is your invites arriving fashionably late.

Set your RSVP deadline for about 3-4 weeks before the big day so you'll have plenty of time to finalize seating charts, meal counts, and vendor details—without completely losing your mind. Aim to send out your invitations 10-12 weeks ahead of the wedding. And if your date lands near a holiday or during peak travel seasons—like summer vacations or the holiday hustle—consider mailing them even earlier to give your guests extra time to plan.

Good ol' snail mail has become a bit unpredictable these days. Delays, lost envelopes—it happens. Build in some extra time for your save-the-dates and invitations to make it safely to your guests, and consider sending digital reminders just in case.

Let's explore the world of digital invitations—because plenty of modern couples are going that route, and honestly, they're kind of fantastic. Digital invites are sleek, fast, and eco-friendly (Mother Nature sends her thanks). No waiting on the mail, no postage drama, and no worrying about an invitation getting lost between the sofa cushions of your cousin's house.

You can customize them beautifully, complete with animations, music, or whimsical artwork that show off your personalities. Plus, managing RSVPs becomes a breeze—your guests can just click a button, and you'll instantly know who's coming, what entrée they want, and whether they're bringing an unexpected plus-one.

They're also a lifesaver if you're on a tight timeline. Need to let people know your date ASAP? Digital invitations can be in everyone's inboxes the same day you design them. Talk about efficiency! If you're looking for something modern, budget-friendly, and a little less paper pile–inducing, digital invitations might just be your new best friend.

9

LIGHTS, CAMERA, I DO

Before you can schedule that dreamy engagement session in a golden field or atop a city rooftop at sunset, there's one very important task: book the right photographer. Makes sense, right?

Yet this isn't simply about hiring someone with a fancy camera and a slick website. It's about finding a person who sees the world—and your love story—the way you do.

Are you drawn to traditional, posed portraits? Obsessed with candid, unfiltered moments where raw emotion shines through? Maybe you're swooning over those dreamy, film-style images with nostalgic tones and soft focus. Whether your heart beats for light and airy, bold and editorial, or dark and moody vibes, there's a photographer out there for you. As your planner, I consider it my mission to help you find "the one"—photographically speaking, of course.

I'll admit, this is one of my favorite parts of the job: getting to know you, your partner, your story, your style—and then playing matchmaker with a photographer who fits both your aesthetic and your vibe. When I nail it on the first try? Picture a full-blown happy dance happening in my head. Possibly even a celebratory high five with myself.

Here's the real secret: the photographer you choose will be right there with you during some of the most personal, emotional, and joy-filled moments of your wedding day. You have to genuinely like this person—not just their rates or their Instagram grid, but them. Their personality, presence, and energy. Because no fancy filter or trendy preset can hide an awkward vibe between a couple and their photographer. Comfort breeds confidence, and confidence leads to incredible photos.

Let's talk editing style for a moment—that matters more than you might think.

Traditional / Classic: Posed, timeless, and formal. Think family portraits, staged couple shots.

Photojournalistic / Documentary: Candid, in-the-moment storytelling. Captures events as they happen with minimal interference.

Editorial: Magazine-style, dramatic, and fashion-forward. Focused on composition, lighting, and elegance.

Fine Art: Artistic, romantic, and creatives. Emphasizes mood, beauty, and visual storytelling.

Lifestyle: Natural and lightly posed. Candid, but slightly curated to look relaxed and authentic.

Cinematic: Moody lighting, dramatic tones, often inspired by film. May use wide shots, storytelling angles, and rich edits.

Dark and Moody: Uses shadows, muted colors, and deep contrast. Emotional and intimate, often with a rustic or dramatic vibe.

Light and Airy: Bright, pastel tones with soft highlights. Dreamy, romantic, and whimsical.

Black and White: Timeless and emotional. Focuses on contrast, texture, and moment.

Vintage / Film-Inspired: Mimics old film photography with grain and soft color palettes. Evokes nostalgia.

Once you've nailed down the photography style that makes your heart skip a beat—whether it's light and ethereal, moody and romantic, or crisp and classic—share that vision with your planner. It's the best way for us to pair you with photographers whose work aligns with your aesthetic and whose vibe meshes perfectly with yours.

Try to keep your shortlist to no more than two photographers. I know, that might sound restrictive, but trust me—it saves you from drowning in decision fatigue and endless late-night Instagram stalking. A focused approach helps you make a confident choice without spiraling into a sea of second-guessing. Trust your gut—and your planner's expertise!

Review Full Galleries: Instagram might look glamorous, but remember—it's only the highlight reel. Ask to see full wedding albums so you can check for consistency. Can your photographer handle all lighting situations and capture both big moments and little details without missing a beat?

Prioritize Personality Fit: This one's huge. You're going to spend your entire wedding day with your photographer practically attached to your hip. It's essential that you mesh well. Do they make you feel comfortable? Are they calm, professional, and upbeat? The vibe matters because comfort equals better photos—and less awkward smiles.

NOT JUST PRETTY PICTURES: THE LOWDOWN ON PHOTOGRAPHY PACKAGES

Hours of Coverage: Think about what moments you want documented. Are you planning a first look, private vows, or dreaming of pretty flat-lay shots with all your wedding details?

Pro tip: Aim for a package that allows your lead shooter to start coverage about 1.5 to 2 hours before the ceremony. That way, they can capture:

- Getting ready moments—hair, makeup, and all those little details
- Flat lays of invites, rings, accessories
- Candid moments with your bridal party (because who doesn't love adorable PJ pics and bubbly toasts?)
- First looks (which, by the way, can be with anyone—partner, bridesmaids, parents, grandparents, or even your fur baby)
- Pre-ceremony portraits of the couple, family, and wedding party. I'm all for accomplishing all formal photos beforehand so you can spend cocktail hour laughing with your guests instead of feeling stuck in a photo shoot. Sure, portraits are important, but genuine smiles and laughter are even better when captured in real time during your celebration.

Consider Starting Coverage Earlier If:
- You're getting ready at a different location from your ceremony
- You want full hair and makeup coverage
- You're planning emotional first looks, letters, or gift exchanges
- You've got a big bridal party or elaborate flat lay plans

Or Start Coverage Later If:
- Getting-ready shots aren't your thing
- You'd rather allocate more time for the reception coverage
- You're having a short ceremony or an elopement-style day

LITTLE DETAILS, BIG IMPACT

Second Shooter Availability: I can't recommend this enough. A second shooter means more coverage, more variety, and an overall fuller story of your day. While your main photographer focuses on capturing the big moments—like your vows or first kiss—the second shooter is catching candid laughs, tears, and all those sweet behind-the-scenes glimpses.

It's like giving your photographer a sidekick to ensure nothing gets missed—and it saves them from having to sprint across the venue like a marathon runner in formal wear. The result? More peace of mind, more perspectives, and a richer visual narrative.

Engagement Session Inclusion: Don't be shy about customizing your package. Many photographers include engagement sessions, but if a friend already snapped those shots for you, no problem! Talk to your planner about swapping it for something else.

You could trade the engagement shoot for bridal portraits, a post-wedding family session, or even an extra hour of coverage on your wedding day. Or, if you simply don't need it, see if removing it can lower your cost. Remember—packages aren't set in stone, and most photographers are open to crafting something that suits your unique plans. A little flexibility can go a long way toward making the most of your investment.

Check Reviews & Referrals: Dive into reviews to see how others felt about working with them. Look for praise about their professionalism, responsiveness, and how they handled any surprises that cropped up during wedding days.

Consider the Photographer, Not Just the Portfolio: One last tip—if your chosen photography studio employs multiple shooters, confirm exactly who will be capturing your big day. You deserve to know whose lens you'll be looking into when you say "I do."

PLANNER INSIGHT: We're basically matchmakers, connecting our clients with the creative pros who'll bring their wedding dreams to life. When it comes to photographers, we're balancing both style and budget. Keep in mind that photography packages are rarely one-size-fits-all, so don't hesitate to ask about customizing. Maybe your bride doesn't need printed albums or giant canvas art for the living room wall. Perhaps she only wants coverage for the ceremony and reception, plus digital access to all those gorgeous shots.

That said, always approach these conversations with kindness and respect for our talented photographer friends. Their artistry is worth every penny, and pricing reflects years of experience and creative dedication. If you need to discuss adjustments, do it with grace and professionalism. The ultimate goal? A joyful couple and a photographer who feels valued, appreciated, and fairly compensated. It's a win-win—and that's the picture-perfect ending we're all aiming for.

CHOOSING A VIDEOGRAPHER - PRESS PLAY ON FOREVER

Match Their Style to Your Vision: Look at their portfolio and ask yourself: does it feel like you? Common styles include:
- Cinematic (dramatic, polished)
- Documentary (real-time storytelling)
- Highlight Reel (short, emotional recap)
- Vintage / Super 8 (nostalgic, artsy)

Watch Full Videos, Not Just Highlights: A 2-minute Instagram clip might be amazing — but ask to see full wedding films to assess pacing, audio quality, and emotional flow.

Ask About Audio: Clean, clear sound makes a huge difference. Ensure they mic the ceremony, vows, and speeches properly.

Understand What's Included: Get clarity on:
- How many hours of coverage
- How many videographers
- Turnaround time
- Length of final video
- Raw footage availability

Check for Vibe Compatibility: This person will be with you all day — you want someone who feels professional, calming, and respectful.

Read Reviews and Ask for Referrals: Past clients often mention things like responsiveness, attitude, and how well they worked with the photographer.

Make Sure They Work Well with Your Photographer: They'll share space, so it's best if they can collaborate rather than compete.

BRIDE-TO-BE SECRETS: GUT FEELINGS + PLANNER MAGIC:

When it comes to choosing your photo and video team, follow your instincts—and lean on the expertise of your planner. We truly do have your best interest at heart. If you've opted for a day-of coordinator rather than full-service planning, no worries—reach out and ask for their trusted recommendations. Most seasoned planners have preferred professionals they love to work with, and your venue likely has a vetted vendor list as well, which is a helpful starting point.

HERE'S A TRUTH BOMB:

Do not hire someone just because they're inexpensive or looking to build their portfolio. Your wedding is not the place for someone's trial run. Photography, especially, is an investment worth every penny—because when the party's over, the cake's been devoured, the music has faded, and the flowers have wilted, your photos are the one thing that sticks around to remind you how fabulous it all was.

If your photographer hasn't worked at your venue before, ask (or have your planner ask) that they arrive early to scout out the best spots and lighting. Trust me—no one wants their first look photos happening next to the industrial dumpster or under flickering neon lights. A little prep goes a long way for a smooth, confident day.

Now, let's talk videography. It may seem like a quieter role, but it's just as important. Think of your videographer as the silent superhero of the wedding world, working around the photographer to capture all those moving, emotional moments. Just be prepared: you might have to walk the same path, kiss your partner, or laugh like a lunatic more than once so they can "get the shot." But hey—that's all part of the magic of turning your day into a mini movie worthy of popcorn and replays.

PLANNER INSIGHT: One of the most crucial parts of your role is being an excellent listener—especially when it comes to your couple's photography and videography preferences. Often, their wish list emerges organically during the welcome meeting or even earlier in the consultation phase. Pay close attention to their personalities, communication styles, and the words they use to describe their vision. These subtle clues will guide you toward creatives who are the right fit—not just in style, but in energy and approach.

Be ready to navigate a wide spectrum of creative personalities. Photographers and videographers each bring their own unique flair, and it's your job to bridge the gap between artist and client seamlessly.

Start with budget discussions. There's no sense connecting your couple with vendors far outside their price range. Honor their financial comfort zone and seek professionals whose work falls within it.

Next, consider style. Whether your couple dreams of light and airy images, rich editorial tones, or cinematic film vibes, tailor your recommendations to match their aesthetic.

Once you've curated a thoughtful shortlist, coordinate introductions. Schedule consultations with your top two choices to keep the process focused, efficient, and enjoyable. Your mission? Pair your couple with a creative team that feels like an extension of their celebration. When you nail the match, it's a win for everyone—and a moment worthy of a happy dance behind the scenes!

LENS LEGENDS

The Novice Photographer
After a few years in the world of weddings, most planners naturally find themselves gravitating toward a core group of trusted creative partners—the ones who "get it," show up prepared, and deliver consistently. But every now and then, especially when working with a budget-conscious bride who may have hired you later in the planning process, you find yourself in a different kind of scenario—one where you're expected to create magic with a team you didn't help assemble.

Often in these cases, the photographer is someone sourced from a high-volume studio or budget vendor list—likely underpaid and overbooked. They show up, do the job, and follow a checklist. Nothing more, nothing less. And while I respect that we all start somewhere, as a planner, this situation forces me to take on a more hands-on role than usual.

I'm not a fan of micromanaging—but when the photographer doesn't know the venue, the couple, or the flow of the day, I find myself having to step in and steer the ship. It's frustrating, not because they're new, but because it takes me away from my own responsibilities: managing the event and caring for my clients. Too often, I catch the telltale look—the wide-eyed "what's next?" stare—and while I respond with grace and guidance, inside I'm calculating how to keep things on track without overwhelming the bride.

That's when I call on my assistant to shadow the photographer, manage the timeline, and free me up to focus on the couple's overall experience. And then, I pause and remind myself: we've all been the novice once. With time, experience, and the right mentorship, they'll grow. In fact, it's not uncommon for me to see these very same "what's next" shooters return months or years later—this time as second shooters for some of my favorite pros. And that's always a full-circle moment worth celebrating.

The Prick
As professionals, we're not always graced with dream teams or warm personalities. Every so often, we encounter *that* creative—the arrogant type who exudes superiority, the kind who walks into a space with an ego bigger than their camera lens. You know the one: aloof, dismissive, and convinced they're the only genius in the room.

In my early days, I'd make an effort to bridge the gap—small talk, compliments, attempts at collaboration. But over time, I learned a hard truth: it's not worth the energy. Some personalities aren't looking to connect—they're looking to dominate.

This kind of photographer often comes with a hefty price tag, and with that often comes an inflated sense of self. They typically work with high-end clients and believe that status alone justifies their behavior. But let's be honest—we're all working the same event, on the same timeline, for the same couple. No one person's role outweighs another.

My advice? Do your job exceptionally well. Be professional, be poised, and engage only when necessary. Don't force connection where there's resistance. Respect the schedule, manage the client, and let your calm confidence speak for itself. If a change arises in the timeline or logistics, communicate clearly and directly—but don't get pulled into ego wars or passive battles for control.

Photographers like this tend to operate best when left alone. They thrive on control, so give them space, and focus instead on what truly matters: the couple, the experience, and the seamless execution of a beautiful celebration.

Remember: respect is earned, not demanded. And sometimes, the most powerful statement you can make is to smile, stay in your lane, and let your work speak for itself.

The Favorite

Ah, the picture-perfect partnerships—we all have them. Over the years, I've naturally gravitated toward a trusted circle of photographers who have become more than just colleagues; they've become friends. These are the ones who show up early, know their craft, and create not just beautiful galleries, but a beautiful *experience* for everyone involved. They bring a second shooter or assistant, stay ahead of the timeline, and move with confidence and calm.

When you're working alongside someone who's both skilled and kind, everything flows. There's no need to micromanage, no need to worry if something will be missed. The laughter is genuine, the teamwork effortless. The client can feel it too—this seamless rhythm between vendors that brings lightness to what could easily be a high-stress day.

It's in the silent communication—a glance across the room, a subtle nod, an intuitive understanding of what's needed next. That's the magic of working with your favorite creatives. You don't have to try so hard to make the day a success—it just *is*.

So here's my advice: make yourself talented photographer friends. The kind who care about the couple, the day, and the bigger picture. They're worth their weight in gold—and your event will be better because of them.

THE LOST LENS

It was a warm spring afternoon, the kind that hums with anticipation and excitement. Hair and makeup were nearly finished, the dress was steamed and glowing in perfect light, the flowers had arrived, and I was fully in coordinator mode—straightening menus, checking in with vendors, and making sure everyone was fed and relaxed. Everything was running on time, and, for once, I was even ahead of schedule. Then, the curveball arrived.

The photographer showed up.

Not dramatically late, but just enough to make me start recalculating in my head. He strolled in with his camera bag slung over one shoulder, exuding the laid-back vibe of someone heading to a coffee date instead of capturing one of the biggest days of someone's life.

I took a deep breath, smiled, and greeted him warmly yet purposefully. "Hi! So glad you're here. We've got a full pre-ceremony list to get through—reception details, flat lays, the dress, getting-ready shots, and the bride's first look with her dad. We're tight on time, but I'll help keep things moving."

He nodded and said, "Cool, cool… Where's the dress?"

My stomach dropped a tiny bit. "It's in the bridal suite—right this way," I said, gently steering him in the right direction.

The next fifteen minutes felt like a high-stakes juggling act. I found myself helping him stage flat lays, reminding him about important reception detail shots, and fielding repeated questions like, "What should I do next?" and "Is there a first look?"

Part of me wanted to say, "Yes—and it's happening in ten minutes. And I've already mentioned this twice." Instead, I kept my smile, gave him the next item on the shot list, and enlisted my assistant to help him find what he needed.

Meanwhile, my bride, radiant and serene, remained blissfully unaware that behind the scenes, I was performing a quiet ballet of damage control. That's the goal, after all—keeping any chaos far away from the couple.

The first look finally took place, right on the sun-dappled terrace outside the bridal suite. The bride, radiant in her gown, moved gracefully toward her dad, her veil sweeping behind her like a **silk cloud.** She tapped him on the shoulder, and as he turned around, his face transformed from anticipation into pure, unfiltered joy.

The bride's eyes filled with tears, and thankfully, the camera was pointed in the right direction. Still, I couldn't help but think how much stronger those images might have been if the photographer had arrived prepared—mentally, physically, and logistically.

He wasn't a bad person. Just inexperienced. Probably far more comfortable in a controlled studio than navigating the whirlwind of a wedding day. And while I deeply respect every creative's learning curve, there's a reason weddings aren't the place to "wing it."

That day, I unofficially became the photography assistant—posing people, adjusting angles, and feeding the lens direction it should've had from the start. It wasn't how I'd planned to spend those hours—but it's what the day needed.

The big takeaway? A nice camera doesn't make a wedding photographer. Experience does. When in doubt, hire the pro who shows up early, knows what to ask, and doesn't wait for you to tell them what comes next.

TOO COOL FOR SCHOOL

It was a beautiful Saturday at one of the city's most luxurious hotels—gleaming marble floors, towering floral arrangements, and a guest list dressed to the nines. The vibe was pure high-end elegance, and the pressure to execute flawlessly was even higher.

Enter him—the photographer. *The Prick.*

You could spot the swagger from across the ballroom. Dressed as if he were heading to a GQ editorial shoot, he strolled in with the confidence of someone who'd personally invented the camera. I greeted him warmly, like I do with every vendor, flashing a smile and saying, "Hey there! So glad you're here—let me catch you up on where we are with the day."

He didn't even break stride. "I know where everything is. I'm heading to the bridal suite now," he shot back, barely making eye contact, hauling his gear behind him like he owned the place.

Alrighty then. No updates needed, I guess.

As the day went on, I stayed in my lane, letting him do his thing. When it came time for the first look, I offered, as always, to help set the groom in place and ensure the moment went off without a hitch. Once again, I was met with that cool detachment: "I've got it under control." So, I backed off.

This wasn't shaping up to be one of those collaborative vendor experiences where we laugh through the stress and high-five each other in the ballroom kitchen at the end of the night. Nope. Today, we were simply two professionals sharing the same timeline—working side by side but never quite together.

And, of course, just as I suspected, there were no sneak peeks after the wedding. Want to see the gallery? You'll have to go through the client. This guy's vault is sealed tighter than Fort Knox unless you're the one who signed the contract. No malice—just zero effort to be a team player.

It's a solid reminder that not every vendor experience will be warm and fuzzy. Some creatives prefer to exist on their own exclusive island of ego, and that's fine—as long as the job gets done and the couple is happy.

A FRIENDLY WORD OF ADVICE:

If your planner doesn't recognize the photographer's name, or their vibe feels a little *too* exclusive, trust us to dig deeper and ask the right questions. The most talented vendors are often the kindest collaborators. Because at the end of the day, beautiful photos matter—but so does having a beautifully executed wedding.

WHEN IT ALL JUST CLICKS

Some wedding days practically hum with enchantment from the very start. The sun was shining, a soft breeze whispered through the air, and everything seemed infused with the vibrant promise of spring—a season made for fresh beginnings and unforgettable moments. It was the kind of day planners dream of, and I knew deep in my bones that something special was unfolding.

The couple? Utterly smitten, glowing with delight in their mid-twenties, brimming with gratitude and an infectious optimism. They entrusted us—the entire vendor team—with their vision and their hearts. That kind of trust is the ultimate gift a client can give. When a couple releases the weight of stress and confidently places their day in the hands of their chosen professionals, it leaves room for real magic to bloom.

That morning, our photo and video dream team—some of my favorite humans and brilliant creatives—arrived early, full of quiet purpose. They scouted the venue, seeking out pockets of perfect light and the most breathtaking spots for the day's standout shots. Once settled, we gathered for a quick team pow-wow. No lengthy meetings or micromanaging—just a few nods, a glance at the timeline, and silent agreements shared between professionals who've danced this dance many times before.

From there, the day blossomed like a flower in sunlight.

Because we'd worked together so often, communication became almost telepathic. A single look across the room or a subtle hand signal was all it took to say, "Wrap it up," or "We're rolling now." It was seamless—a behind-the-scenes ballet executed with precision and grace, while the couple remained blissfully present in the joy of their celebration.

When vendors know and respect each other, when there's history and trust woven into the fabric of the team, it creates an invisible current that carries the entire day forward. It makes everything feel lighter, smoother, and more joyful. And that's exactly what this day was, like so many others—a seamless dance where every vendor played their part beautifully.

I've been lucky to witness countless weddings where the team clicks into place like a well-oiled machine, each of us anticipating the next move without needing to speak a word. It's beautiful cohesion, and it makes my heart so grateful. Because the truth is, behind every flawless wedding day is a group of talented, dedicated professionals working tirelessly—and lightheartedly—to work wonders.

I'm endlessly thankful for the incredible vendor partners who help turn dream days into reality, again and again. A symphony of professionals in perfect harmony. No egos, just a shared commitment to creating something beautiful.

It was the kind of wedding you hold close long after the lights dim and the last song fades—a reminder that the true magic of weddings often happens behind the scenes, carried on the quiet currents of collaboration and love.

ENGAGEMENT SESSION: ON TRACK TO FOREVER

Sifting through my closet, I tried valiantly to piece together outfits we already owned. Practical? Yes. Realistic? Not for a shopaholic like me. Anyone who knows me could've predicted what happened next—I found the perfect excuse to buy not one, but two new dresses.

The first was a breezy lavender lace number with delicate spaghetti straps that hugged in all the right places. The second was a classic teal chiffon dress, complete with wispy sleeves and a romantic, effortlessly chic vibe.

And then there was the jewelry—because 2012 demanded it. Bold, chunky statement necklaces were having a moment, and I was fully on board. I paired the lavender dress with a triple-stranded turquoise necklace that practically shouted "Look at me!" and matched the teal dress with rich amber stones for a warm, glowing contrast. Nude heels tied it all together—neutral, but elegant.

John, ever true to himself, kept things clean and casual. We landed on a crisp white collared shirt with soft blue pinstripes and jeans. It felt authentic—and that's all we wanted.

We picked downtown for our shoot, though in hindsight, it might not have been the most merciful choice in August. The moment I stepped out of John's car, a wave of heat smacked me square in the chest—thick, unmoving, radiating off the asphalt like a convection oven. Sunset Train Station, built in 1902, stood quietly in the background, ready to play its part as our historic backdrop.

"Geez, it's hotter than hell," I muttered, fanning myself with my hand.

John shot me a look—he was in long sleeves and jeans while I stood there whining in a sundress. Fair enough. I cracked a grin. "Okay, okay. Let's power through this, and I'll buy you a drink afterward."

Now, if you know John, you know he's not exactly the "photo shoot" type. He was doing this for me. And believe me—I knew it. We bounced from one location to the next, following the photographer's chirpy commands: "Smile here! Okay, now look at each other and laugh!" I could practically hear John's internal eye-roll, but he never complained. He held my hand, kissed my temple, and kept showing up for me, moment after moment.

Halfway through, I pulled off a lightning-fast outfit change. With no open shops or cafés in sight (because naturally, it was a Sunday), the most private spot we could find was a dim stairwell. John played lookout while I shimmied out of my teal dress and wriggled into the lavender lace. It was chaotic, slightly nerve-wracking, and somehow still a thrill. "John, hurry! Zip me up!" We were laughing so hard; my mascara nearly ran.

I stuffed the teal dress into a bag, adjusted my necklace, and we emerged into the heat once more. We ended the session at the train itself—a towering, powerful locomotive stretching behind us like something out of a vintage movie reel.

There's just something symbolic about trains: movement, transitions, fate. They run on tracks already laid—destined paths. Was it fate that brought John and me to this moment, hand in hand, ready to merge our journeys? I'd like to believe so. I've always been a believer in soulmates, and while I know many people settle for what simply "works," I never did. I married the person who feels like home. John is my once-in-a-lifetime.

"Are you brave enough to hop onto the tracks for one last shot?" our photographer asked, eyes twinkling with mischief.

I glanced at John, grinned, and grabbed his hand. "Yes! Let's do it."

"Hell yeah," he said with a smirk.

And just like that, I knew—we'd both surrendered to the moment.

I picked my way carefully across the wooden beams, heels wobbling on the gravel.

"Stop right there!" the photographer called. "John, pick Jen up and kiss her like you mean it."

And he did.

Right then, as if the universe was in on our love story, a yellow train thundered past behind us, blurring into streaks of motion. The photo turned out like a scene from a vintage movie poster—romantic, cinematic, and utterly timeless. That moment wrapped our session. As promised, we celebrated with cold drinks and full hearts.

A few weeks later, our gallery arrived. If you've ever waited on engagement photos, you know that delicious mix of nervousness and hope—that what felt magical in person would look just as amazing in photos. And it did. All of it. The heat, the sweat, the stairwell costume change, the track-top kiss. Every wild, hilarious, and heartfelt moment was absolutely worth it. Because now, we have it all, forever.

WHY ENGAGEMENT SESSIONS ARE WORTH IT

Let's be real—feeling natural in front of a camera doesn't come easily for most people. Very few couples are accustomed to being professionally photographed, and suddenly finding yourselves the center of attention can feel, well... a bit awkward.

That's why an engagement session is worth its weight in gold. It's not just about capturing pretty pictures—it's about easing into the experience, building a connection, and freezing a sweet, fleeting chapter of your love story in time.

Think of your engagement shoot as a dress rehearsal for the big day. It gives you and your partner a chance to relax, shake off any camera jitters, and discover which angles and poses feel most natural. The more comfortable you are in front of the lens, the more authentic—and stunning—your wedding photos will be.

It's also the perfect time to bond with your photographer. You'll get a feel for how they direct, how they capture spontaneous moments, and whether their energy meshes well with yours. And trust me, chemistry matters.

Your photographer will be by your side through some of the most intimate and emotional moments of your wedding day. Getting to know them ahead of time can make all the difference between stiff, posed images and photos brimming with genuine joy.

Plus, engagement photos are wonderfully versatile. They're perfect for save-the-dates, your wedding website, guest books, reception décor, or even holiday cards. They make thoughtful, sentimental gifts for family or can serve as a fun and stylish way to announce your engagement on social media.

This is a once-in-a-lifetime stage—you're not just dating anymore; you're engaged! It deserves to be celebrated and documented.

Another perk? Engagement sessions tend to be far more laid-back and creatively flexible than the wedding day. There's no strict timeline, no worry about wrinkling a gown, and no pressure to squeeze everything into a packed schedule. It's your chance to choose a location that truly means something to you—a cozy coffee shop, the hiking trail where you got engaged, the stoop of your first apartment.

One of my favorite examples? A couple who made weekly date-night stops at 7-Eleven for slushies. For their engagement shoot, the bride wore a playful white mini dress and a short veil, both of them rocked heart-shaped sunglasses, and they posed in the back of a pickup truck, clinking slushy cups before sharing a kiss. It was quirky, joyful, and perfectly them.

Engagement and bridal portrait sessions are also a brilliant excuse to schedule your hair and makeup trial. It's a chance to see how your chosen look photographs—and how it holds up under heat, wind, or spontaneous dance breaks.

While engagement sessions are often included in many photography packages, if they're not, consider adding one. Think of it as an invaluable test run.

If the photos come back and you're not completely thrilled, it's the perfect opportunity to have an honest conversation with your photographer. Maybe it's the editing style, maybe it's the posing. Either way, you'll have the chance to fine-tune things before the big day—or explore other options if needed.

In the end, engagement photos aren't mandatory—but they're undeniably meaningful. They're about more than just aesthetics. They're about comfort, connection, and confidence. And when those three things fall into place, that's when the real magic happens.

10
CUE THE MUSIC

It was one of those rare moments in the whirlwind of a wedding day when everything had finally hit its stride. Dinner was served, the toasts were wrapped, and the dance floor was just starting to wake up. My assistant and I slipped out to the back porch with a few other vendors, grateful for a five-minute breather. We let the cool evening air wash over us, savoring the satisfaction of a job well done—so far.

And then, I froze.

"Do you hear that?" I asked, eyes wide with alarm.

My assistant glanced at me, then at the others, confusion all over their faces. "No… what is it?"

"It's nothing," I said, pausing mid-sentence. "Literally. I hear no music."

I tilted my head slightly, straining to confirm the unsettling realization. The hum, the beat, the pulse of the party—gone. In its place: silence. That dreadful, momentum-killing silence that slowly drains the energy out of a room.

We bolted.

Back through the doors, into the reception hall, and there it was—a quiet room that nearly shattered my wedding-planner soul.

Guests were looking around, puzzled, their conversations growing louder in an attempt to fill the void. The vibrant energy we'd spent hours cultivating had evaporated in seconds.

At the DJ booth, we found him—frantically twisting knobs, clicking through his laptop, sweat beading on his forehead. He was clearly wrestling with a tech meltdown, and more alarmingly, he didn't seem to have a backup plan.

Cue planner mode.

I hustled to the booth, leaning in and asking, as calmly as humanly possible, "Need me to plug in a backup playlist?" He nodded, still battling his gear. Blessed be Spotify Premium. I pulled out my phone and plugged in my "emergency wedding vibes" playlist. As the first familiar beat pulsed through the speakers, the guests exhaled collectively and began swaying back into party mode. Disaster averted.

Here's the moral of the story: tech fails happen. Always, always have a safety net—a filler playlist, a contingency plan, something. Because silence at a wedding? It's not golden. It's a buzzkill.

Music isn't just background noise at a wedding—it's the secret sauce, the emotional glue, the invisible hand guiding the entire vibe of the day. From the very first note, it tells your guests exactly what kind of celebration they're stepping into: elegant and formal, laid-back and fun, or romantic and dreamy. It creates a soundtrack for every moment, transforming an ordinary timeline into a cinematic, unforgettable experience.

Few things spark memory and emotion the way music does. The songs you choose will forever be stitched into your memories—and your guests'—so that years from now, hearing that one track instantly transports everyone back to your big day.

Your music choices also speak volumes about your story and style as a couple. It's one of the easiest (and most fun) ways to sprinkle your personalities throughout the celebration. During the reception, music breathes life into the crowd and draws people to the dance floor. An experienced DJ or band knows how to read the room and keep guests of all ages engaged—even Uncle Jay who swears he "never dances."

Music is also the hero of those quiet in-between moments: guest arrival, cocktail hour, dinner. Silence can feel painfully awkward—like crickets chirping in an empty ballroom. Music smooths those gaps and keeps the mood flowing seamlessly. An experienced DJ or musician can guide the energy from dinner to dancing, and gracefully ease things toward the final song of the night. Simply put: music is the heartbeat of a wedding.

But how do you choose? String quartet, jazz trio, solo guitarist, pianist, or cellist? Maybe a jazz ensemble to set the perfect cocktail hour mood? And let's not forget the eternal debate: live band or DJ? Oh, and does your DJ also double as the MC, or is that a separate gig? Spoiler alert—despite what you might hope, not all DJs wear that second hat, as we've learned the hard way more than once.

Though we haven't *quite* seen it all, we've witnessed moments of musical brilliance, perfectly average performances, a few serious vibe killers, and yes, some downright disastrous soundtracks. So, take a deep breath, pour yourself a cup of tea—or let's be honest, a glass of wine—and get comfy. You'll want to savor this chapter.

Future planners, think of this as your masterclass in navigating the unpredictable world of wedding music. Brides, this is your all-access, backstage pass to the highs, lows, and lessons learned from real weddings—where every note counts.

JENNIFER CRAFT

WALKING DOWN THE AISLE, ONE NOTE AT A TIME

No DJ? No Problem—famous last words. Flashback to 2011—back before AirPods existed to make life easier. I was fresh out of college, eager to prove myself as a wedding planner's assistant, when I somehow volunteered to be the "music woman"—a.k.a. the human iPod—trapped inside a tiny chapel music closet. Yep, the closet. The one with the thick, fancy wooden door that effectively turned me into a soundproofed prisoner.

Missy, the lead planner, looked me dead in the eye and said, "Okay, Jennifer, when I text you 'GO,' you play the bride's song."

"Got it," I said, trying not to let my voice crack. Why was I nervous? Because this wasn't just any playlist—this was the literal soundtrack to someone's wedding ceremony. Screw this up, and I might as well have handed in my planner badge on the spot.

So there I was, sitting alone in the dark, like a wannabe DJ in solitary confinement, gripping my phone like it was a life raft. I couldn't see or hear anything happening outside, and my only company was the occasional cricket chirp and the sound of my own pulse.

Missy shut the door behind her with the softest click, leaving me alone with my thoughts—and a phone buzzing in my hand. I thought, *Okay, maybe I'll just crack the door a bit. No one will notice.* Spoiler alert: they definitely did not notice, but I absolutely heard my own echo.

Then the texts started rolling in:

Missy: "Lining bridal party up soon."

Me: thumbs up emoji. Cool. I was basically a covert operative waiting for my mission. I sat there twiddling my thumbs, imagining myself as the DJ superstar I might one day become.

Missy: "Play family song."

I hit play and instantly felt like a game show contestant on the brink of elimination. No pressure, right? After what felt like an eternity (okay, three minutes tops), my moment finally came: pressing play on the bride's song. Who knew being a human iPod could be this stressful?

Missy: "GO."

I pressed play on the bride's song, bobbing my head awkwardly to the beat like a sleep-deprived dance party.

Missy: "Fade."

I carefully lowered the volume, feeling like a smooth operator trying not to ruin a sacred moment. Then came the long wait. I sat there listening to dead silence, convinced someone was about to burst in and accuse me of ruining the ceremony.

Finally, I heard the officiant announce, "Presenting the new Mr. and Mrs.!"

I slammed the play button on the recessional music and felt like I'd just won Olympic gold in "Music Closet DJ-ing."

As the chapel emptied, I stumbled out of my wooden prison, took a deep breath, and immediately pivoted into ushering guests like nothing out of the ordinary had happened.

Fast forward a few years, and the venue eventually upgraded that music closet with a small window so whoever was running the music could actually see the ceremony. Also, professional DJs now show up armed with cameras, monitors, and all sorts of tech wizardry, making cueing music less like a high-stakes guessing game and more like a smooth dance.

WEDDING WISDOM: Hire a professional for your ceremony music, or just in general. I know—it sounds obvious. But trust me, you do *not* want your assistant doubling as the DJ in a soundproof closet with no clue what's happening outside. If you're a coordinator, pack three radios—one for the DJ, one for your assistant, and one for yourself. Because nothing kills a vibe faster than dead silence when the processional song should be playing. Remember: the soundtrack to your big day is not the time to improvise.

DROPPIN' BEATS—AND COMMENTARY

Early in my career as a solo event coordinator, I learned quickly that DJs come in all shapes and styles—including those who fancy themselves not just masters of music, but also of running commentary.

Picture this: you're onsite, coordinating solo, juggling a thousand moving parts, and you quietly give the DJ a heads-up that the buffet, cake cutting, or special dances are about to begin. You even remind him gently what to say, suspecting he might be a bit green. And then, instead of waiting for your carefully timed cue, he seizes the microphone and proceeds to announce private logistical updates to the entire room.

"Don't go anywhere — we've got more stuff coming up."

"So, the coordinator just told me to say... (insert any behind-the-scenes info)."

"Hope you're all hungry. Smells good, right?"

"Alright folks, time for the part where you watch them cut the cake and feed it to each other." "Make some noise if you're ready to party!!"

Cue my skin crawling. Truly, it's peak cringe. Why broadcast every behind-the-scenes detail over the mic? Sometimes, the smartest move is simply silence paired with smooth music. My motto: more music, less chatter.

Don't get me wrong—I'm all for the essential announcements: introducing the couple or wedding party, inviting parents to the dance floor, or guiding guests for speeches and toasts. But the cake cutting? I'd much rather keep that moment low-key, letting it unfold naturally instead of turning it into a spectacle.

One major pet peeve of mine? DJs announcing table numbers to the buffet over the mic. That task belongs to the coordinator or catering team. It's far more elegant—and far less disruptive—when a professional discreetly visits each table to invite guests, ensuring a seamless and gracious flow instead of turning dinner into a cafeteria roll call.

When DJs start narrating logistical details meant for vendor ears only, it can shatter the elegant or intimate atmosphere. A good DJ or MC keeps the energy up without oversharing backstage chaos. Short, confident, well-timed announcements are gold — and silence with great music is often the best choice of all!

COORDINATOR INSIGHT

Set Expectations Early: Once the DJ has finished setting up, gather them for a quick chat. Go over your expectations calmly and clearly. If you have to, read the timeline out loud so there's no confusion.

Confirm They Have—and understand—the Timeline: Don't assume they've studied the timeline you sent weeks ago. Walk them through the key moments—grand entrance, speeches, first dance—and make sure you're both on the same page.

Clarify Mic Duties: DJs new to weddings often either talk too much or freeze up completely. Let them know exactly who's announcing what, in what order, and how you'll cue each transition. Confirm who's handling the mic—will it be the DJ, you, or someone else? Lock this in at least 60 days out.

A little prep now saves your wedding from turning into a live DJ commentary. Because at the end of the day, guests came to hear the music—not the DJ's blow-by-blow narration.

Verify they have organized a playlist in timeline order, including:
- Ceremony (prelude, processional, recessional)
- First dance and parent dances
- Cake cutting, bouquet toss, and other key moments

Coach Them on Tone: If the DJ starts giving off "nightclub hype-man" or "game show host" vibes during dinner, gently steer them back on course. For example, you could say: *"We're going for warm and polished right now. Save the party energy for the dance floor later."*

Establish a Silent Signal: If you don't have radios or an assistant, create a discreet hand signal for transitions (like "wrap it up," "cut the music," or "start the next track"). It's far better than shouting across the room mid-reception.

Communicate What's Off-Limits: Let your DJ know ahead of time about anything you'd prefer to avoid—like surprise announcements, guests grabbing the mic unplanned, or dance music starting during dinner. Clear communication keeps everyone in sync and protects the vibe of the day.

Arrive early and confirm they have backup gear—extra mics, cords, and batteries. Make sure the mic actually works in your space, and that they've sound-checked both speech and music levels.

Inexperienced DJs can get flustered quickly. A calm, confident coordinator helps keep them grounded. Check in regularly, but don't hover. Let them know you're their point person if they hit a snag.

CUE THE CHAOS ... TOO SOON

Oh, wouldn't it be nice if MCs actually *listened* to us coordinators? How hard is it to wait for our cue? Apparently, for some, the microphone is just too tempting—a siren's call to unleash their inner talk show host. Maybe they just love the sound of their own voice, or maybe they enjoy filling awkward silences with… more awkwardness.

It's 2015, and I'm the rookie planner clutching my clipboard for dear life. Things are going pretty smoothly. We've got a band—live music is my absolute favorite. Nothing beats the vibe of a live band jamming on stage.

According to my timeline, speeches are due in about ten minutes. I mosey up to the band leader, our unofficial MC. "Hey, it's almost time for speeches. Give me a shout when you're ready to go." He gives me a cool "Roger that."

The room is packed tighter than a can of sardines—250 to 300 guests eagerly waiting. My assistant and I exchange a knowing look and I flash the MC a big thumbs-up.

"Alright, ladies and gentlemen," the MC's voice booms like he's hosting a game show, "it's time to raise your glasses to the newlyweds! First up, our maid of honor, Tracy!"

Applause explodes as Tracy steps onto the dance floor. The couple looks radiant.

Tracy's speech is sweet and heartfelt—cue a few sniffles. Then the best man takes the floor and cracks, "They say a best man's speech should be like a mini skirt: short enough to keep it interesting, but long enough to cover the essentials."

The crowd laughs, the MC chuckles along, "So true, so true! Thanks, Brad. Last but not least, the father of the bride would like to say a few words."

And then… nothing. Crickets.

I scan the room like a hawk, mouthing *Where is Dad?* to my assistant.

The mother of the bride shoots me a look that could melt steel: *Why didn't you leash him?*

Whispers and murmurs ripple through the crowd like a low tide. *Where is he? Little boys' room?*

Minutes drag on. I'm mentally rehearsing my apology speech when finally—glory be—Dad strolls in at the back of the room, grasping a beer like it's his life raft. He weaves between tables like he's dodging an invisible obstacle course, mumbling, "Right here! Coming, sorry, sorry!"

Cue me facepalming, thinking, "Welcome to wedding coordination—where the unexpected is expected and the chaos is part of the charm." Because every great wedding comes with a little "Dad's gone rogue" energy.

LOST DAD AT THE DANCE

It was a gorgeous spring day in the Texas Hill Country—sunshine warming the air, wildflowers in bloom, and the kind of perfect weather that makes you feel like you've stepped into a living postcard. The ceremony had just wrapped, and guests streamed effortlessly into the cozy indoor bar lounge, where margaritas were flowing and appetizers were being devoured with gusto. Family photos were snapped in record time, leaving ample opportunity for the couple's portraits, which turned out downright swoon-worthy.

As the grand entrance time approached, I made my rounds, checking in with parents, helping guests find their tables, and ensuring everything was humming along like a well-tuned orchestra. Each wedding pulses with its own rhythm, shaped by the venue, the season, and the couple's vibe—and tonight's rhythm was meant to flow seamlessly from the bride and groom's grand entrance into the dining space, then into the first dance, followed by those cherished parent dances.

The first dance was pure romance—the couple wrapped up in each other, surrounded by warm smiles and sun-kissed light. Riding the wave of that sweet moment, the DJ smoothly announced the father of the bride for his turn on the dance floor.

Only problem? Dad was nowhere to be found. The bride shot me a look sharp enough to slice through fondant—a dagger-eyed glare that screamed, *"Where is he?!"*

In that instant, my heart dropped into my shoes. I mouthed, "It's okay," while trying to radiate calm, but internally I was already plotting my search-and-rescue mission.

With a swift wave of my hand to signal *pause the panic,* I dashed off to track down the elusive father, who seemed to have evaporated into thin air. Pretty soon, I had half the staff conscripted into the hunt—because this wasn't just a missing wedding guest anymore. This was officially a high-stakes episode of *Where in the World is the Father of the Bride?*

I couldn't help thinking: Should we start equipping dads with GPS ankle bracelets? Or maybe hand out "Please Stay Put" wristbands at the rehearsal dinner? Honestly, these are grown adults—why is it so impossible for them to stay in one place on their child's wedding day?

Yet somehow, the blame always lands squarely on my shoulders. Because between the last time I saw Dad and ten minutes later, he'd apparently decided to go off-script and take a mysterious stroll stage left.

At the end of the day, wedding coordination isn't just about timelines and table linens—it's about herding humans, tackling curveballs, and transforming little fiascos into stories everyone will laugh about... eventually. Preferably once the father of the bride is safely back on the dance floor, where he belongs.

BRIDAL BRAINSTORM: Weddings are joyful celebrations filled with laughter, love, and unforgettable moments—but they're also events that demand a bit of thoughtful coordination behind the scenes. One of the most important things you can do for yourself is to communicate clearly with your family and friends about their roles, especially if they'll be giving speeches or participating in special dances.

Don't assume your loved ones automatically know what's expected of them or when their moment will arrive. Gently but firmly let them know in advance that they're on the schedule to speak, toast, or perform during the reception. Giving them time to prepare heartfelt words—or rehearse a few dance moves—ensures they'll feel confident and ready when the spotlight hits.

Sometimes, people freeze up or get anxious simply because they didn't expect to be called on.

By setting expectations early, you'll help avoid surprises and ease the pressure on everyone—including yourself. A well-prepared speech or dance isn't just about the performance; it's a chance to honor your special day with sincerity and warmth that your guests will remember.

So, take a moment to check in with your chosen speakers and dancers before the big day. Send a friendly reminder, share the timeline, and offer any helpful tips or encouragement. When everyone's prepared, the day unfolds seamlessly, allowing genuine emotion to shine and making your celebration all the more enchanting.

COORDINATOR'S CORNER: No matter how many times you've scanned the room or chatted with the VIPs, they'll always find new ways to surprise you—especially once the nerves kick in. Suddenly, someone realizes they just can't hold it for ten more minutes and makes a mad dash to the restroom like it's a sprint to the finish line. Classic.

To keep the day running as seamlessly as possible, make it a point to check in with everyone scheduled to speak. Give them a friendly, "Hey, your big moment's coming up soon—time to warm up those vocal cords!"

Show them exactly where they'll be standing (preferably not next to the bathroom door) and run through a quick overview of what to expect. Bonus points if they've got a drink in hand—champagne, a cocktail, or even a mocktail—to help transform their speech into a heartfelt toast rather than a stiff lecture.

But be ready—because curveballs are practically guaranteed.

You'll hear gems like, "I already gave a toast last night, thanks!" (Accompanied by a sly wink) or, "Hey, can I add my own speech to the lineup?" right in the middle of the reception.

To avoid last-minute chaos, sit down with the couple a few weeks before the wedding to confirm how flexible they want to be about surprise speeches. And get yourself a list of the no-mic-zone VIPs—those who, for everyone's sanity, should absolutely not be handed the mic.

That way, you won't be blindsided when Uncle Bob suddenly declares himself the keynote speaker. In the end, embrace the madness with a smile—you're the air traffic controller of love, laughter, and the occasional potty break!

TOSSING BOUQUETS AND TIMELINES

We did everything right. I mean, we went through the timeline, rehearsed the cues, even whispered sweet nothings to the schedule before the event. I thought we were all on the same page. Spoiler alert: I was wrong.

There we were—my rockstar assistant and I—hanging out with the venue manager on the side porch, enjoying a well-earned breather from the blaring music. The venue's basically a giant glass box, so you'd think the DJ could spot us through the windows. Nope. He knew exactly where we were but apparently decided to launch a covert operation instead.

Bouquet toss? Scheduled for 9:00 p.m. We casually stroll back inside, head to the DJ booth, and check in like pros.

"How's it going? The dance floor looks amazing, everyone's having a blast! It's 8:30 p.m.—let's plan the bouquet toss when you see the perfect moment to clear the floor."

The DJ casually replies, "Oh! Sorry, forgot to tell you—we already did that."

Cue my jaw hitting the floor. "Wait, what? You already did that?"

"Yeah, the bride came up and said she was ready to get it over with."

At this point, my brain is scrambling for a polite yet firm response, so I say, "Well, I wish you'd given me a heads-up so I could be in the room to actually see it happen."

"Oh, no worries! The photographer and videographer were there," he shrugs, looking apologetic but utterly unfazed.

"Okay, fine. It's done. The bride looks happy, so there's that," I say, trying to find the silver lining. "I'll be just over there if you need me. Oh, and please promise me you'll check in before the last song so we can coordinate the send-off."

As we walk away, Mikaela gives me the 'did-that-just-happen?' look. The moral of the story? You can plan every detail and cue every moment—but the DJ? The DJ might just freestyle the night away.

PLANNER'S PLAYBOOK: Long before you even arrive on-site, walk the DJ through the run-of-show and make it absolutely clear that nothing goes live without your go-ahead.

"For everyone's sake, let's agree that all major moments—like the first dance, bouquet toss, and toasts—need to come from me first, not just when the mood feels right."

Being too casual leaves the door open for improvisation. *Be polite but direct:*

"Please don't start any formalities unless you've confirmed with me directly."

"We're running on a timeline, not on instinct—let's keep things coordinated."

Establish a simple, unmistakable signal.

"When I give the thumbs-up, that's your cue to start. Until then, hold tight—even if people are asking."

Watch for "Hero Syndrome": Some DJs believe they're "saving the party" by skipping protocol. Gently but firmly remind them that orchestrating the flow is your job, not theirs.

"I know you've got fantastic instincts, but when it comes to timing, I need us in sync."

If you suspect your DJ has a tendency to freestyle, build in a few flexible buffer points in the timeline. That way, if they jump the gun, it won't completely derail the key moments.

HERE FOR THE VIBES, NOT THE SCRIPT

"What do you mean you don't give announcements?" I asked, blinking rapidly and trying to mask my internal freak-out behind a calm, coordinator exterior.

"Oh, no ma'am," he said casually, like he was politely declining an extra breadstick at Olive Garden. "I don't MC. I just play the music."

Cue internal screaming.

"Okay… see, that's not great for me," I replied, keeping my smile firmly in place even as my soul quietly exited the building. "I'm the coordinator, not the MC—and traditionally, this falls under your job description."

He shrugged. "I guess I can make an exception… but bear with me."

"Perfect," I said, powering through the panic. "Let me whip up a quick script—just to be safe. And please, don't make any announcements unless my assistant or I are standing right next to you giving the universal 'thumbs-up of approval.'"

"Yes ma'am."

Crisis (barely) averted.

Now, picture me: early twenties, fresh-faced, and still semi-terrified of microphones. Asking me to MC an entire wedding? Hard pass. I'd rather alphabetize 200 escort cards—twice. Fast-forward to today, and I'll snatch that mic like it is karaoke night and I'm five cocktails in. Age plus experience equals unstoppable MC energy.

I've had to hop on the mic more times than I can count—especially when an officiant forgets to tell people what to do after the ceremony. (You'd be shocked how many guests just sit there waiting for an encore performance.)

Suddenly, I'm striding back to the altar once the couple and wedding party have exited.

I plaster on my best cruise director smile and channel pure confidence:

"That was a gorgeous ceremony! If you're part of the family, please stay behind for photos. Everyone else, follow me to happy hour—there's a margarita with your name on it!"

Imagine me leading 250 guests through what feels like an airport terminal: out the garden, down a winding path, up a few stairs, through the lobby, past a couple of suspiciously large potted plants… and ta-da! Cocktail hour achieved.

It's honestly hilarious how quickly people lose all sense of direction at weddings. Guests turn into lost puppies in formalwear. This way to the ceremony. That way to the restrooms. No, sir, the appetizer table is not an all-you-can-eat buffet. The one thing they *can* find without fail? The bar. Every. Single. Time.

Over the years, I've heard the dreaded "I don't make announcements" line countless times. Brace yourself: it's always from a club

DJ—a friend-of-a-cousin-of-the-groom who spins on weekends and thinks he is just there to play the beats.

WEDDING DJS NEED TO BE DOUBLE-THREATS: masters of music and wizards with a microphone. Meanwhile, we coordinators are juggling timelines, family dynamics, wardrobe malfunctions, and tracking down Aunt Carol's lost shoe. We do not have time to be your backup hype squad.

PLANNER PRO TIP: Always confirm before actual event day—that your DJ is also willing (and able) to serve as the MC. Don't rely on what the couple *thinks* their DJ does. Ask directly: *"Will you be making announcements throughout the night?"* If they hesitate, start writing a script. If they flat-out say no, find someone else who will. And no—you shouldn't be that person. You've already got enough on your plate, like keeping the bride's dress bustle from un-bustling every five minutes or tracking down Grandma who wandered off during family photos.

BRIDE BEST BET: Hire a *wedding* DJ—not your cousin's roommate who spins at a downtown lounge on Thursdays. A professional wedding DJ offers far more than just music. They bring structure, seamless transitions, an online music planning portal, and the experience to keep things moving even when the dance floor suddenly empties out. They've got contracts, professional gear, backup gear, and (gasp) insurance. A great DJ doesn't merely play the party—they *are* the party. And that's an investment worth making.

REAL INSTRUMENTS, REAL VIBES

Live music, you can't beat it! A band brings a unique energy that no DJ or playlist can quite replicate: the warmth of live instruments, real-time interaction with the crowd, and a vibrant atmosphere that pulses through the room. Jazz trios, string quartets, and acoustic sets add sophistication and charm, effortlessly elevating the mood, especially during the ceremony or cocktail hour.

Live performers often engage guests, encouraging dancing and participation, which makes the celebration feel even more memorable and dynamic. Bands can adjust tempos on the fly, extend songs, or tailor their setlist to perfectly match your vibe—whether that's romantic ballads, upbeat funk, or classic rock.

Watching talented musicians perform isn't just music—it's a show and a soundtrack woven into your day. Many bands are also willing to learn and perform a special first dance song or meaningful request, adding an extra layer of intimacy and personalization.

Another perk? Many wedding bands offer an impressive range of genres, from Top 40 hits and country favorites to soulful pop tunes and classic oldies covers, seamlessly switching styles throughout the night to keep guests of all ages entertained.

So how do you choose the right band for your wedding? **Start by defining your style:**
- Elegant and romantic? A jazz band or string ensemble could be the perfect fit.
- High-energy dance party? Look for a pop, funk, or soul band to keep the floor packed.

- Laid-back and indie? An acoustic or folk-style group might be your vibe.
- A touch of country? There's no shortage of talented country bands ready to bring the twang.

Ultimately, the right live band doesn't just play music—they create an unforgettable experience that becomes part of your wedding's magic.

Check the reviews and watch full length videos, better yet - go seem them live if you are local to their area. The vocals and stage presence make or break a live band. Make sure the singer in the video is the one performing at your wedding. Ask directly: "Will the same lead vocalist be there on the event day?"

GET A CLEAR CONTRACT AND MAKE SURE IT COVERS

- Start and end times
- Number of musicians
- Setup needs (space, power)
- Breaks (do they provide music during them?)
- Cancellation/refund policy
- Green room requirements
- Special requests in their rider?
- Stage requirement (elevated stage and size?)
- Ask about backup plans—what if someone gets sick? Severe weather plan?

Band rider is a document attached to a band's performance contract that outlines their specific requirements for a show. A rider helps ensure the band has everything they need to perform smoothly, and it helps venues prepare in advance. There are usually two main parts:

Technical Rider
Details all the **equipment, stage setup, and tech requirements** the band needs, such as:
- Number of microphones, monitors, DI boxes
- Size of stage
- Soundcheck times
- Lighting preferences
- Backline (amps, drums, etc.)

Hospitality Rider
Outlines the **comfort and catering requests** for the band backstage:
- Food and drink (e.g., snacks, meals, water, alcohol)
- Dressing room setup
- Towels, mirrors, Wi-Fi access
- Security or parking arrangements

Talented bands will often learn your first dance song (sometimes for an additional fee), take a few requests, and adjust their set lists based on the crowd's energy. Most groups are happy to learn two to four custom songs, but you'll need to give them at least four to six months' notice. Bonus tip: Ask which songs they recommend for keeping the dance floor packed all night.

Not all bands bring their own PA systems, microphones (especially for speeches), or lighting. Confirm whether their equipment meets your venue's sound restrictions and space requirements. While most bands provide basic gear, if you'd like to use their digital music for your ceremony or cocktail hour—and need an additional speaker setup, microphone, or a band member to manage the soundboard—that typically comes at an extra cost.

Stellar bands can book up 12 to 18 months in advance, especially for prime dates. If live music is high on your priority list, don't wait too long to secure your dream band!

A TOUCH OF CLASS, A SOUND OF LOVE

Your wedding ceremony is, after all, the very reason you're gathering—to promise to love one another for the rest of your days. So why not make those thirty minutes deeply meaningful? I understand if hiring live musicians feels out of budget, but there are creative ways around that.

So often, my couples hesitate to ask family members to contribute to the wedding in a meaningful way. But remember: you never know unless you ask. Looking back, I'd bet gracious Aunt Sally, who sponsored a guitarist for her sweet niece's ceremony, is thrilled she got to play a part in such a momentous occasion.

Live string instruments, piano, or guitar bring a warm, resonant sound that instantly elevates the atmosphere—perfect for poignant moments like walking down the aisle or exchanging vows. Many musicians can craft custom arrangements of your favorite songs—be it classical pieces, pop hits, or even beloved movie scores—adding a unique and personal touch to your ceremony. Compared to recorded tracks or larger ensembles, strings or solo guitar offer a soft, romantic vibe that's ideal for indoor chapels, outdoor gardens, or intimate spaces.

Live musicians don't just provide music; they add a refined, timeless presence to your ceremony. Guests not only hear the notes but also witness the artistry in real time. Skilled musicians can seamlessly synchronize music with your processional, vows, and recessional. They're also adept at improvising transitions if your timeline veers off track, adjusting volume and tempo on the spot.

Another advantage? A solo guitarist or string trio requires minimal space and power, making them perfect for smaller venues, outdoor settings, or historic buildings with specific limitations.

Given enough notice, musicians are often delighted to learn special songs meaningful to you as a couple. And even if you don't have a specific tune in mind, their extensive repertoire of exquisite pieces ensures you'll find selections that make your ceremony unforgettable.

CENTER STAGE

There's a quiet magic that unfolds during the dances—moments that feel almost suspended in time. The first dance between a couple is often the first chance they truly pause amidst the whirlwind of the day to simply be together. The way they lock eyes, share whispered words only they can hear, and sway in rhythm to a song that holds special meaning…it's intimate, vulnerable, and breathtaking. It's not merely choreography—it is emotion woven into music.

Every time I witness it, I'm struck by the profound weight and beauty of that moment. If I allow myself to be still and truly watch their faces, it often brings tears to my eyes.

Then come the parent dances—mother and son, father and daughter. These moments are steeped in history and memory. You can see it in the gentle way a mother rests her head against her son's shoulder or the tender grip of a father holding his daughter as if she were still five years old, twirling in the living room. It is joy intertwined with nostalgia; pride wrapped in tenderness. These dances express what words often cannot: "I love you," "I'm proud of you," "I'll always be here."

As a planner, I've witnessed countless first dances and parent dances—but the emotion never loses its power. Sometimes, when a beloved parent is no longer here to share in the joy of a wedding day, another cherished family member—a devoted aunt, uncle, or sibling—steps in to fill that role. These moments carry a poignancy all their own, transforming the dance into a tribute that blends remembrance with celebration. It's deeply touching to witness someone step forward with love and grace, honoring the absent parent while creating a memory that is uniquely beautiful and profoundly meaningful.

Each one is uniquely personal yet universally moving. They remind me of the true meaning behind every detail we carefully orchestrate—the timelines, the rehearsals, the song choices. Because in those few minutes on the dance floor, time seems to slow, hearts open, and love—real, enduring love—takes center stage.

BEATS YOU'LL LOVE, BANTER YOU'LL TOLERATE

Let's be honest—everyone loves live music. There's just something irresistible about a sizzling saxophone solo or a vocalist belting out *Don't Stop Believin'* like it's 1981 that makes your heart race and your feet hit the dance floor. Bands bring an energy, nostalgia, and charisma to a wedding in a way no playlist ever could.

But let me set your expectations right now:

Just because someone can sing *At Last* with Etta James-level soul doesn't mean they're also a seamless, timeline-obsessed emcee. In fact, most vocalists aren't born announcers—they're artists. They live for chord progressions and key changes, not timeline cue points.

So yes, the music will be phenomenal. The transitions, though? Anticipate the occasional stretch of silence. Picture this: We're rolling into toasts—champagne is bubbling, emotions are running high, and all eyes turn to the stage.

The band leader announces, "Please welcome the Maid of Honor!" and then…

Crickets. Literal chirping, because the mic wasn't switched on or the sound guy decided it was the perfect moment to grab a plate of sliders.

Or imagine the best man finishing his speech with a punchline worthy of a mic drop—and… nothing. No follow-up music. No gentle swell to carry the moment forward. Just dead air so silent you could hear a boutonnière hit the floor.

Why? Because they're not DJs.

They're not hovering over digital soundboards, ready to cue up the next track with split-second precision. They're busy warming up their vocal cords, tuning guitars, or making sure the keyboard player hasn't wandered off for a whiskey refill.

When you hire a band—especially one in the $5,000–$10,000 range—you're paying for incredible live music, not necessarily for flawless event flow with a seasoned MC.

Now, if you're shelling out $15,000 or more for a top-tier band, that's another ballgame entirely. You should expect tight transitions, a dedicated MC, DJ-style tracks during breaks, and microphones that don't sound like they were bought at a garage sale.

Make sure your contract clearly spells out exactly what they'll handle—because the last thing you want is to be awkwardly announcing the cake cutting yourself, shrimp taco in hand. Here's the good news: most guests won't notice the gaps. They're too busy sipping cocktails, taking selfies, and raving about the food. I'm keenly aware, though. Whenever the flow falters, a tiny piece of my Type-A planner soul quietly dies inside

PLANNER'S PLAYBOOK: If you're working with a band, **over-communicate.** Walk through the timeline in detail. Clarify who's handling announcements, who's managing the mic during toasts, and what the plan is when the band takes a break. Find out if they have a DJ playlist or someone overseeing transitions. If they mention "a guy with a laptop," perfect—introduce yourself, become best friends, and maybe offer him a snack so he doesn't vanish halfway through a speech.

Also, be prepared for occasional pauses. Not every moment needs to be filled with music or chatter, but be ready to jump in with a cue if things start to feel awkward. (Or grab the mic yourself and unleash your inner awards-show host—trust me, you'll get more comfortable with practice.)

SAVVY BRIDE TIPS: If you're hiring a live band (which—yay! Great choice!), make sure you ask the right questions:

- Who's handling announcements?
- Is there someone managing music during breaks?

What's the setup for toasts and special moments?
Above all, don't make assumptions. Just because someone has a microphone and loads of charisma doesn't mean they're eager—or experienced enough—to MC your big day. Bands often prefer you have the singer (or a designated hype-person) to help cue important moments.

Live bands bring an unforgettable energy—but keep your expectations realistic when it comes to smooth production. Pair incredible music with a solid plan and a reliable support team, and you'll enjoy the best of both worlds: music you'll love and transitions so seamless you'll hardly notice them.

A STRING IS A WISH YOUR HEART MAKES

Once upon a time, we had the absolute delight—and a dash of pixie-dusted wonder—of being part of a Disney-themed wedding that truly felt like stepping into a storybook. The couple, self-declared Disney superfans, curated every detail with care, from delicate castle motifs hidden in the stationery to table names inspired by their favorite animated films.

But the real showstopper? A live string quartet performing an exclusively Disney repertoire throughout the entire ceremony.

The moment the first notes floated into the air; the atmosphere shifted. The ceremony space was light and airy, bathed in natural sunlight streaming through sheer draping. Florals in soft dusty blue and blush pink spilled from towering arrangements and delicate aisle markers, filling the air with a subtle, sweet fragrance. The entire scene felt like a dreamy watercolor painting, ethereal and serene.

Guests visibly softened as the opening chords of "A Dream is a Wish Your Heart Makes" whispered through the space. It wasn't just a ceremony—it became an immersive, emotional experience. People mouthed the lyrics, dabbed tears from their eyes, and squeezed their partner's hand as if waiting for the story's happily-ever-after.

When the bride glided down the aisle to "A Whole New World," the collective gasp was palpable—a moment where time seemed to pause. Who knew violins playing "Can You Feel the Love Tonight" could elicit such tender emotion? And yet... they absolutely did.

Each musical choice was intentional and touching. "Beauty and the Beast" underscored the vows, wrapping the moment in nostalgia and romance. The recessional closed on a playful note with "You've Got a Friend in Me," sending guests out into cocktail hour grinning and humming along.

And the best part? Every single guest—yes, even stoic Uncle Charles—was utterly charmed. The children believed they'd stumbled into Disneyland itself. The grandparents grew misty-eyed, reminiscing about trips with their own kids to see these beloved films. And the couple? They positively glowed. Because their ceremony didn't merely reflect them as partners—it reflected them as dreamers, romantics, and proud Disney aficionados in the best possible way.

The delicate harmonies, elegant arrangements, and the sense of pure enchantment the quartet delivered transcended mere music. For half an hour, they wove a world that was familiar yet magical, timeless yet deeply personal. It felt as though, for a fleeting moment, we were all inside a living fairytale.

It was a seamless blend of romance, whimsy, and artistry—and proof that when couples stay true to who they are, the result can be absolutely unforgettable. This wasn't just a wedding. It was a once-upon-a-time moment brought vividly to life.

DANCING INTO FOREVER

The lights dimmed to a soft amber, casting a golden glow across the polished floor as music drifted into the room. All eyes gravitated toward the couple — both striking, statuesque brunettes, poised as though they'd stepped straight from the pages of a bridal editorial. She moved like poetry set to motion; her gown sculpted to her figure in lines of effortless grace. It was the kind of dress that required no introduction: sleek, timeless, utterly destined for her. A daring thigh-high slit whispered of drama—and delivered it in every step.

Their first dance unfolded not as a casual sway, but as a choreographed story — passionate, intimate, meticulously synchronized. Each movement revealed layers of their connection: playful glances, elegant spins, laughter only the two of them could hear.

When the chorus rose, he lifted her high, strong and certain, as though the music had been written solely for their moment. Her dress spiraled around them like a silken ribbon caught in a gentle breeze, the slit parting in perfect rhythm to reveal fleeting glimpses of motion and allure.

He guided her into a seamless twirl, time seeming to slow in the hush of the crowd's admiration. As the final note shimmered and fell away, she folded into his embrace. Their lips met in a kiss so tender, so cinematic, it felt not merely like the perfect ending to a love story — but the breathtaking beginning of one.

FROM TEARS TO CHEERS

One of my favorite moments at any wedding is when a parent dance takes an unexpected turn. It often begins exactly as you'd imagine—sweet, gentle, and steeped in emotion. A father slowly sways with his daughter, or a mother cradles her son close, both wrapped in a quiet bubble of reflection and pride. Guests look on with soft smiles, some discreetly dabbing tears from their eyes.

The song playing is tender and significant—perhaps tied to childhood memories or a special family moment—and for a brief, wistful stretch of time, the world seems to pause. It's all about love, the passage of time, and the journey that led them to this day.

Then, in the blink of an eye, everything changes.

The slow melody fades away, the lights shift to a livelier glow, and suddenly an upbeat rhythm bursts through the speakers—playful, vibrant, and delightfully unexpected. And that's when the magic unfolds: the father busts out a moonwalk, the mother starts shimmying like she's auditioning for a music video, and the groom jumps in, nailing full choreography—and the crowd goes absolutely wild.

Laughter echoes through the room, phones fly into the air to capture every second, and jaws drop in joyful disbelief. What began as a tender, heartfelt moment transforms into a full-blown celebration, overflowing with personality, humor, and pure delight.

These moments are surprising, yes—but also profoundly moving in their own way. They speak volumes without words, saying: "We know how to savor life. We know how to have fun. And we're doing it together."

It's surprises like these—equal parts emotional and electrifying—that capture the very heart of a wedding. They remind us that love isn't just sentimental; it's playful and vibrant. It's not only about tradition; it's about authentic, personal expression. Watching a parent and child share that journey on the dance floor—first through tears, then through uproarious laughter—is the kind of memory no one ever forgets. And as a future mother of the groom, I'm already planning to pull off something just as fun—because if I don't, I might simply dissolve into a hot, crying mess instead.

11

FORKS, FIZZ AND FROSTING

FORKS

When it comes to wedding planning, catering is one of the most memorable—and sometimes complex—elements to get just right. Food shapes the atmosphere of the event and plays a crucial role in how guests experience the day; after all, a well-fed crowd is a happy one.

The first step is to define your wedding style and service format: will it be an elegant plated dinner, a relaxed buffet, trendy food stations, or even a cozy family-style meal? Your choice should reflect the overall tone of your event and align with your priorities, whether that's sophistication, guest interaction, or simplicity.

It's equally important to consider your guest count and budget early in the process. Catering costs often scale with headcount, so having a clear estimate helps prevent last-minute surprises. Ask potential caterers for detailed proposals that include service staff, rentals (if needed), and any additional charges, such as cake-cutting fees or corkage. And don't overlook dietary needs—be sure there are delicious options for guests who are vegetarian, gluten-free, or managing food allergies.

Tastings are a must. They offer insight not only into the flavors but also the caterer's presentation and attention to detail. Pay close attention to taste, plating, and portion sizes. It's also wise to ask how they handle timing, temperature control, and logistics, especially if you're working with a non-traditional venue that lacks a full kitchen. An experienced caterer will help you craft a realistic timeline and may offer advice on meal pacing or which appetizers hold up best during cocktail hour.

Lastly, consider adding personal touches. Incorporating a signature dish, late-night snacks, or desserts that honor your cultural background or love story can make your menu feel intimate and distinctive. Exceptional catering doesn't merely satisfy hunger—it sparks connection, conversation, and a sense of celebration.

BEFORE SIGNING WITH YOUR CATERER, BE SURE TO CLARIFY:

Do you provide staff for the full duration of the event—including cleanup? Don't assume! Some caterers only stay through dinner service and leave before dessert or reception cleanup. Make sure you understand:
- How long the staff will stay
- If they assist with bussing tables during dancing
- Who handles trash, rentals, and post-dinner breakdown

Is cake cutting included in your service? Believe it or not, many caterers charge extra for this.
- Will your staff cut, plate, and serve the cake (or put it on a dessert table)?

- Is that fee already included?
- If not, what's the additional cost?

Do you provide water stations and beverage service separate from the bar?
Especially important for outdoor or hot-weather weddings.
- Is there a self-serve water station?
- Who sets it up and refills it?
- If the bar line is long, will guests still have access to water?

What kind of plates, utensils, and service ware do you provide?
Styrofoam vs. ceramic, plastic cutlery vs. silverware—big difference in guest experience.
- Are real plates and cutlery included?
- If not, what are the upgrade options?
- Do they match your event style or theme?

Who is responsible for bussing tables, taking out trash, and cleanup at the end of the night? This is where corners often get cut.
- Will they clear tables throughout the night?
- Do they take out trash and handle food waste?
- Do they help pack up leftover food or rentals?

Trash Duty is Not in My Job Description
Get all of this in writing—either in your contract or in a clear, documented email. If it's not spelled out, it's not guaranteed. The last thing you want on your wedding night is discovering your caterer has ghosted after dinner, leaving your coordinator and your family to clear plates and slice cake in formalwear.

HERE'S A GOLDEN RULE I LIVE BY: always hire a full-service caterer. And by full-service, I mean a team that stays at least an hour after the grand send-off to clean up, bus tables, haul out trash, and leave the kitchen looking like it never hosted a 200-person chicken marsala marathon.

Why? Because nothing annihilates that just-married glow faster than realizing you, your assistant, or—heaven forbid—the mother of the bride is hauling garbage bags into the moonlight in a ballgown. Trust me, I've witnessed it, and it's about as glamorous as a soggy bread roll welded to a tablecloth. We're talking half-sipped wine glasses, abandoned plates of mashed potatoes, and a vibe that's less fairy tale and more culinary crime scene. Nobody wants that as their parting memory of the day.

If you're fortunate enough to be working at a reputable venue, chances are they've seen this horror show play out and now enforce strict policies. These venues often provide couples with a list of vetted caterers who actually stick around until the last crumb is cleared and every trash bin is empty. To that, I say: bless them.

However, if your couple opts for a venue that allows outside catering—be it their favorite taco truck or Uncle Larry's "famous BBQ"—this is where you, dear planner, must hold the line.

HERE'S WHAT YOU SHOULD DO:

Require a cleanup clause in the catering contract: Don't settle for a vague "yes, we clean up." Get specific. Will they bus guest tables? Haul trash to the dumpster? Scrape plates, wipe counters, and leave the kitchen looking like it's never hosted a single bread roll? If the answer's no, it should be a hard pass from you. And if they're unwilling, line up a third-party cleanup crew to handle the aftermath.

Get clear about the timeline: Make sure the caterer knows disappearing after dinner is not an option. They stay until the bitter end—at least an hour after the send-off. That extra time ensures everything gets cleaned without frantic chaos during the final moments of the event.

Confirm who's handling rentals and disposables: If the caterer's using real plates and glassware, find out who's washing, packing, or returning them. If it's disposables, clarify who's dealing with the Styrofoam apocalypse. Spoiler alert: it shouldn't be you.

Check with the venue about their standards: Some venues require caterers to mop floors, remove trash, and lock up the kitchen before they leave. Share those requirements with your caterer upfront so no one's pointing fingers later.

Because when the last sparkler fizzles out and the couple drives off into newlywed bliss, you deserve to be high-fiving your team, sipping a mocktail, and basking in the afterglow of a job well done—not elbow-deep in leftover salad, rummaging through an industrial fridge, and wondering why someone decided to stash a half-eaten cupcake inside.

YOU GET WHAT YOU PAY FOR

Let's talk about food. Specifically, the kind of food you serve to 120 guests after a long, hot, emotional wedding day.

My bride was working with a tight budget. Totally understandable—weddings are expensive, and every couple has to make some tough choices. But one of the corners she decided to cut was catering. She chose a very inexpensive vendor who promised buffet-style service, bussing, and a water station. On paper, it sounded fine. Not glamorous, but perfectly functional.

I did my part. I confirmed everything in advance:

✔ Buffet? Confirmed.

✔ Staff to bus tables? Confirmed.

✔ Water station? Confirmed in writing. (You know I had screen grabs at the ready.)

Flash forward to the big day. The ceremony is lovely—a pop-up rain shower adds a touch of drama, there's a bit of hair frizz, makeup touch-ups, and the kind of humid Southern air that makes everyone a little glassy-eyed.

Guests are parched after photos and the outdoor heat. I swing open the reception doors, ready to welcome everyone inside—and immediately, my heart stops. There's no water station.

Just a long, slow, sweaty line at the bar, where guests are desperately waiting... for water.

People aren't even asking for cocktails yet—they're simply trying to hydrate. And they can't.

I whirl around to my assistant and hiss, "Where is the water station?!"

She blinks and says, "The caterer told me they don't set up water stations."

Excuse me?!

I speed-walk back to the kitchen, pull up my email thread, and show the catering captain exactly where I confirmed the water setup in writing. Not in a snippy way, but in a firm, professional "this is not optional" way. They scramble to assemble it.

Eventually, pitchers and glasses appear—but not before several guests are fanning themselves with dinner menus and shooting me looks that could wilt the floral centerpieces.

Crisis semi-averted… and then dinner is served.

Oh. My. Goodness.

The plates—if you could call them that—were flimsy Styrofoam. Each guest received one tiny enchilada and a single lonely fajita strip. A spoonful of rice. No sauce. Nothing green in sight unless you counted the handful of shredded iceberg lettuce tossed on top. It was like a sad school lunch… at a wedding.

I wanted to cry. The couple was embarrassed. Guests were puzzled. Because there's being budget-conscious, and then there's underfeeding 120 people who've been sweating and sipping cocktails in formalwear for hours.

And let me be clear: I don't share this to shame anyone. I share it because it's important. Food matters. Not just because people expect a good meal—but because service matters. Hydration matters. The quality of the experience matters. Guests don't expect filet mignon on a shoestring budget—but they do expect to be fed, have access to water, and feel looked after.

HERE'S THE GOLDEN NUGGET FROM ALL THIS:

Cheap catering isn't always affordable. It can cost you in guest experience, comfort, and the overall vibe of your reception. If you're not sure where to save and where to splurge, talk to your planner (hi, that's me). Because trust me, it's far better to simplify your menu than to cut corners with a vendor who disappears when you need them most. And please—for the love of your guests—always confirm the water station.

THE CATERER WHO VANISHED AFTER DINNER

In my early years as a wedding coordinator, I learned a lesson the hard way — and let me tell you, it stuck. The day had been smooth. One of those rare weddings that felt like sailing on a calm lake. Just enough breeze to keep things interesting, but overall? Easy. Dinner was served, toasts went off without a hitch, and we were gliding right into the cake-cutting like seasoned pros.

The photographer captured every sweet moment — the couple laughing, gently feeding each other cake — and I whisked the cake into the kitchen to have it sliced and plated for guests.

That's when I hit a wall.

I asked the catering team to start cutting, and they looked at me as though I'd just requested, they build an entirely new cake from scratch.

"Oh, we don't do that," one of them said.

Excuse me?

They explained the couple hadn't paid for cake cutting.

Now, let me pause here: If the couple doesn't pay for cake cutting, guess who ends up wielding the knife? The coordinator. Every. Single. Time.

Without missing a beat, I said, "Fantastic. Can someone grab me a pair of food-safe gloves?"

And there I was, back in the kitchen, cutting cake like it was my side hustle, trying to keep the slices neat and photogenic while guests began drifting toward the dessert table. To their credit, the caterers helped me set the plated slices out for guests to grab. It wasn't ideal, but we made it work.

Fast forward a bit. I stepped away for a quick bathroom break, and when I returned to the kitchen — it was spotless.

And empty. Gone. They'd vanished.

I immediately called the catering lead.

"Hey, where's your team?"

"Oh, we leave after dinner. That's what the client paid for."

No bussing. No trash service. No breakdown assistance. Just… gone.

And there I was, standing in the middle of the reception, glasses piling up, half-eaten cake plates abandoned on tables. Guests were still dancing and having the time of their lives — blissfully unaware that behind the scenes, my smiling face (and a few kind-hearted family members) had officially become the impromptu clean-up crew.

Because someone has to do it. And no, it wasn't in my job description. But there was no way I'd let the bride's grandma sit down to sticky tables littered with crumpled cocktail napkins.

THIS IS THE INVALUABLE TAKEAWAY

I carry forward, and the advice I give all my clients who didn't select a full-service catering company: **Ask exactly how long your caterer stays — and what they're responsible for while they're there.**

Cutting the cake? Bussing tables? Taking out the trash? Those tasks aren't always included.

You do *not* want to discover this when the catering team is already halfway to the freeway, chafing dishes clanking in the back of the van.

That night, I became a cake-cutter, plate-passer, and busser. And while I'll always step in when needed, you'd better believe I now confirm every single post-dinner service detail in advance. **In writing.** Because disappearing caterers? That's a lesson learned — and never forgotten.

ARE Y'ALL ALMOST HERE?

It's 2021, and John and I are in Rockport, Texas—a laid-back Gulf Coast town where the breeze is salty, the pace is leisurely, and people still call you "doll" without a hint of irony. We're onsite for a 300-person Polish wedding (yes, 300), handling coordination, florals and décor, and even a photo booth. Basically, the full wedding marathon.

It was all hands-on deck. My amazing in-laws, Joe and Gail, came along for the ride. Even my little Jameson helped decorate the day before. It was a family affair in every sense.

The day unfolded smoothly. We got the bride down the aisle on time, photos were rolling, and the Catholic ceremony included a break—giving us just enough time to hustle over to the convention center and start receiving vendors before the crowd arrived.

Appetizers were DIY, lovingly prepared by the family. There was a shrimp station (a bold choice in the coastal summer heat, but okay) and a table piled high with snack mix. A little iffy, but hey—it's Rockport. We were rolling with it.

But then... where were the caterers?

Guest arrival time was looming, and the catering team was nowhere in sight. I called the lead:

"Hi Becky, are y'all almost here?"

"Yes, doll, we're right around the corner."

Okay. Deep breath. Yet I'm not seeing trucks. I'm not seeing staff. It's just Becky and her husband. I ask, "Where's the rest of your team?"

"Oh, they'll be there. Don't worry—we do this all the time."

Cue the skeptical side-eye.

There we were in a coastal town, staring down 300 hungry guests and a Polish family primed for a party—and just two people about to serve dinner. I was sweating, praying, and running backup plans in my head.

And then… they absolutely crushed it.

I'm not exaggerating: they rolled in, got to work, and within thirty minutes had an entire kitchen set up, a buffet staged, and food hot and ready to go. I blinked, and suddenly it was showtime. Not only that—they had dinner served to all 300 guests within forty minutes.

It was seamless. It was fast. And it was delicious.

Guests were raving. The family was ecstatic. The bride never heard a single whisper of doubt. Becky and her husband? Total pros. Like hospitality heroes with Southern accents.

And here's the thing:

Yes, as planners, we're trained to worry. We confirm, double-confirm, and brace ourselves for the unexpected. But every once in a while, someone comes along who reminds you that experience trumps appearances. That laid-back doesn't mean unprepared. And that some people genuinely know exactly what they're doing—even if they don't show up with an army in tow.

Always confirm. Always prepare. But never underestimate the quiet confidence of a vendor who says, "We do this all the time." Because in Rockport, Texas? They absolutely meant it.

WHY DROP-OFF ISN'T ENOUGH

Ah, restaurant caterers. Bless them—they know how to make delicious food, but sometimes forget that weddings are a far cry from takeout orders with table numbers. This particular story hails from my early years as a solo coordinator.

Like many tales that begin with, *"I noticed a few red flags during confirmations,"* it required quick thinking, a sturdy backbone, and that professional smile you wear when you're silently screaming inside.

It was a sweet spring wedding. I was reviewing final details and running through confirmations with vendors—a last round of *"Are we all good?"* before showtime. I called the caterer, and immediately my stomach began to twist. They were a beloved local restaurant, but the truth became painfully clear: they were planning to simply drop off the food. That's it.

No staff. No serving tools. No plates, napkins, or silverware. No one to bus tables. No plan for cleanup. Just brisket and sweet tea.

Delicious? Absolutely. Disaster waiting to happen? Also, yes.

I reached out to the couple and gently said, *"Hey, we need to talk through a few critical details."* I explained this wasn't a full-service catering setup—it was essentially dinner delivery with a tea station. I rattled off the essentials they'd still need: buffet tables, chafing dishes, serving utensils, dinnerware, napkins, cups, staff to clear tables and trash, and a kitchen crew to handle cleanup and resets. The whole nine yards.

They pushed back—hard.

"But they said it would be fine!"

"It's just food for 75 people. How complicated can it be?"

"Can't someone else help with the cleanup?"

That's when I stepped into my "friendly but firm" mode.

I said, *"Look—as your coordinator, I manage logistics, timeline, vendors, and the flow of the day. I am not bussing tables or scraping barbecue sauce off rented linens. Respectfully, that's not my role."*

Eventually, logic prevailed. We hired a catering staffing team through the restaurant to handle service and cleanup. We secured all the necessary rentals—from plates and napkins to serving trays and trash bins.

Come wedding day, everything flowed seamlessly. Guests were served hot, fresh food without a hitch. Tables were cleared efficiently. The couple enjoyed their meal in peace, completely unaware of how close they'd come to culinary chaos.

Later, the mother of the bride approached me, eyes glistening with grateful tears, "Thank you for being our rock. I had no idea weddings were this complicated. I'm so grateful you made sure everything ran smoothly."

CAPERS, CHEERS, AND THE CASE FOR ONE VENDOR

When it came to planning the food and drinks for our wedding, John and I knew two things for certain: we were working with a budget, but we wanted the entire day to feel like we weren't.

Our tasting lived up to every bit of its promise—it was absolutely delicious. From the moment we arrived, we were greeted by friendly smiles and ushered into a cozy little dining room that already felt like a celebration. It was clear we were in good hands.

We sampled several dishes, but the second I tasted the chicken piccata—with its bright, lemony sauce and briny pops of capers—I was completely sold. I'm a sucker for capers. I may or may not have batted my lashes and sweetly requested extra on my plate (spoiler: I totally got them).

While we couldn't stretch our budget to cover full porcelain place settings, we got creative. We opted for what I like to call the half-and-half setup: glass goblets, decorative charger plates, linen napkin, and polished flatware. The dinner plates were clear acrylic with a silver edge, displayed beautifully at the buffet. Were they fine porcelain? No. But honestly, who's scrutinizing the plates when the food is divine and the drinks are flowing?

Speaking of drinks—that's where we made one of our smartest decisions. Early on, we chose to use the same company for both catering and bartending, and it was a choice that paid off in spades.

One of the best perks of hiring a *single vendor* to handle both catering and bar is how wonderfully streamlined everything becomes. You've got one team, one timeline, and one captain steering the ship—which means far fewer emails clogging your inbox at midnight. The service itself feels seamless, with food and drinks flowing effortlessly because the crew behind the scenes is already operating in sync. Plus, shared staff means a shared vision: everyone's on the same page about the vibe, the pacing, and how to keep guests feeling like royalty.

It's often more cost-effective too, sparing you extra delivery fees, multiple contracts, and the kind of headaches only spreadsheets can cause. And let's not forget crisis control—because if something goes sideways, like running out of ice or realizing someone forgot the extra cups, there's no "not our department" nonsense. They just handle it. And frankly, that kind of teamwork is worth its weight in gold—or at least in top-shelf tequila.

And let's talk about the bar itself: we are firm believers in the open bar philosophy. I've never been fond of pay-as-you-go bars, especially when your guests have invested their time, energy, and travel dollars to share in your celebration. It simply feels gracious to treat them to a drink—or three.

Our bar was lively, our plates were cleared, and our hearts were full. To this day, I still recommend Absolutely Delicious Catering to my couples. They made us feel like royalty—even on a beer-and-wine budget.

FIZZ

Planning the bar for your wedding isn't just about picking drinks—it's about creating a seamless, enjoyable experience for your guests while staying mindful of budget and logistics.

The first decision is choosing your bar type: open bar, limited bar, or pay-as-you-go. An open bar is the most guest-friendly but also the priciest. A limited bar—offering beer, wine, and perhaps a couple of signature cocktails—is an excellent way to balance warm hospitality with cost control.

Once you've settled on your bar style, think about your crowd. If your guests love craft beer or tequila-based cocktails, tailor the menu accordingly. Featuring signature cocktails is a stylish, wallet-friendly way to make your celebration feel distinctly you. Consider choosing drinks that reflect your personalities or a special memory you share—but ensure they're simple and quick for bartenders to pour so the line doesn't become a traffic jam. **Pre-batching cocktails can be a great option to keep service moving efficiently.**

Don't forget to clarify whether your venue or caterer provides bar service or if you'll need to bring in a licensed bartender and supply your own alcohol. If you're supplying the alcohol yourself, work with your bartender or planner to calculate quantities based on your guest count and event duration—typically, plan for about one drink per person per hour. And always provide plenty of non-alcoholic options like infused water, soda, or mocktails for guests who don't drink or want to pace themselves.

Lastly, ensure that alcohol service wraps up in line with your venue's regulations and timeline. A well-timed coffee station or a late-night snack offering can help transition guests from party mode to farewell hugs. When thoughtfully planned, your bar can be both a dazzling focal point and a seamless part of your celebration.

QUESTIONS TO ASK YOUR BARTENDER BEFORE BOOKING

What's included in your service? Not all bartending packages are created equal.

- Do you provide the alcohol, or do we need to provide it?
- Do you include mixers, garnishes, ice, straws, napkins?
- Are bar tools, coolers, and tables included, or do I need to rent those separately?

How many bartenders will be on-site, and for how long?
The number of bartenders matters, especially for larger guest counts.

- How many staff will you bring for my guest count?
- Do you offer additional support staff (e.g. barbacks)?
- Is there an overtime fee if the reception runs late?

Do you help with alcohol quantity recommendations?
Most couples have no idea how much to buy. A good bartender can help.

- Will you provide a customized shopping list if we supply the alcohol?
- Can you suggest signature cocktails or help us build a basic menu?

Do you carry liquor liability insurance?
This is big. Many venues **require** this and won't let uninsured vendors serve alcohol.
- Are you licensed and insured to serve alcohol in this state?
- Can you provide a copy of your liability insurance?

Do you handle setup and cleanup of the bar area?
You don't want to find yourself bussing cocktail glasses or hauling out bags of ice at midnight.
- Will you set up and break down the bar?
- Do you clean up trash/glassware at the bar area?
- What do you need from us to make this run smoothly?

If your bartending team seems vague about any of the above—or they don't ask questions about your venue, timeline, or guest count—that's a red flag. A great bartender is part mixologist, part logistics pro.

SHAKEN, STIRRED... AND OUT OF ICE?

Ah yes, the great cocktail catastrophe of 2022. Picture this: The sun was shining, chairs were perfectly set, the timeline was on point, and the vibes? Immaculate. That is, until we discovered the bartending company had arrived… brimming with enthusiasm, charm, and a cute bar sign they'd found on Etsy—yet armed with virtually no ice or mixers.

I'm making my rounds: checking vendor arrivals, ensuring the florals aren't wilting, and giving my signature nod of encouragement to the nervous groom. Eventually, I wander over to the bar to greet the bartenders. They're all smiles, busily arranging coolers and cocktail tools.

"You're off to a good start!" I remark. "Let me know if you need anything."

The head bartender flashes me a casual thumbs-up and replies, "Will do!"

Fast-forward thirty minutes. Guests are arriving for ceremony when one of the servers comes over, whisper-shouting: "We've got a situation."

The bar situation? A comedy of errors: zero ice (well, two shy little gas-station bags), a couple of half-used margarita mixes, and not so much as a fizzy mixer or a garnish to save the day. Oh—and the signature drink? The spicy margarita? They'd forgotten the jalapeños.

So essentially… they had tequila. And vibes. That's it.

I blinked. Took a deep breath. Blinked again.

"Didn't we go over a supply list?" I asked calmly, already knowing the answer.

"Well, yeah," the bartender stammered, now sweating a bit more than before. "But we thought the couple was bringing the ice and mixers."

No. Nope. Negative. Not today.

Cue my assistant sprinting to the nearest gas station to buy all the ice in stock while I frantically texted the bride's cousin (mercifully, a professional bartender himself) to help us pull off a makeshift bar miracle.

We salvaged cocktail hour with a much more *"streamlined"* drink menu—read: choose your spirit and pick from three mixers we managed to procure on the fly. And yes, the guests still had a blast. But I'll never forget the moment a guest took a sip of a gin-and-Sprite and remarked, "Well, this is different."

WHERE'S THE BOOZE?

There's nothing quite like setting up a beautiful wedding and suddenly realizing… the alcohol is MIA. It was two hours before guests were set to arrive. Florals were fluffed, candles glowed, and the ceremony chairs stood in perfect rows. But something was off.

That's when the bartender approached me, concern etched on his face despite his best efforts to stay chill: "Hey… just wondering if the alcohol delivery is running late?"

I stared at him. "It should've been here an hour ago."

Cue the internal panic.

I sent my assistant off to call the number listed on the delivery invoice. She was the picture of calm—far cooler than me—and managed to get the driver on the line. Turns out, his truck had broken down enroute. And the worst part? All the alcohol was sitting in the back of a hot vehicle somewhere on the outskirts of town.

Then, a glimmer of hope: "Backup truck is on the way," the driver assured us. "Should be there soon."

Let me tell you—I stared down that gravel road like it was the red carpet at the Oscars. And sure enough, with thirty minutes to spare before the ceremony began, a dusty white van rolled in like a hero—packed to the roof with everything we needed.

The bartenders sprang into action, icing bottles as if they were vying for Olympic gold. Champagne chilled, whiskey cooled, mixers lined up like little soldiers at attention.

By the time guests drifted from the ceremony to cocktail hour, the drinks were perfectly cold, and not a single person knew how close we'd come to serving room-temperature rosé in paper cups. Planner crisis averted. Bartenders redeemed. Guests blissfully unaware. And me? I'd say I earned every glorious sip of that post-sendoff pinot.

SIP, SIP, HOORAY!

Let's flip the script and talk about a bar story that *actually* went off without a hitch. Because while we planners are excellent at troubleshooting, nothing makes us happier than when everything simply *works*.

Most days are great, honestly, but it brings me back down to earth when I reminisce about the learning years. Those early days were full of surprises and lessons learned the hard way—which makes smooth events like this one feel even sweeter.

It was a lovely fall day—the kind with crisp air and a gentle breeze that makes everyone feel festive. We were at one of our favorite hill country venues, the kind that requires couples to choose from a curated list of trusted caterers and bartending companies. And let me tell you, that policy is a lifesaver. It keeps our job smoother, the couple stress-free, and the entire day running like clockwork.

After a beautiful ceremony, guests were ushered into cocktail hour and greeted by a showstopper: a margarita wall. Rows upon rows of colorful glasses, each brimming with perfectly pre-batched margaritas, waiting like little jewels to be plucked off the display. It was festive, fun, and the perfect icebreaker as the party got underway.

From the very start, everything was seamless—confirmations, load-in, setup, and service. The bartending team was an absolute dream. Friendly, efficient, and always two steps ahead, they kept glasses full and guests smiling. There was zero waiting, zero confusion, and not a single hiccup in sight.

The magic combo? A hosted bar, delicious pre-batched cocktails, and a crowd that was enthusiastic yet respectful. It's the trifecta that keeps the good vibes flowing without chaos.

By the end of the night, the couple was glowing, the guests were happy, and our vendor partners were high-fiving each other behind the scenes.

So, here's a massive thank-you to the venues who insist on working with true professionals. You make our jobs happier—and help ensure that, sometimes, everything really does go perfectly. Cheers to that!

BRIDE BONUS: HERE'S WHAT MAKES THE BAR EXPERIENCE TRULY MEMORABLE

Beyond prebatched drinks and a hosted bar, there are so many ways to elevate the guest experience and make your bar the place to be.

Start with signature cocktails—give them clever names inspired by your love story, your pets, or your favorite vacation spots. Add a custom cocktail menu with cute illustrations, and don't forget personalized drink stirrers or cocktail napkins (bonus points if they include a fun fact or cheeky quote).

Now let's talk ambiance: a beautifully styled bar with florals, candles, or a killer backdrop turns your drink station into a photo-op. Charismatic bartenders who know how to work a shaker—and a crowd—make all the difference.

If you really want to wow, bring in a flair bartender or offer something unexpected like smoked cocktails, frozen margaritas, or espresso martinis served late-night.

And don't leave your non-drinkers hanging—thoughtful mocktails and a hydration station with infused waters will keep everyone refreshed. The best bars are where drinks are cold, the design is hot, and your guests can't stop talking about it.

FROSTING

The wedding cake is more than just dessert—it's a statement piece that weaves together your celebration's style, flavor, and tradition. Whether you envision a towering showstopper or a small, elegant cutting cake, the key is to start planning early. Connect with potential bakers at least 4-6 months in advance—especially during peak wedding season—to secure availability and allow time for tastings, design consultations, and custom details.

When selecting flavors, think beyond classic vanilla. Many couples choose multi-tiered cakes featuring different flavors on each tier to delight a variety of palates. Popular pairings include lemon cake with raspberry filling, chocolate with salted caramel, or almond cake with amaretto buttercream.

Don't forget about texture and structure. Talk to your baker about how moist or dense you'd like the cake layers to be, as well as the textures of fillings and frostings. Also discuss structural integrity—particularly important for outdoor weddings—to ensure your cake will stay stable and beautiful throughout the event.

Visually, your cake should enhance your wedding aesthetic without replicating it exactly. Share your color palette, floral choices, attire details, and overall vibe with your baker so they can craft a design that feels cohesive and personal. Inspiration can come from anywhere: the lace on your gown, flowers used in your bouquet, or cherished patterns and family heirlooms.

Lastly, don't overlook the logistics. Confirm whether your venue allows outside cakes if you're hiring an independent baker, and clarify who will handle the cutting and serving. If you're considering a ceremonial "cutting cake" paired with sheet cakes behind the scenes, rest assured your guests will be none the wiser—and it can be a savvy way to manage costs.

Whether simple or intricate, the most unforgettable wedding cakes are those that reflect your unique style, tastes, and the spirit of who you are as a couple.

QUESTIONS TO ASK YOUR WEDDING CAKE BAKER

Can I schedule a tasting — and is it included in the price?
Tastings are where you find out if the cake actually tastes as good as it looks.
- How many flavors can we try?
- Is there a tasting fee?
- Can we mix flavors in different tiers?

Do you deliver and set up the cake at the venue?
You do not want Aunt Jane driving a three-tier cake in a heatwave.
- Is delivery included in your pricing?

- What time will you arrive to set up?
- Do you bring extra décor (like florals or cake stands), or do we supply those?

What is your pricing structure — and are there extra fees?
Wedding cakes can have hidden costs.
- Is the price based on number of servings, design complexity, or both?
- Are there fees for special flavors, tall tiers, gold leaf, etc.?
- Do you charge extra for cutting or packing leftover cake?

Can you work with our wedding theme and design?
Your cake should feel reflect your wedding's style.
- Can I show you inspiration photos or my vision board?
- Do you offer custom designs?
- Can you match our colors, florals, or vibe (boho, modern, classic, etc.)?

How do you handle outdoor weddings and heat-sensitive ingredients?
If your wedding is outdoors or in a warm climate, this is crucial.
- Can you recommend designs or fillings that hold up in heat?
- Will the cake be refrigerated before setup?
- How long can the cake sit out before it starts to wilt or slide?

Always get everything in writing: including flavors, design sketch, delivery time, and any allergy accommodations.

LOVE IS SWEET, TAKE A TREAT

If a traditional tiered wedding cake isn't quite your style, there are plenty of delicious and creative alternatives to consider. A popular option is a cupcake tower, which allows for a variety of flavors and makes serving easy, while still creating an impressive display. Dessert bars have also become a favorite, featuring an array of sweet treats like cookies, brownies, macarons, mini tarts, and cake pops, giving guests plenty of choices and adding a fun, interactive element.

For couples who prefer savory over sweet, a cheese wheel "cake" stacked with wheels of cheese and served with crackers, bread, and fruit offers an elegant and unique alternative—perfect for rustic or wine country weddings.

Donut towers or walls are trendy and playful, offering glazed or filled donuts arranged in a tiered display or hanging setup that appeals to guests of all ages. Seasonal pies or tarts provide a cozy, homey vibe and work especially well for fall or rustic-themed celebrations. An ice cream or gelato bar is ideal for warmer weather, allowing guests to customize their desserts with various toppings and flavors.

For those seeking something more traditional but still distinctive, a croquembouche—a French tower of cream-filled profiteroles held together with caramelized sugar—makes a stunning centerpiece. Macaron towers offer a delicate, colorful, and sophisticated alternative, especially for smaller or more intimate weddings.

Cheesecakes in a variety of flavors can also replace a traditional cake, sometimes offered as individual mini servings. Lastly, specialty desserts tailored to dietary needs, such as vegan, gluten-free, or allergen-free treats, ensure all guests can enjoy a sweet ending that fits their preferences. Whatever your taste or wedding style, there's a cake alternative to suit every celebration.

SMART QUESTIONS TO ASK YOUR DESSERT VENDOR
(That Aren't About the Desserts)

Styling matters, and those Instagram-worthy displays don't build themselves.
- Do you offer display rentals?
- What kind of trays, risers, or signage is included?
- Can I see photos of past setups?

You do not want your aunt arranging mini cupcakes in the final 15 minutes.
- Is set-up and display included or do I need to assign someone?
- Do you need a diagram or guidance from my coordinator?
- How much time do you need for setup?

You don't want to be stuck with 14 glass cake stands the next morning.
- When are the rentals due back?
- Who returns them—us, the planner, or someone from your team?
- Do you charge a security deposit?

Presentation and freshness matter.
- Will everything come boxed individually or in bulk?
- Do you use insulated or refrigerated transport?
- Should I have someone on-site to help unload?

Super helpful for guests (especially with common allergies).
- Do you label gluten-free, nut-free, or vegan items?
- Can you customize signage to match our theme?

Dessert bars can be tricky—too much or too little is easy.
- How many pieces per person do you recommend?
- Should I plan for one of each item, or just a few varieties?
- Do you offer bulk pricing or pre-set packages?

SWEET STRATEGY: Here's a little insider wisdom to save your wallet—and your waistline: don't over-order your cake or desserts. Let's say your guest count is 150—that doesn't mean you need 150 slices of cake or 150 individual desserts. Plenty of guests skip cake altogether (hard to believe, I know) because they're too busy tearing up the dance floor or clutching a cocktail. Nine times out of ten, we end up with enough leftover cake to start a small bakery. Save your money (and your fridge space) by ordering a bit less than your headcount. Your baker or caterer can help you hit that sweet spot—pun fully intended.

THE DESSERT TABLE THAT DOES NOT REFILL ITSELF

At the final venue walk-through, everything was falling into place. The bride was glowing, her mom was beaming, and I was mentally checking off my list like the seasoned planner I am.

Then she said it.

"Oh yes—we're going to have the cutest dessert table!" the bride beamed, already picturing a Pinterest-worthy setup, overflowing with pastel macarons, tiny cupcakes, and maybe even a donut wall.

"That sounds adorable!" I said with genuine enthusiasm. "Who's setting it up?"

She smiled confidently. "Oh, my aunt will—no problem."

"Perfect!" I replied, nodding. "Just make sure Auntie knows she's officially in charge of this sweet little project—so she's not surprised when she's mid-mimosa and suddenly being asked to unwrap ten dozen cake pops and organize a tower of mini cheesecakes."

Also me, silently: *Wait—who is Auntie? Is she dependable? Does she own cake stands? Will she bring a tablecloth or are we doing this on a bare six-foot folding table from the venue's back closet? Does she have serving tongs? Napkins? A game plan?*

Because here's the thing: a dessert table might *look* effortless when it's lit by candles and surrounded by guests swooning over salted caramel tarts—but behind the scenes, someone has to *place* each of those confections, unwrap the bakery boxes, arrange the risers just so, and ensure no one grabs a brownie with their bare hands. Auntie might be lovely, but if she's also wrangling flower girls, sipping bubbly, or just not briefed properly, things can go sideways fast.

Fast forward to wedding day. Cocktail hour is in full swing, guests are floating from conversation to conversation with drinks in hand, and I do a quick loop to check on details.

That's when I see it: the dessert table.

Except... it's not there.

I finally locate the "dessert table," which turns out to be a folding table draped in a wrinkled linen, with a few bakery boxes stacked on one end. The "cutest dessert table" is still very much in box form. No display. No signage. No tiers, no trays. Just a faint whiff of sugar and the distant sound of my sanity unraveling.

I ask around and eventually find Auntie—who is lovely, by the way—but completely unaware that she was the chosen one for this mission. "Oh, I thought someone else would handle it!" she says, casually sipping her sweet tea.

Cue the deep breath.

So, my team and I did what we always do—we pivoted. We opened boxes, borrowed trays from the caterer, folded napkins into makeshift doilies, and built a charming little display in under ten minutes flat.

But here's the kicker: no one was assigned to refill the table. So once guests descended, the desserts disappeared like magic—and never returned. That "cute dessert table" was a fleeting moment of glory and then… poof. Just crumbs.

MORAL OF THE STORY: dessert tables are not self-sustaining ecosystems. They require care, attention, signage, and a designated dessert czar. Otherwise, your adorable cookie tower becomes a sad little crumb graveyard before the first dance is over.

THE SECRET LIFE OF WEDDING CAKES

It's 2017. The music is thumping, the dance floor's alive with energy, and I'm weaving through the crowd on my usual rounds, getting the cake table ready for its big, sweet moment.

Music hums through the speakers, the lights glow warm and golden, and laughter bubbles around the room as guests swirl on the dance floor. Perfect!

The couple steps up to the cake table, hands intertwined, faces flushed with joy. Cameras flash like paparazzi as they share a sweet moment—grinning, laughing, and gently nudging each other while they pose for photos. They lean in, slice the cake together with that iconic first cut, and cheer erupts from the crowd.

Then… they wander off, champagne flutes in hand, blissfully unaware that the towering confection behind them isn't going to magically slice itself into neat little pieces.

I stand there, scanning the room as the DJ slides into another song. Guests are beginning to drift toward the cake table, curiosity and sugar cravings pulling them closer. The energy shifts—a ripple of expectation, like sharks circling for chum.

And I'm left looking around, wondering: *Where's the caterer? The family friend who said they'd handle it? Anyone?*

Crickets. Just the glow of fairy lights, the smell of buttercream, and me—suddenly realizing the cake might soon become my problem.

It was a classic case—the caterer wasn't paid to handle the cake cutting. Awesome. That left me scanning the room for Auntie, who was supposedly "in charge" of this whole operation. But where is she? Oh, right—she's out on the dance floor, living her best life, arms in the air, perfecting her Wobble like she's auditioning for a music video.

Picture 28-year-old me, posted up at the cake table ready to go with my food-safe gloves on and cake-knife in hand, suddenly promoted to pastry surgeon. I'm doing my best to carve tidy slices of buttercream bliss for a crowd growing increasingly restless.

And those guests? Oh, they were silently judging me with laser eyes. I swear I could *hear* their thoughts:

"Go faster."

"Why is this taking so long?"

"Has this woman never cut a cake before?"

I'm sweating buttercream bullets. The cake is oddly dense, the frosting's clinging to the knife like its life depends on it, and my slices look more like modern art than elegant dessert. I try to fan them out on trays like a bakery pro, but deep down, I know—this was *not* the job I signed up for.

And yet, since then, it's happened more than once. Someone forgets to assign a cutter. Or they assign Cousin Janet, who has no idea she's on duty. Or worse—who's had a little too much "celebration" and is in no state to handle cutlery. And suddenly, it's me again, elbow-deep in frosting while a line of sugar-deprived guests refuses to budge until cake is in hand.

But these days? Oh, I've learned.

I always ask:

"Who's cutting the cake?"

"What's their name?"

"Can I have their number?"

I treat the cake cutter family member like a vendor now—confirmed, contacted, and fully briefed. Because if no one's ready when the music fades and the sweet tooths kick in…

Well, that cake's staring at me. And I am *not* doing it again without a slice of hazard pay—and maybe my own piece of cake to go with it.

SLICE, SLICE BABY

There's nothing I love more than when a full-service caterer is in charge of the cake cutting. It's pure delight. Seamless, polished, and downright magical.

Imagine: The glow of candlelight flickers across an all-white reception, accented with soft hints of beige and warm tan tones. The room feels like a cloud—elegant, romantic, and brimming with quiet anticipation.

I'm there, cake knife in hand, gently coaching the couple, who are beaming but slightly nervous. I position them just so for the cameras and lean in with a grin.

"Okay, you two—this is your first team-building exercise as husband and wife. Don't forget to smile!"

They laugh, shoulders relaxing, as guests gather around in a semicircle, phones poised, waiting for that iconic moment. The couple makes the first slice, gently feeds each other a bite, and seals it with a sweet kiss. The crowd erupts in cheers, and just like that, they're whisked off to the dance floor for their first dance, wrapped in the glow of twinkle lights and love.

Here's the part that feels like a secret show only planners get to see: the catering squad swoops in like dessert virtuosos. They tackle that cake with precision and speed that rivals a Super Bowl halftime show. Boom, boom—slices are cut, plated, and elegantly arranged onto gleaming trays. They're weaving through the crowd, offering delicate plates of cake like dessert wizards, each piece looking as perfect as the first.

It's flawless. The guests barely have time to wonder where the cake went before a slice appears in their hands. The energy stays high, no messy interruptions, no stress—just pure wedding magic.

And that, my friends, is why I always say: thank goodness for professional caterers who treat cake-cutting like the beautiful, delicious art form it truly is.

12

THE PRETTIES

Inspiration vs. Reality

Let's talk about Pinterest. It's an incredible tool—a place where ideas spring to life, where color palettes are born, and where couples fall head over heels for the look of their dream day. I truly love it, for the most part. It helps you put language to your vision—what you're drawn to, which styles resonate, and how you imagine your day unfolding.

But here's the truth no one likes to talk about:

Pinterest is a highlight reel, not a blueprint. Many of those swoon-worthy photos you're pinning come from styled shoots—which, by the way, involve zero guests, no surprise weather hiccups, and absolutely no budget stress. They're also heavily filtered or edited; that moody, cinematic vibe you love? Thank the photographer's post-production wizardry for that one.

Let's not forget those jaw-dropping floral arrangements—they're either crafted on luxury-level budgets or made of faux blooms designed purely for the camera. Oh, and all those images bathed in dreamy golden-hour light? That's the result of hours of meticulous setup and a complete lack of real-world chaos. Mood boards and inspiration photos are wonderful for sparking ideas—but real life comes with price tags, weather forecasts, and dance floors that suddenly turn into a slip-and-slide because someone spilled a drink.

And that's perfectly okay! Social media, in general, is still a wonderful source of inspiration. But as your planner, it's my job to help bridge the gap between those dreamy images and your real-life wedding—with your budget, venue, vendors, and timeline in mind.

REAL VS. FAUX FLOWERS

Here's a common pitfall I see all the time: those lush, cascading bouquets or jaw-dropping ceiling installations you fall head over heels for often feature silk flowers. They photograph beautifully but don't always deliver the same magic in person—especially when viewed up close.

Even more important, many couples assume those looks can be replicated with real blooms, without realizing the dramatic price difference. (Spoiler alert: that overflowing tablescape bursting with garden roses and orchids? It can easily run into thousands—per table.)

That's not to say we can't create something extraordinary—we absolutely can. But it happens by setting realistic expectations and collaborating thoughtfully and creatively with your florist and design team.

FILTERS & EDITING MAGIC

Let's talk about those dark, moody tones or ethereal, light-and-airy images you're swooning over. That's editing magic at work, not reality. The candles didn't glow quite that golden, the linens weren't quite that pristine, and the sky might not have been that impossibly blue. Your photographer will certainly add their own artistic touch in post-production, but it's important to remember that most of what you see online has been filtered through multiple layers of digital enhancement.

A LITTLE COLOR TRUTH

Here's the honest truth: what you see on a screen doesn't always match what you'll get in person. Colors can shift dramatically depending on lighting, filters, and even your phone's brightness settings. That dreamy blush pink you've pinned? It might read a little peach—or even beige—in real life. Whenever possible, I always recommend viewing physical swatches or samples. It's the most reliable way to ensure that what you envision is what actually appears on your wedding day.

WHERE DO WE GO FROM HERE?

Let's use inspiration boards the way they're meant to be used: as a foundation, not a blueprint. We identify the vibe, the colors, and the feeling you're hoping to evoke—and then craft a version that makes sense for your wedding, your budget, your style, and your priorities.

And the best part? That version is yours. It's not a carbon copy of someone else's curated fantasy. It's your real, beautiful, joy-filled day—and that's what truly matters. Because in the end, no one remembers how closely your bouquet matched a photo on your phone. They remember how they felt in the room with you—the warmth, the joy, the love that radiated from every detail.

The lasting memory is how that bouquet looked stunning in your hands as you walked down the aisle, how its colors complemented your dress and the entire setting, and how it seamlessly tied into the overall vision of your day. It's not about replicating an image; it's about creating a moment that feels authentically yours. And that's the kind of beauty people truly carry with them long after the last petal has fallen.

THE PLUM THAT WASN'T

The bride's vision? Shades of purple.
Her favorite word? Plum.

She said it at least a dozen times during our design meetings: *"Plum bridesmaid dresses. Plum ribbon on the bouquet. Plum dahlias, please."*

It was perfect. Elegant. A rich, romantic tone that pairs beautifully with soft lilac and creamy neutrals. The florist and I were completely aligned—at least, so we thought.

Fast forward to our floral sample review. The bride walks in, sees the mock-up, and pauses. Her eyes lock on the "plum" dahlias in the centerpiece.

She tilts her head. *"Hmm… these look kind of… red?"*

The florist and I glance at the flowers, then at each other.

To be fair, they *were* plum—at least by floral industry standards. A deep, wine-colored hue with a hint of burgundy undertone. But the bride's version of plum? Definitely more purple. Less red. Cooler in tone.

It was one of those moments where no one was truly "wrong," but we were absolutely not on the same page. Thankfully, it was an easy fix. We swapped in purple scabiosa and deep-toned lisianthus, and kept the dahlias out of the main arrangements. No drama, no tears. Just a gentle reminder that color is subjective—and sometimes wildly so.

In the end, the bride was overjoyed with how it all came together. Her bouquet glowed with perfectly plum blooms, the bridesmaid dresses shimmered in the exact shade she'd dreamed of, and the entire design felt cohesive and undeniably her.

Because in the world of weddings, plum might mean merlot to one person and eggplant to another—but when we finally nailed her vision, it was pure perfection.

BLUSH VS. BUBBLEGUM

Behold, blush. The darling of wedding palettes everywhere. It's the color of soft romance and dreamy elegance—a wisp of pink, not a shout. It was the bride's absolute favorite shade and a major star of her wedding vision.

We had every detail meticulously planned: ivory linens, gold flatware gleaming like jewelry, and delicate blush napkins folded just so at each place setting, complete with custom ivory menus kissed with gold foil. The mock-up was flawless. The mood board? Swoon-worthy.

Then… delivery day arrived.

I'm breezing through the reception space, doing my usual quick once-over while the rental crew is unpacking box after box. All seems normal until one of the staff holds up a napkin—and I stop dead in my tracks.

No.

No, no, *no*.

That is not blush. That is bubblegum.

We're talking full-on, cotton-candy-at-the-carnival, Barbie's-lip-gloss pink. It practically glowed under the lights. I swear I could hear it humming the theme song to an '80s teen movie.

I felt my soul leave my body for a second.

In my calmest planner voice (which, to be clear, was about two octaves higher than usual), I told the team: "Okay, let's pause on setting those out." Meanwhile, my brain was shrieking: *This is not a baby shower. Abort! Abort!*

One frantic phone call, a backup order placed at lightning speed, and a few mild heart palpitations later, we had the correct blush napkins rushing to the venue. The new linen napkins arrived just in time, and no one—not even the bride—ever knew how dangerously close we'd come to transforming the entire reception into a retro gender reveal.

Blush is not universal. What one vendor calls blush might actually baby pink, dusty rose, or in this particular case—Pepto-Bismol. These days, I double-confirm every linen by physical sample or at the very least, a photo under natural light. Because in weddings, a shade off can be a mile away. I've sworn off any repeat run-ins with bubblegum pink. I'm now a firm believer in specifying shades—think sugar pink, barely pink, or champagne pink.

JUST LIKE PINTEREST

Sandy and Sean were one of those couples you instantly adore. Kind, gracious, and deeply in love—not just with each other, but with the idea of tailoring a wedding that felt intimate, elegant, and brimming with meaning.

They chose a hidden Hill Country resort for their micro wedding. The vibe was pure moody romance: deep burgundy hues, inky black accents, and enough candlelight to make any fire marshal sweat. It sounded stunning on paper—but I knew we needed to have *the talk*. During our floral design meeting, I leaned forward and gently brought it up.

"So, let's chat about burgundy," I said, smiling. "It's a gorgeous color, but here's the thing—it doesn't always behave. Sometimes it leans purple, sometimes red. It can shift depending on the flower variety, the season, even the grower."

Sandy tilted her head thoughtfully, then gave me a small, certain smile.

"I trust you," she said simply. And I believed her.

That trust meant everything.

Fast forward to wedding day.

We'd transformed the dining room into something out of a midnight fairytale. Layers of candles flickered on every table, casting pools of golden light that danced across black taper candles and antique brass accents. The air smelled faintly of warm wax and fresh blooms. Florals spilled from urns and vases in lush, dramatic waves—shades swirling between burgundy, black cherry, and delicate hints of deep plum. The effect was rich, romantic, and just mysterious enough to feel like a secret worth keeping.

After their first look, and before guests arrived, I led Sandy and Sean to the dining room for a private sneak peek. Sandy stepped inside, and for a moment, she just stood there, her eyes sweeping slowly across the room as candlelight shimmered on her gown. She drew in a breath, eyes wide, and whispered, "Oh… this looks just like Pinterest."

And that right there—that was *it*. That's why I do what I do.

That's why I sift through color swatches and samples. Why I spend hours explaining color theory, hunt down the perfect candleholders, and reroute floral shipments at the eleventh hour. Because when a bride walks into her wedding space and feels like her vision has stepped off the screen and into real life—even more beautiful than the board she built on her phone—that's magic.

Moments like this aren't luck. They're built through countless tiny decisions, one flower at a time, one honest conversation, and a whole lot of trust that quietly says: "You've got this."

A FLORAL WONDERLAND

Every so often, a bride arrives with an exceptionally vivid vision. She doesn't merely want pretty flowers; she dreams of stepping into a floral wonderland—a place where blooms are not simply décor but the very soul of the celebration. That was the vision for this wedding, and the expectation was set high.

She envisioned a palette of pinks and delicate peaches, accented with dusting of burgundy and the faintest kiss of lavender. The atmosphere would be romantic, whimsical, and utterly full—a space where flowers seemed to dance in the air and spill like poetry across every surface.

When floral design lands in a bride's top three priorities, the stakes become exhilaratingly high. Because flowers do more than sit in vases. They set a mood. They transform blank rooms into breathtaking landscapes. They saturate the air with fragrance, paint the space with color, and weave an emotional thread through every moment. Florals craft an ambiance so powerful that each bloom, each petal, holds meaning.

For this wedding, we curated a lush tapestry of texture and variety: billowing hydrangeas, fragrant garden roses, delicate butterfly ranunculus, dahlias, and unexpected flashes of coral peonies. The ceremony space blossomed with floor-level floral meadows, towering ground arrangements, and suspended blooms that seemed to float in midair. The reception became nothing short of a secret garden brought indoors, where every table overflowed with nature's artistry.

After their first look, I guided the couple toward the ballroom for a private reveal. They stepped inside and fell still, eyes wide as the room seemed to embrace them.

"This is incredible."

"More than we ever dreamed."

In that instant, the months of meticulous planning, countless emails, color swatches, mockups, and late-night design tweaks fused into one perfect reality. The bride's eyes shimmered with tears. The groom simply repeated, "Wow," as though language itself fell short.

Moments like these never lose their magic for me. I could recount hundreds of stories just like this one—and I've lived through countless variations—but each time, the feeling is fresh. There's an electric hush that fills the room when a couple stands there, taking it all in, realizing their vision has materialized before them. It's pure, unfiltered joy.

Because behind every stunning floral installation captured in a wedding photograph lies a world of trust, collaboration, and thoughtful artistry. And when flowers rise to the top of the priority list, it's never just about centerpieces. It's about weaving enchantment. It's about creating wonder. It's about turning a dream into something you can step into—and never forget.

THE GROCERY STORE FLORIST

Madeline hired me just a few months before her wedding—a classic "day-of" coordination booking with a tight timeline. As always, I dove in right away, confirming vendors across the board. Photographer? Fantastic. DJ? Reliable. Catering? All set.

Then came the florist.

If you've never worked with a grocery store florist, let me give you a glimpse behind that particular curtain. It's a very different experience. You show up in person, fill out a paper order form (yes, paper), and hope that what you picture in your mind is what actually arrives on the wedding day. There's no email confirmation, no design proposal, and no cell number for a delivery driver. Everything hinges on whichever kind soul happens to be staffing the floral counter that day.

Calling to confirm the order felt like dialing a rotary phone back in 1993. Several calls and a few marathon hold sessions later—during which I practically memorized the store's weekly specials—I finally reached someone willing to confirm the date and drop-off time.

Wedding day arrived.

The flowers showed up—barely on schedule—and were left in a cardboard box in the venue's kitchen. There was no setup, no instructions, just a stack of boxes and a printed invoice. My assistant and I rolled up our sleeves and started unboxing the bouquets.

Then I saw it: the bridal bouquet. My heart sank.

The dahlias—which, by the way, were out of season—drooped so sadly, their petals dropping like confetti. Heat had already taken its toll, leaving the bouquet wilted and lifeless before the ceremony even began. I stood in the kitchen, bouquet in hand, mind racing for a solution, when the mother of the bride passed by and caught sight of it.

She froze, her expression falling, "Oh no… is that Madeline's?"

I met her eyes and said, "I'm going to fix this."

She didn't question me. She just nodded, a flicker of hope lighting her face.

While my assistant stayed behind to handle the rest of the setup, I grabbed my keys and dashed to Hobby Lobby. I made a beeline for the floral aisle and selected the highest-quality faux dahlias I could find—deep, vibrant blooms that looked convincingly real.

Back at the venue, I carefully dismantled and rebuilt the bouquet, blending silk stems seamlessly among the struggling real flowers. Fluffing, taping, and rewrapping, I worked until it looked… presentable. When I finished, it was beautiful. You'd never have known which blooms were real and which weren't. While I was at it, I gave the bridesmaids' bouquets a little rescue operation of their own.

Later that evening, the mother of the bride pulled me aside, gratitude shining in her eyes. "You saved the day," she said. "I'm telling everyone you were also the florist." In that moment, something shifted inside me. I realized I was exhausted from rescuing low-budget floral mishaps and from standing in kitchens trying to coax life back into wilting blooms.

I didn't want to merely react anymore. I wanted to create. That day was the catalyst for branching into floral design—not because I needed one more task on my plate, but because I knew I could elevate the experience. With artistry. With intention. And with flowers that would never arrive abandoned in a cardboard box.

BLACK TIE, WHITE BLOOMS, AND EVERYTHING IN BETWEEN

There's something undeniably timeless about a black-and-white wedding. It doesn't chase trends or beg for attention. It doesn't rely on color to make a statement. Instead, it speaks with elegance and murmurs in the glow of candlelight.

This particular celebration was the very definition of classic sophistication — black tuxedos, sleek satin gowns, crystal-clear goblets, and an abundance of pure white florals. Roses, hydrangeas, peonies, orchids... we layered them into the design like stanzas of poetry.

The tables became a sea of soft petals and flickering flames. Candles of varying heights danced along flowing white chiffon runners, casting a warm, golden glow that shimmered against the blooms, reminiscent of fireflies weaving through a summer evening in the hills.

We kept the palette pristine and the timeline precise. The couple placed their trust in the flow we designed together, and it showed. From the moment guests arrived to the final champagne toast, every transition felt natural, seamless, and beautifully elevated.

There was a moment just after dinner when I paused at the edge of the room and took it all in: the gentle murmur of conversation, the delicate clink of glassware, the glimmer of candlelight reflected in champagne flutes, and the music slowly building as the dance floor beckoned.

Everywhere I looked, people were glowing.

The couple? Radiant.

Their parents? Overflowing with gratitude.

Guests? Effusive in their praise.

"This feels like a dream."

"Every detail is perfect."

"This is the best wedding I've ever been to."

You never expect those words, but when they come, you tuck them away in your heart.

Because amid all the timelines, floorplans, linen counts, and floral stem substitutions, it's moments like this that make it worthwhile. This is the reward. A flawless evening. A room shimmering with radiance. A triumph where meticulous planning transforms into an unforgettable memory.

A NEW CHAPTER IN BLOOM

In 2020, like so many others, I found myself at a crossroads. The world had shifted, weddings were evolving, and I started asking myself some big questions—one in particular: *How can I increase my income while staying in the space I already love?*

As a planner, I was already immersed in the details, working side by side with my brides. I understood their vision, their vibe, their color palette—sometimes before they even said it out loud. And as a naturally creative person, the idea of diving into floral design didn't intimidate me; it felt like a natural next step.

Not everyone shared that perspective. Some said, *"You can't do both."* I thought to myself, *"Watch me,"* and took matters into my own hands.

I began offering floral services to the brides I was already guiding—nothing flashy, just thoughtful designs tailored to what I knew they truly wanted. To my delight, they embraced it.

Some brides loved that I could handle both planning and florals, streamlining their process and ensuring every detail felt cohesive. Others preferred I stick to coordination only, and I respected that completely.

But what happened next still feels like a blessing: the floral side of our business began to bloom—quietly, steadily, beautifully. A few years later, it had grown enough for my husband, John, to retire from his day job and join me in JC Events full time.

Now, we're side by side—my soulmate and I—bringing wedding dreams to life together. Sure, we have our moments (what couple doesn't?), but working with him feels natural. It feels right. Every wedding we design is a reflection of love, and now, we get to create that magic as a team. I wouldn't have it any other way.

Looking back, stepping into floral design wasn't just about creativity—it was about growth. About trusting my instincts, leaning into what felt natural, and believing that "you can't" is never the final word.

What started as a practical solution—to serve my brides better and expand my business from within—became something so much more. It became the next chapter of JC Events. The chapter where John joined me full time. The chapter where we built something beautiful together.

Today, we get to bring wedding dreams to life—hand in hand, petal by petal, plan by plan. And it quite literally makes my heart and soul feel happy and full, knowing that I can take a vague idea and transform it into something beautiful that my couples and their families will cherish forever. I can't help but smile knowing... this is exactly where we're meant to be.

13
HEART AND HUSTLE

When people think of a wedding planner, they often picture someone surrounded by swatches, seating charts, and timelines, calmly coordinating the chaos of a big event. And yes, that's certainly part of it. But the reality is, wedding planning is an intensely personal and emotionally layered **experience**—and planners frequently find themselves stepping into far more roles than most people ever realize.

We're not just logistics experts; we're problem solvers, peacekeepers, creative directors, budget analysts, and sometimes even part-time therapists. If you're considering a career in wedding planning, here's some candid advice from someone who's lived the beautiful, the brutal, and everything in between.

THE LOGISTICIAN

At our core, we are masters of orchestration—conductors of a beautifully intricate symphony of moving parts. A wedding may appear seamless on the surface, but behind every elegant moment lies a meticulously crafted timeline, **multifaceted** communication, and weeks (or months) of behind-the-scenes coordination.

We're the ones ensuring the florist doesn't arrive too early, the DJ knows exactly when to cue the processional music, the rentals get delivered to the correct entrance, and the photographer is fully briefed on the timing for the first look.

We read contracts like novels, spot fine print that others might miss, and make sure no detail slips through the cracks—right down to confirming that the bartender brings a wine opener or that the officiant has a functioning microphone. When a groomsman forgets his tie, the cake arrives leaning slightly, or an unexpected downpour forces the ceremony indoors, we don't panic—we pivot. We adapt in real time, finding creative solutions while shielding the couple from the stress.

To guests—and often even to the couple—it all looks effortless. And that's the magic. They get to remain fully immersed in the moment, laughing, celebrating, and soaking in the **bliss**, because we've already carried the weight behind the scenes. While others are sipping cocktails or dancing the night away, we're quietly steering the flow, smoothing over hiccups, and ensuring the celebration unfolds exactly as envisioned (or as close as humanly possible). That quiet, invisible management is the very heartbeat of what we do.

THE CREATIVE VISIONARY

We're also design consultants—creative interpreters of vision, emotion, and atmosphere. Couples often come to us with vision boards brimming with dreamy inspiration, screenshots, and wonderfully vague ideas like "romantic but modern" or "boho, but not too boho." It's our job to take those abstract feelings and transform them into tangible, cohesive design decisions that bring their story to life.

From selecting the perfect floral palette and table settings to refining the layout of the ceremony space or choosing linens that subtly tie the theme together, we shape environments that reflect the couple's personality—not just look beautiful.

Yet it's never only about aesthetics. It's about flow, functionality, and the guest experience. We consider how guests will navigate the space, how lighting will shift from day to night, and how music, décor, and timing create a full sensory journey. We think holistically, connecting every detail so nothing feels like an afterthought.

Whether it's choosing between a soft drape or a structured arbor, or ensuring the signature cocktail signage complements the menu suite, we guide couples toward decisions that serve the bigger picture.

Often, we're not merely blending colors and textures—we're blending people. A bride who adores sleek minimalism may be marrying someone who envisions rustic charm. Families may have strong opinions. Culture and tradition can carry significant weight. It takes both an artistic eye and emotional diplomacy to honor those diverse influences while crafting a vision that feels seamless and authentic to the couple.

Great wedding design doesn't shout; it speaks softly and deliberately through every detail. And we're the ones quietly orchestrating that creative harmony, transforming vision into reality.

THE BUDGET MANAGER

No matter the size or style of the wedding, money matters—it's one of the most significant factors influencing every decision. As planners, we become trusted financial guides, helping couples navigate the often-overwhelming task of balancing their dream wedding wish list with the realities of their budget. It's not about stifling creativity or fun; it's about making intentional choices that maximize impact without causing stress or regret.

We sit down with couples to understand their priorities—what elements they're willing to invest in and where they're open to compromise. Perhaps they envision a gourmet menu but are willing to simplify floral designs, or maybe a breathtaking venue is non-negotiable while other décor details can be scaled back. By clearly mapping out what truly matters, we help couples stretch their dollars in thoughtful, strategic ways.

Along the way, we're vigilant for red flags—contracts hiding sneaky fees, vendors lacking transparency, or plans poised to spiral beyond budget. We ask the tough questions, offer candid feedback, and suggest cost-effective alternatives that maintain style and quality. Often, the best value isn't simply the lowest price, but the vendor or choice that delivers reliability, flexibility, and peace of mind.

Ultimately, our role is to advocate for value, not just cost savings. We help couples invest in experiences and services that will create cherished memories, all while ensuring their financial footing remains secure. Because a truly joyful, stress-free wedding day is about more than a beautiful moment—it's about feeling confident, cared for, and supported from the first planning meeting to the last dance.

THE FAMILY MEDIATOR

Weddings are joyful celebrations, but they can also become a hotbed of strong opinions and conflicting emotions—often arriving from every direction. Families bring their histories, expectations, and sometimes unresolved tensions, all converging on what is meant to be an impeccable day.

Whether it's the mother of the bride with a very specific vision for the flowers, the groom's aunt insisting on a particular seating arrangement, or divorced parents struggling to find common ground, planners frequently step into the role of neutral, calming mediators.

This aspect of the job calls for a unique blend of emotional intelligence and diplomacy. We listen attentively to everyone's concerns and wishes, validating feelings while maintaining focus on the bigger picture. We know when to gently steer conversations away from conflict and when to hold firm boundaries to protect the couple's vision.

Often, our presence alone helps defuse tension, offering a calm, organized voice that reminds family members—and sometimes even the couple—of what truly matters. At the heart of our mediation is a single focus: helping everyone remember why they're gathered in the first place.

Weddings are about celebrating love, connection, and new beginnings. We guide families back to that core purpose, encouraging compromise and kindness so the day remains joyful and inclusive rather than stressful or divisive. While we can't resolve every disagreement, our role is to create an environment where love stays at the forefront, and where every person feels heard, respected, and part of something beautiful.

THE THERAPIST (UNOFFICIAL, OF COURSE)

You might think my job is mostly about vendor calls, floral mock-ups, timeline, floor charts and color palettes. And yes—it absolutely is. But tucked into all of that is another unofficial, yet essential, hat I wear: **therapist**.

Okay—not a licensed one, obviously. But make no mistake: wedding planning is an emotional rollercoaster. When people are navigating one of the biggest days of their lives, the stress, the pressure, and the expectations all bubble to the surface. Regularly.

I've had brides call me sobbing from the parking lot because their mom won't stop criticizing their dress. Grooms have texted me in the middle of the night, needing reassurance that their surprise or dance will go off without a hitch. I've comforted teary-eyed dads realizing their little girl is truly growing up, and I once spent 30 minutes listening to a mother of the bride unpack family drama before we even touched on reception linens.

And you know what? That's part of the job.

We hold space. We listen. We offer practical advice when we can, but more often, we simply let them talk—sometimes vent, sometimes spiral, sometimes just release. I always say it's not just about the day itself; it's about everything that led up to it. The relationship, the family dynamics, the history. Wedding planning cracks all of that wide open, and we're the ones who help people navigate it with grace—and maybe a few deep breaths.

Over the years, I've become better at this part. Life experience helps. You grow more grounded, calmer, more intuitive. You learn when to give a pep talk and when to simply nod and hand over a tissue. You recognize when someone's frustration isn't really about the seating chart at all. You become the safe space they didn't even know they needed.

And no—none of this is written into the contract. But it's one of the most human, meaningful parts of what we do. The best planners aren't just skilled with logistics—they're skilled with people. I feel deeply honored that couples trust me enough to be there for the big moments and the emotional in-betweens.

Wedding planning isn't just a checklist; it's a journey of the heart for so many people. Be steady. Be kind. Be the calm in the chaos. (And keep a stash of emergency tissues in your bag—trust me on that one.)

ON HER OWN TWO FEET

She didn't want him there. From our very first meeting, the bride had been upfront about her complicated relationship with her father. Estranged for years, he hadn't been a part of her life, and she didn't plan on making space for him now—not even on her wedding day.

Yet families are families, and after persistent, not-so-subtle persuasion from relatives who "just wanted peace," she reluctantly agreed to invite him. "Fine," she told her sister during one of our meetings, eyes weary. "He can come. But he's not walking me down the aisle."

I nodded in understanding. No judgment. No second-guessing. Just support.

"You don't owe anyone anything," I told her, meaning every word.

On the wedding day, emotions ran high—as they always do—but she held her ground. Her hair fell in soft, polished curls, and her dress, flowing and ethereal, skimmed her figure with graceful movement. Her bouquet was a mix of gentle blooms and bold colors, reflecting her perfectly. She took one final look in the mirror and exhaled deeply.

She then turned to me and said, "Let's do this."

Music began to play, guests rose from their seats, and she stepped into the light—alone. No father on her arm. No borrowed tradition to steady her. Only her.

There was a moment, halfway down the aisle, when everything seemed to pause. The music swelled, her eyes remained fixed ahead, but I could see it—the courage, the vulnerability, and the quiet pride, all layered beneath her soft, resolute smile. In that instant, she wasn't merely walking toward her future husband; she was reclaiming every step of her own story.

I stood tucked just behind the door, misty-eyed, heart pounding, so proud of her I could have burst.

Later that night, after toasts were given and cake had been cut, she found me. Her makeup was slightly smudged, her shoes abandoned somewhere under the table, but her spirit radiated joy.

She wrapped me in the biggest hug and whispered, "Thank you. For everything. For just… letting me do it my way."

Support doesn't always mean fixing problems. Sometimes, it's about holding space, quietly cheering them on, and standing ready in the wings—steady, devoted, and firmly on their side.

Because sometimes, the bravest walk down the aisle is the one a bride takes on her own.

WHEN THE BRIDESMAID BAILED

There's always that one curveball in wedding planning—and for this bride, it arrived dressed in dusty blue chiffon and drama. About three weeks out from the big day, my phone rang. It was the bride. Her voice trembled, raw and brittle.

"She dropped out. Just like that," she said, barely holding it together.

Her bridesmaid—supposedly her best friend since middle school—had backed out. Claimed the wedding was "too much" for her to handle.

Too many group texts. Too many dress fittings. Too much emotional energy. And so, with a vague apology and a trail of emotional wreckage, she bowed out.

The bride was devastated. Not because she needed one more person in her bridal party, but because this friend had been someone she expected to stand beside her. Literally. When she came to me, she was unraveling—second-guessing herself, wondering if she'd been too much, too demanding, too anything.

Cue my unofficial therapist hat.

I sat her down, looked her straight in the eyes, and said:

"Let's get one thing straight—you are not too much. She was simply not enough."

Bridal party drama is far more common than people realize. I've witnessed adults throw tantrums over spray tans, shoes, and hairstyles. But this was different. This was heartbreak, a deep fracture in a lifelong friendship. And I could feel how deeply it cut.

So, I did what I always do: I listened. I reminded her that her wedding wasn't defined by the one person who couldn't show up—but by the many who would. I reassured her that standing at the altar isn't about matching dresses; it's about being present, wholeheartedly.

The bottom line? If someone couldn't show up in that way, they weren't meant to be part of her day. "Better this happen now than three days before the wedding or halfway through the reception," I told her. "Now we make a plan. We move forward. We protect your peace."

And that's exactly what we did.

When the wedding day arrived, her tribe—though one person smaller—radiated happiness. The laughter was genuine, the vibe was strong, and the bride herself? Utterly unshakable.

Later that night, she found me, cocktail in hand, eyes sparkling, glow unstoppable.

"You were right," she said. "I didn't need her there. Thank you for being my anchor."

People will reveal their true colors during wedding planning—and that's okay. It's not your job to carry those unwilling to carry you. Let them go, hold your head high, and surround yourself with those who truly celebrate you, not merely tolerate you. Because sometimes the best therapist is the one holding the timeline—and a Tide pen.

MONSTER-IN-LAW, PARTY OF ONE

There's always one. The opinionated aunt, the flaky bridesmaid, the overly involved sister. But truly, nothing—and I mean nothing—compares to the dreaded monster-in-law.

I was deep into planning with one of my brides when things started to go off the rails. Not because of the vendors or the timeline, but thanks to the mother of the groom. My bride already wasn't exactly sipping mimosas with her future in-laws, and tensions had been quietly brewing.

Then came the comment—the kind that makes your jaw drop and your blood pressure skyrocket. The mother of the groom informed my bride: "I'll be wearing black to the wedding. As if I'm in mourning."

Oh. No. She. Didn't.

Cue the panicked phone call. My bride was devastated—hurt, frustrated, and trying desperately not to let it overshadow the entire wedding. She vented while I listened. She cried a little. I reassured her a lot.

Then she said, "I just feel like my fiancé needs to step in and handle this. It's his mom."

Couldn't agree more. And I added—half joking but entirely serious— "If I need to call the monster-in-law myself, I'll happily do it. I'll even put on my 'customer service voice.'"

Being a planner sometimes means navigating family landmines. It's making sure one woman's passive-aggressive fashion statement doesn't hijack an entire celebration. In the end, the groom stepped up. The mother-in-law dialed it back. And yes—she wore navy instead. A win, if you ask me.

More importantly, it was a reminder: weddings aren't just about flowers, seating charts, and perfectly placed candles. They're about people, emotions, decades-long family baggage, and future hopes. Often, a planner's true superpower is knowing when to say: *I've got your back—even if I have to make the call no one else wants to make.*

Family dynamics have a sneaky way of showing up on wedding day—sometimes subtly, sometimes like a marching band. As a coordinator, your job isn't to referee every fight but to stay cool, classy, and calm. When drama erupts—and trust me, it will—listen to your bride. Validate her feelings. Remind her she's not alone. You're there to advocate for her and keep the peace.

You might not be able to change a mother-in-law's mind, but you can set boundaries, reinforce the couple's vision, and be the poised presence when emotions run high. And when all else fails? Be ready to make that phone call—gracefully and professionally. With just enough backbone to remind everyone whose day it really is.

WHEN HAPPILY EVER AFTER NEEDS A REWRITE

Weddings stir deep emotions. Often, they reveal truths couples weren't entirely prepared to face.

Several brides have called, texted, or emailed me with the words that bring everything to a screeching halt:

"We're canceling the wedding."

My immediate response is always a phone call—not as a planner seeking details, but as someone who genuinely cares. I want to hear her voice, check in on her well-being, and make sure she's okay.

Over the years, I've heard every possible version of the story:

"It's not our time."

"We're working on ourselves."

"He/she cheated."

"He doesn't want to get married at all."

"He's just not my guy."

On some occasions, it's the groom who calls me to say it's over. Other times, he simply reaches a breaking point, overwhelmed by the stress and expectations.

Weddings can amplify the pressure on a relationship. While some people rise to meet the moment, others realize they're not ready. It's raw and emotional. Yet the truth is, a breakup isn't always the worst outcome.

I've witnessed what happens after. Brides have come back to me—sometimes years later—with a completely different glow, a new partner, and an entirely different energy. We never dwell on the past or reopen old wounds. Instead, we begin anew: a fresh chapter, a different love story, a brand-new beginning.

That's my calling—helping people move forward, celebrating what's right for them. When the time is right, I'm here to craft a wedding that's everything they've dreamed of. No judgment. Just genuine delight.

Here's my best advice: take a deep breath and lead with compassion. When a couple says they're canceling, the instinct is to jump into logistics—vendor calls, contract terms, retainers, and refunds. Yet before tackling any of that, pause. Remember: you're not simply coordinating an event; you're guiding people through one of the most emotionally complex seasons of their lives.

Sometimes the decision is mutual. Other times, it's heartbreak. It might stem from family pressures, fear, or betrayal. Whatever the cause, the couple's first need is grace—not policy, not panic, but a human connection. Make the phone call. Ask how they're holding up. Let them talk. Be the calm in their storm.

When they're ready, help them navigate the next steps with professionalism, empathy, and dignity. Because even if the wedding doesn't happen, how you show up in those moments stays with them. If you're in this business long enough, you learn that canceled weddings still shape stories—and sometimes lead to the most beautiful beginnings of all.

THE EMERGENCY RESPONDER

We carry sewing kits, stain remover, breath mints, bobby pins, backup timelines, and not merely a Plan B—but sometimes Plans C and D. Our bags are stocked with solutions before problems even appear. Because even the best-laid plans hit snags, and we're here to smooth them out.

Whether it's a last-minute wardrobe malfunction, a splash of red wine on a white dress, an unexpected downpour, or a vendor running late, we step in swiftly and calmly. We handle every hiccup with a steady hand and a strategy, shielding the couple from stress and allowing them to stay fully immersed in their moment of celebration.

Embracing any array of responsibilities isn't just part of the job—it's the very essence of what makes this work profoundly rewarding. Every role we inhabit, from crisis manager to gentle confidant, is an opportunity to support our couples in meaningful ways. We're not simply orchestrating an event; we're guiding people through one of the most significant and emotional transitions of their lives. We witness vulnerability, delight, and hope—and in those moments, we become more than planners. We become anchors of steadiness in a sea of excitement and nerves.

Of course, it can be exhausting—physically, mentally, and emotionally. The hours are long, the details relentless, and the stakes high. Yet it's also immensely fulfilling. When the music rises, vows are spoken, and the couple finally walks down the aisle hand in hand, we know our work helped make that moment possible. Not only through meticulously crafted timelines or breathtaking décor, but through compassion, finesse, and an unwavering commitment to excellence. That's the magic of wedding planning—being the quiet force behind a day that becomes a cherished memory.

Let's dive deeper into what it's truly like to be a wedding planner. There's an undeniable allure to this world—flowers, fashion, fairytales, and the privilege of helping people live out one of the most luminous days of their lives. For a new planner just starting out, the vision is vivid: crafting beautiful celebrations, working with grateful couples, and being surrounded by sheer happiness. And yes—there is happiness. Yet there's also hustle, hard lessons, and the sobering truth that this is a business, not merely a dream.

THE ZIPPER THAT GAVE UP

It was one of those rare, blissful wedding days when the universe seemed perfectly aligned. Hair and makeup were gliding along on schedule. A soft, cheerful playlist drifted through the bridal suite like a gentle breeze. The bride was positively radiant—glowing so brightly she could have lit the entire room—and the bridesmaids were swirling around her in matching satin robes, sipping champagne, snapping selfies, and floating like a living vision board brought to life.

Then, from behind the bathroom door, came a piercing shriek. "OH NO!"

Cue the imaginary record scratch.

I set down my clipboard and made my way—calmly, because sprinting kills the vibe—to the epicenter of the drama. There, frozen like a mannequin with her arms stiffly outstretched, stood the maid of honor. The zipper on her dress had given up entirely. Not just stuck—obliterated—split open from waist to shoulder, exposing the underlayers like some couture disaster. Her face was a perfect storm of horror and helplessness.

Around her, the bridesmaids hovered like startled birds, whispering nervously, unsure whether to cry, laugh, or rummage for safety pins. Meanwhile, my hand was already diving into my trusty emergency kit like a surgeon reaching for a scalpel.

"Deep breaths," I said, my voice steady as I threaded a needle. "I've got this."

And I truly did.

I worked from inside the dress, stitching tiny, invisible seams with the precision of a seamstress, while the bridesmaids looked on in wide-eyed awe, murmuring things like, "Slay. Absolute slay!" and "How do you even know how to do that?!"

Truth is, I've saved more zippers than I can count—and funny enough, "seamstress" doesn't even appear on my business card.

Ten minutes later, the maid of honor emerged looking immaculate. The dress fit even better than before, and we collectively dubbed the impromptu rescue "invisible tailoring." I made a mental note to stock extra thread in my kit, just in case fate decided to test me again.

She walked down the aisle right on time, radiant bouquet in hand, the freshly sewn seams holding strong. The bride never suspected a thing. The guests remained blissfully unaware. Even the photographer was left slack-jawed when I shared the story afterward. Crisis averted. Honor restored. Zipper conquered.

THE GREAT GROOMSMEN SHOE SWAP

You know the phrase *"It's always something"*? Well, on this particular wedding day, *something* arrived in the form of the wrong shoes. The groomsmen had crystal-clear instructions: wear caramel brown dress shoes to match the vibe—warm, polished, slightly rustic, and perfect for our Hill Country setting. But of course, there's always *one*.

This particular groomsman showed up in a pair of shiny black shoes. Not just slightly off—**totally** off. The kind that gleamed under the lights and clashed horribly with the tailored suits, throwing off the entire coordinated look we'd spent weeks curating.

This wouldn't have been the end of the world... except it was time for photos. Group portraits. Detail shots. The kind of images destined to live in frames, albums, and family slideshows for decades. Panic began to creep in as I scanned the room, mentally flipping through potential solutions.

And that's when John—my husband, my rock, my unofficial co-pilot on wedding days—stepped in like a hero emerging from the wings.

Without missing a beat, he casually walked over and said, "What size are you?"

The groomsman blinked, still confused. "Uh… 10.5."

"So am I," John grinned. "Here. Take mine."

And just like that—**swap.**

Caramel brown for shiny black. The groomsman slipped into John's shoes like Cinderella heading to the ball, while John casually laced up the black pair as if nothing unusual was happening. The camera clicked on, capturing shot after shot in perfect harmony, caramel brown shoes adding polish to the rustic scenery.

When the "I Dos" were spoken and final formal photo was captured, they swapped back like seasoned pros exchanging a secret handshake.

Crisis averted. Photos saved. And John? Officially a legend.

It's moments like that—small, spontaneous, and brimming with quiet heroism—that remind me how lucky I am to have him by my side. Yes, we plan weddings. Yes, we manage logistics and craft floral installations. But sometimes? We also swap shoes behind the scenes to save the photo gallery. And that, right there, is what true teamwork looks like.

THE BOUTONNIERE BACK-UP PLAN

On wedding days, there's a rhythm to everything—florals arrive in careful waves, counts get checked off clipboards, and personal flowers are distributed like delicate tokens of honor. Corsages for mothers. Bouquets for bridesmaids. Boutonnieres to the men's suite.

Except… when the math doesn't quite add up.

It started like any ordinary pre-ceremony prep. The groom and groomsmen were suited up, the photographer was capturing crisp detail shots, and I was sifting through the floral boxes when it hit me: we were short.

Not by one.

Not by two.

But by three boutonnieres.

Whether it was a miscount, a last-minute lineup change, or a communication slip somewhere along the way—we'll never know. What I did know was that I couldn't let anyone walk down that aisle looking as if they'd been left out of the celebration.

So, I improvised. Fast.

My eyes scanned the room until they landed on a trio of bud vases, each holding a perfect little clutch of ceremony blooms—ranunculus, spray roses, bits of textured filler. I gently dismantled them, pairing blooms together, adding a flourish of greenery snipped from a nearby arrangement.

One by one, I crafted three fresh boutonnieres on the spot. Wrapped in floral tape. Secured with a pearl-tipped pin. Labeled with names and passed off as if they'd been part of the plan all along.

No one ever knew.

Not the photographer.

Not the guests.

Not even the florist—unless they're reading this right now… in which case, surprise!

It's these quiet, behind-the-scenes pivots that keep a wedding running seamlessly. Because personal florals aren't just pretty—they're deeply symbolic. Everyone deserves to feel seen and included as they step into that aisle moment.

Always triple-check your boutonniere count—and remember, bud vases might just be your secret floral first aid kit. They should absolutely be verified during your florist confirmations, because when the unexpected strikes, they can save the day.

EMERGENCY KIT: SMALL, BUT MIGHTY

The real MVPs of a wedding day? Sorry, champagne tower—you're gorgeous, but you're not it. The true heroes are safety pins, band-aids, and bobby pins. Seriously. Here's the bubbly lowdown.

Safety Pins: These little metal marvels have saved more wedding days than I can count. Bridesmaid dresses? Held together. Broken bustles? Fixed. Rogue straps? Tamed. Flower girl sashes? Secured.

I've safety-pinned suspenders back onto a groomsman who decided they were 'too annoying' five minutes before photos—and yes, I've even pinned bow ties into place. Another time, I had to rescue a mother-of-the-bride's shawl after she insisted it was "just for looks"… until it started slipping off and she was two seconds from a wardrobe malfunction five minutes before family portraits. Fashion fails fast. Safety pins save faster.

Band-Aids: Weddings might look glamorous, but they're filled with tiny tortures: new shoes, mystery paper cuts, jagged nails, blisters from dancing like no one's watching. I keep band-aids in every size, shape, and shade—neutral tones, heel-specific ones, even super-hero-themed (because kids get rowdy).

Bobby Pins: Want a sleek low bun to survive Texas wind? Need a veil to withstand gusts of drama (and literal wind)? Bobby pins are your new BFFs. I've re-secured hair, headpieces, veil combs, and—

my personal claim to fame—a cake topper that kept sliding off like it was trying to make a run for it. (It worked. Do I recommend it? Nope. Desperate times, my friends.)

If you ever see me sprinting across a venue clutching three tiny items in my palm, just know: a dress is being rescued, a blister is getting tamed, or someone's hair is about to be saved from certain doom. And that, folks, is the real secret sauce inside a wedding planner's emergency kit.

BONUS MVPS YOU'LL BE GLAD YOU PACKED:

- Stain remover pen
- Seltzer water + cloth for wine spills
- Super glue (for heels, décor, you name it)
- Zip ties (yes, seriously—miracle workers for décor and last-minute fixes)
- Lighter (for candles and sparkler send-offs)
- Tape (clear tape and trusty gaffer tape)
- Extension cord + phone chargers
- Portable steamer + distilled water
- Extra copies of the timeline
- Contact list + contracts for all vendors
- Snack bars or crackers
- Breath mints
- Blotting papers — essential in warmer months; brides glow, we manage the shine
- Fashion tape — because strapless dresses love to misbehave
- Deodorant wipes — perfect for last-minute freshen-ups

- Earring backs — tiny and always disappearing
- Lint roller — because black tuxes plus white pet hair is a photo nightmare

PLANNER VS. COORDINATOR: KNOW YOUR ROLE

One of the biggest mistakes new wedding pros make is blurring the line between a *wedding planner* and a *wedding coordinator*. Sure, those titles might sound interchangeable to the average person—but in practice, they're worlds apart. Getting super clear on your offerings—and how you communicate them—means less confusion, happier clients, and a much calmer you. Think of it this way:

A **planner** is in it from Day One. You are shoulder-deep in budget spreadsheets and color swatches, hunting venues, vetting vendors, reading contracts with a magnifying glass, managing the budget, weighing in on design decisions, troubleshooting family drama, and coaxing your couple through every emotional high and low. You're their expert, guide, confidant, and—yes—sometimes their unofficial therapist. This level of service takes time, emotional bandwidth, and extreme organization—and it deserves to be priced accordingly.

A **coordinator**, on the other hand, is like the brilliant conductor who steps in once all the musicians are seated and the instruments are tuned. You're not composing the symphony—you're making sure the performance goes off without a hitch. Coordinators typically jump in around 6–8 weeks before the big day, gather all the plans the couple has set in motion, confirm vendors, build the timeline, layout, run the rehearsal, and keep the wedding day on track. It's still a hugely important job—but a distinctly different one.

Here's the catch: if you don't clearly define your role, people will expect everything. They'll think they've hired a full-service planner when all they've booked is coordination. And if you're not careful, you'll end up doing the work of both—for the price (and stress level) of one.

Be crystal clear in your packages. Spell out exactly what's included—and what's not. State it in your contracts, your calls, your emails, and your pricing sheets. Define it early and reinforce it often. This isn't just about protecting your time and energy—it's about ensuring a seamless client experience. The sooner you clarify precisely what you offer—and share it confidently—the smoother your client relationships (and your sanity) will be.

So, whether you're wielding spreadsheets or running rehearsals, remember: your role is essential—but it's not interchangeable. Know your lane, own it proudly, and price it like the pro you are.

Let's shine a light on a topic that can feel awkward for new planners: **pricing**.

If you're serious about being a professional, you need to price yourself like one. This isn't a hobby. This isn't a favor. This is a business. And if you're offering high-touch, customized, emotionally invested service, your pricing should reflect that. You're not Wal-Mart. You're not even Nordstrom. You belong—ideally—in the Louis Vuitton, Chanel, Gucci, or Hermès lane: curated, intentional, premium. Your time and talent are luxury items, not clearance-rack deals.

It's tempting, especially in the early days, to set your rates low just to fill your calendar. You think, *"If I charge less, people will say yes. I'll get experience, build my portfolio, and eventually I'll raise my prices."* It sounds logical, right? But here's the hard truth: the clients who hire you because you're cheap will expect the most, respect you the least, and drain more time, energy, and sanity than you ever imagined.

Bargain-seeking clients often come with strings attached. They want extras for free. They micromanage every detail. They question your value at every turn. And when something inevitably goes sideways (because it always does), they're the first to place blame. Suddenly, that "great opportunity" becomes an exhausting, demoralizing experience—and that's not the foundation you want to build your business on.

Pricing yourself properly isn't arrogance—it's sustainability. You can't deliver exceptional service if you're perpetually burnt out, overextended, or quietly resenting what you're being paid. Know your worth. Account for your hours, your behind-the-scenes prep, your experience (even if limited—your training counts), your overhead, and your emotional labor.

Remember: the clients who recognize your value will never flinch at your rate. They're investing in peace of mind, in artistry, in expertise. They're not looking for the cheapest—they're looking for you. So be the Gucci of planning. Deliver excellence. Stand behind your brand. And never, ever apologize for charging what you're worth.

BRIDEZILLA ON A BUDGET

Oh, those rookie days. The scrappy, wide-eyed version of me who said yes to every opportunity with a hopeful heart and an underpriced contract. She found me on Facebook. A mutual friend tagged me under one of those "Anyone know a wedding coordinator?" posts with the ever-encouraging words: "Highly recommend!"

I was flattered, excited, and fresh enough in the industry to take on just about anything. So, when this bride reached out and said,

"My budget is $800—can you do it?" I said… yes. Bless my ambitious little heart.

Now, to be fair, it was a unique venue—brand new, trendy vibes, and honestly, a great opportunity for exposure. But here's the kicker: she expected me to bring an assistant. Not just that—she expected me to pay for the assistant out of my $800 fee. Did I mention she was having 300 guests? Three. Hundred.

There's a general rule in our world: one coordinator per 150 guests to keep the chaos manageable. But in this case? It was just me, myself, and my $800 mistake. First, came the adventure of the dress bustle. To be fair, she had a French bustle and about a million layers of tulle and lace. A gorgeous gown, but basically a textile Rubik's cube.

Her bridesmaids? Totally bailed. One was touching up her lip gloss. The others had slipped off to happy hour, leaving me solo — and, naturally, the bridesmaid with the instructional video was among them. I was under a mountain of fabric, head practically inside the bride's skirt, searching for color-coded ribbons that may as well have been part of a NASA launch sequence.

Meanwhile, the bride is standing there, arms out, tapping her foot. "What's taking so long?" she snaps.

I popped my head out from the folds of tulle and gave her my best calm smile. "Hang tight, hon. That bustle has more hidden tricks than a magician's hat. She was not amused. But hey, eventually, I got it done. The dress was bustled. The bride stomped off (somewhat gracefully) to rejoin her guests, and I emerged sweaty but victorious, hair full of static and bobby pins.

Next up? The cake saga. Because naturally, in the universe's ongoing comedy routine, she informed me her aunt would be in charge of cutting the cake. Fabulous. I love when family pitches in—until that family member is halfway through her chicken and rice and the bride is giving me side-eye like, "Why hasn't the cake been cut yet?"

It was 8:30 PM. Cake-cutting time, according to the timeline. But dinner had run long (because, you know, serving 300 people with a short-staffed catering team takes a minute), and her aunt—the official cake cutter—was still working on her entrée.

The bride is panicking, visibly annoyed, and I'm calmly trying to explain, "Don't worry, the cake's safe. Let's let your aunt clear her plate before we put her on slicing duty." She didn't love that answer. But what was I supposed to do—halt dinner service, grab a knife, and start carving the cake myself while the aunt watched mid-bite?

TAKEAWAY: Sometimes the true price of saying yes is your time, your sanity, and your assistant's hypothetical paycheck. Sometimes the red flags don't start waving until you're too deep to back out. That wedding taught me that experience comes at a cost—and that I definitely undercharged. But it also taught me how to set boundaries and trust my instincts. If 23-year-old me knew what I know now, I'd have done things differently. Still, I'm grateful for those early lessons. They built the backbone I stand on today—and gave me some pretty entertaining stories for cocktail parties.

THE POWER OF THE PING

If you want to know one of the not-so-secret secrets behind a flawless wedding day, here it is: **confirmation.** It's not glamorous. It's not thrilling. But it's absolutely essential. And it's the difference between chaos and calm, disaster and seamless delivery.

In the weeks leading up to an event, never—**never**—assume people will just remember what you discussed weeks or months ago. They won't. Everyone's busy, distracted, and in the wedding world, juggling ten flaming batons at once. That's why confirmation is your best friend.

Reconfirm the timeline. Reconfirm the rental delivery and pick-up windows—and that vendors have a load-in map. Reconfirm the DJ's arrival, the getaway car's departure, and the florist's setup instructions. Double-check what the caterer is bringing (and what they're not). Even reconfirm with your couple—because in the final week, even they forget things they swore were handled. Sometimes details shift for no reason other than a late-night Pinterest binge.

Over-communication isn't annoying. It's professional. It's a sign of leadership, meticulous attention to detail, and a proactive mindset that vendors respect and clients desperately need. You're not being a pest; you're being the adult in the room—the one holding all the strings and keeping them from turning into a giant knot.

Think of it like this: every time you confirm a detail, you're eliminating a potential crisis. You're giving vendors a chance to ask questions they didn't even know they had. You're catching last-minute changes before they morph into last-minute emergencies. You're aligning expectations, setting the tone, and showing that you're running the show—in the best possible way.

Create systems for this. Use email templates, checklists, shared timelines. Schedule a "confirmation week" before every wedding where you run through every detail and check off every vendor conversation. And please, get it in writing. Phone calls are great, but follow-up emails are gold.

Ultimately, confirmation isn't just about logistics—it's about building trust. When everyone knows you've got it covered, they can breathe easy. And when they breathe easy, the wedding flows like magic. Not because you got lucky—but because you were prepared.

CONFIRMATION ISN'T A ONE-AND-DONE DEAL— IT'S AN ONGOING CONVERSATION.

As a coordinator, you'll quickly learn that a single check-in with a vendor rarely covers everything. Multiple follow-ups are your secret weapon for ensuring that no detail slips through the cracks.

Think of each vendor as a crucial piece of a complex puzzle. Missing even one tiny detail—like who's providing the lapel mic or what time linens will be down for the florist—can trigger a domino effect of issues on the wedding day. And trust me, no one wants to deal with a panicked sound technician scrambling for equipment or a florist arriving before tables are covered.

After that initial confirmation email, make it a habit to circle back several times.

HERE ARE SOME QUESTIONS YOU'LL WANT TO ASK IN THOSE FOLLOW-UPS:

- *Do you need anything from us to make setup easier?*

Tables, linens, power sources, special parking permits, etc.

- *Who is responsible for specific equipment?*

For example, does the venue provide the lapel mic and sound system, or is that on the DJ or AV company?

- *Have you had a chance to meet with the client directly?*

This is crucial. Sometimes vendors and couples skip the final meeting, which can lead to misunderstandings about expectations, timing, or style. If it hasn't happened, arrange it or at least facilitate a detailed exchange of notes.

- *Are there any last-minute changes or concerns we should know about?*

Asking this question regularly gives vendors an opening to voice issues before they become emergencies.

Multiple confirmations aren't just about logistics—they're about building relationships. Every follow-up is an opportunity to show professionalism, anticipate challenges, and prove that you're the person who's got it all handled. Vendors appreciate clear communication—it makes their jobs easier, and in turn, helps them deliver their absolute best.

Remember, the best coordinators don't just confirm; they reconfirm, triple-check, and occasionally send one last "just making sure!" email at midnight. That level of diligence protects you, your clients, and everyone involved. It's the difference between a smooth, memorable celebration and a day derailed by avoidable hiccups. Because in weddings—and in life—it's always better to be the person who over-asks than the one left saying, "Wait… who was supposed to bring the cake knife?"

THE ONE WHERE THE MARIACHI LEFT EARLY

Every wedding planner has *that one vendor*. The one who dodges emails like they're competing for gold in the Email-Evasion Olympics. The one who you *know* you need confirmation from in writing—but somehow always manages to finalize details with a breezy "Yeah, sounds good!" over the phone.

Picture the vibes: a perfect summer wedding. The sun sinking low, golden hour light spilling over the ceremony lawn. Guests laughing over cocktails, the gentle clink of glasses punctuating the air. The bride is practically vibrating with excitement about her surprise mariachi band—scheduled to burst into song at 5:30 PM sharp as she and her new husband exit the chapel.

I'd sent email after email to the bandleader. Nada. Silence as loud as a church bell. Finally, I got a text: "Got it. 5:30." Not exactly ideal, but hey—I screenshotted it. Just in case. (You know where this is headed.)

Wedding day arrives. At 5:00 PM, the mariachi band rolls up in full regalia. Giant sombreros. Gleaming trumpets. Guitars strapped over shoulders. It's like a scene from a telenovela, and for a split second, I'm thinking—wow, early? That *never* happens. My assistant, Carissa, and I actually burst out laughing because no musician has ever shown up ahead of schedule in the history of time.

Turns out, it wasn't early. It was the *wrong* time. They thought they were performing from 5:00–6:00 PM. Not 5:30–6:30.

And we didn't realize the miscommunication until 6:00 PM when the bandleader strolls over, wiping sweat from his brow, and says: "Okay, we're wrapping up now—do you have the final payment?"

I stare at him. He stares at me. My assistant and I exchange that look—equal parts panic and murderous calm. I say, "Wait… what? You're booked until 6:30."

The mariachi leader shakes his head. "Nope, I was told 5:00 to 6:00."

But guess what we pulled up faster than you can say *Cielito Lindo*? That glorious little screenshot:

"Got it. 5:30."

We showed him the proof, explained the mix-up, and begged them to keep playing. They agreed to stay another 15 minutes, but they had another gig across town and couldn't finish the full set.

The bride? Let's just say she was *not* throwing roses in my direction. She'd dreamed of that full 60-minute mariachi serenade during cocktail hour. We salvaged what we could, kept the energy flowing, and managed to secure her a partial refund—but the vibe had definitely taken a hit.

HERE'S THE MORAL OF THE STORY: Verbal confirmations mean squat. Texts are barely better. If it's not in writing—officially, clearly, contractually—it *will* come back to bite you. You can triple-check your timeline, decorate your emails with emojis, and gently remind your vendors until you're blue in the face—but if they don't confirm it in writing, that loose thread can unravel faster than a runaway guitar string.

Now? I live by one rule: No email confirmation = no locked-in time.

If I don't have it in writing, I follow up. And follow up again. And *again*. I'd rather be a polite nuisance now than be the one explaining to a bride why the trumpets are packing up halfway through dinner. Because "they said it on the phone" won't help when your mariachi exits stage left mid-salsa solo.

THE RECEPTION RANSOM

Back when I was about 24—green, eager, and willing to work for basically peanuts—I was hired as a "day-of coordinator" by a sweet, young couple. Or perhaps better described: sweet, starry-eyed, and ever-so-slightly clueless. They were lovely people. Budget-conscious. And like many budget-conscious couples, they wanted everything to be over-the-top magical... on a shoestring. We're talking DIY-everything, mason jars galore, and dreams held together with hot glue and sheer optimism.

It was a Catholic ceremony, and they assured me the church coordinator had that part handled, so my job was solely to manage the reception. In hindsight... red flag #1: no walkthrough.

The reception venue was downtown—a modern glass room attached to a restaurant overlooking the Riverwalk. Picture this: floor-to-ceiling windows wrapped in twinkle lights, the river shimmering below, and lush cypress trees filtering the Texas sun into patches of dancing light across the tables. It was gorgeous... but also a logistical circus. Pay-to-park, elevators, and zero margin for error.

I arrived early, hustling to set out the bride's Pinterest-inspired touches. The DJ was untangling a web of cables, the catering staff were placing forks on tabletops like their lives depended on perfect alignment, and the cake—hallelujah—had survived the journey in one piece. So far, so good.

The ceremony wrapped, and about 30 minutes later, guests began trickling in, all smiles and chatter. Cocktail hour passed in a blur of margaritas and mingling. When it was showtime, I gathered the wedding party, nodded to the DJ, and the doors flung open wide.

In came the bridesmaids and groomsmen, arms pumping, grins blazing, dancing down the aisle as if auditioning for a music video, glitter practically trailing in their wake. The bride and groom followed, glowing, kissing, and gliding to their sweetheart table like newly minted royalty. Cue my soft sigh of relief.

Then—bam.

The venue manager beelined toward me mid-dinner, looking like she'd just swallowed a lemon.

"Do you have their final payment?" she demanded.

I blinked. "Excuse me?"

"They haven't paid. The owner says if we don't get it now, we shut it down."

I laughed—nervously—because surely this was a joke, right? Wrong.

Apparently, the couple still owed a significant balance. Not some petty leftover, but a chunk large enough to make a restaurant manager sweat. And this wasn't a rinky-dink venue—this was an upscale spot with real overhead and precisely zero tolerance for unpaid bills.

Naturally, I sprang into damage-control mode.

Rule I live by: Do not disturb the bride on her wedding day.

I headed straight for her parents—thinking, surely, they'd know what's up. Nope. They were clueless, blindsided, and, as it turned out, entirely wallet-less. No checkbook. No emergency credit card. Just a deer-in-the-headlights stare and some frantic rummaging in sparkly handbags.

Next, I started canvassing the room like I was hosting a PBS pledge drive.

"Hi Aunt Susan, Uncle Mike—any chance you're feeling wildly generous today?"

Spoiler alert: No takers.

With no other options left, I had to pull the couple aside. On their wedding day. To tell them their party was about to be evicted if they didn't cough up the cash. To their credit, they were apologetic—but also weirdly casual, like: "Oh, can't we just pay it later?"

Uh… no, sweethearts. This isn't layaway at Target. This is your wedding reception.

I pleaded with the venue manager, practically begging her to call the owner and grant us a one-hour grace period so we could race through the formalities. Miraculously, they agreed. We had sixty minutes—like some twisted wedding-themed game show.

We flew through cake-cutting, first dances, toasts—all while the dark cloud of "you're about to get kicked out" loomed over the glass room. Guests probably thought we had an early bedtime or a noise ordinance. Nope. Just financial doom on the horizon.

The DJ wrapped things up with a few speedy line dances and a polite, "Thanks for coming!" Then… lights up. Game over. I packed my kit in silence, my heart heavy. The sadness wasn't just about the abrupt ending—it was about seeing so much joy fizzle under the weight of something so preventable.

COORDINATOR'S CORNER: You absolutely *must* get a list of all outstanding balances with due dates and remind your couple, their parents, or whoever's holding the purse strings. Every single vendor should be paid no later than two weeks before the wedding. I don't care if the vendor says they'll accept cash day-of—insist on pre-payment or at least an online link. The only cash that should change hands on wedding day is gratuities—and even those should be prepped in sealed, labeled envelopes.

Because let me tell you: the only surprise you want on wedding day is the mariachi band showing up on time—not the threat of your reception getting shut down because someone forgot to pay the bill.

THE CAKE THAT WASN'T OURS

It was a chilly winter day, the tables were set, and the room looked like a dream. Just a few hours to showtime when the cake arrived—towering tiers, intricate piping, delicate florals. Gorgeous.

But… not our cake.

I marched over with my clipboard (aka my wedding-day weapon of choice) and felt my Spidey senses tingle. Yes, the cake was beautiful—but it didn't match the design we'd approved. Ours was supposed to be minimal and chic: soft buttercream edges, elegant simplicity, and a gold-accented monogram. This one, however, was decked out in fondant ruffles and pastel flowers, practically waving jazz hands.

I flipped through my trusty binder and located our original sketch. Turning to the baker, I said, "Sherri, this is stunning. But it's not our cake."

She blinked, glanced at the cake, then back at me—and her face went from serene to sheer panic. "Oh, shoot, Jennifer!" she exclaimed, smacking her forehead. "I am SO glad you caught that—it's in my car! I must've brought the wrong cake in. I need to take this one to the other wedding!"

Yes. You read that right. There was another wedding happening that same day, and somehow, the cakes had staged a secret swap. Because of course they did.

Thankfully, I had the paperwork in hand, and Sherri was honest, fast, and moving like a fondant fairy. She whisked the incorrect cake back to her car and returned ten minutes later with the correct masterpiece: simple, modern, and exactly what the bride had ordered.

No harm done. No one ever knew. The couple later strolled in, laid eyes on the cake of their dreams, and let out gasps of delight so genuine you'd think they'd just been handed keys to a private island. The only person sweating buckets was me—but hey, that's the job.

Always, always print and carry every vendor order—especially for custom cakes. Because when two weddings are happening within a ten-mile radius, the chance of a cake mix-up is as real as buttercream on your blazer.

IT'S NOT ALWAYS GLAMOROUS

It's 2011. Samantha and I found ourselves on our hands and knees picking up thousands of tiny pieces of confetti—by hand. Mind you, I was just the assistant coordinator. Yes, by hand. One broom between us. A single, sad little broom that looked like it came from the dollar bin at a gas station. The venue had a strict no-confetti policy—something we didn't catch until after the grand send-off had already happened.

It was an epic send-off. Slow-motion cheering, glitter raining down, the couple disappearing into the night like movie stars. Gorgeous. Magical. Perfect. And then… they drove off. The guests filtered out. The music faded. And the venue coordinator turned to us with a smile that could cut glass and said, "You'll need to clean all this up. Confetti isn't allowed here."

Cue the horror-movie zoom-in on our faces.

So, there we were—sweaty, sore, dressed in our black-on-black "planner chic" outfits, crawling around the stone patio like glitter-sniffing bloodhounds. Confetti stuck to our clothes, our hands, our hair. Every time we thought we were done, the lights would catch another hidden sparkle, winking at us like, *not yet, darling*.

It was exhausting. It was humbling. It was late. And honestly? It was unforgettable. Because this job—this beautiful, chaotic, emotionally charged job—isn't always pretty. For every dreamy first look, every teary toast, every stunning flat lay that makes it onto Instagram, there are ten behind-the-scenes moments of pure grunt work. Emergency boutonnière repairs in a thunderstorm. Chasing down a missing cake topper. Eating a crushed protein bar for lunch because there's no break and the only other option is half a stale dinner roll left in the staff room.

You don't get into this business because you like weddings. You do it because you love serving people. Those picture-perfect tablescapes owe their existence to endless checklists and behind-the-scenes effort.

If you're in it just for the styled shoots and the champagne, you won't last. But if you can find delight—even when that "delight" means picking glitter out of your hair at 2 a.m.—you'll thrive. Because this job? It's not about being in the spotlight. It's about showing up for the people who are.

PLANNER'S PLAYBOOK: Read the contract. Don't just skim it. Don't assume you know what's allowed because "most venues are fine with this." Actually, read it. Line by line. Because what flies at one venue might be absolutely forbidden at another—and the time to figure that out is before you plan the grand exit, not after the photos are snapped. It's not glamorous, but it's non-negotiable. Knowing the rules before you dream up the big finish will save you (and your team) a mountain of stress—and possibly a hefty fine. That night was sweaty, sparkly, and mildly soul-crushing. But it taught me a lesson I carry into every single event.

HERE ARE JUST A FEW THINGS TO LOOK FOR EVERY SINGLE TIME:

- What kind of send-off materials are allowed? (Confetti, Sparklers, Bubbles, Glow wands)
- Is tape or adhesive allowed on walls, floors, or furniture?
- Are certain décor materials (like real candles, loose petals, etc.) restricted?
- Who is responsible for cleanup—and what does that actually include?
- What are the access times for setup and teardown?

THE ART OF SAYING NO

When you're starting out in business, the urge to say "yes" to every opportunity feels almost irresistible. Each booking seems like a win, every client a chance to prove yourself. Building a portfolio, gaining experience, and expanding your reputation feels essential—and staying busy appears to be the path to success. A truth worth learning early is this: overbooking will break you.

Taking on too many weddings, clients, or responsibilities might look like ambition, but quickly morphs into overwhelm. Calendars, checklists, and support systems all have limits. Spreading yourself too thin causes mistakes to slip through, communication to falter, and quality to suffer. You shift from being the planner who over-delivers to the one barely hanging on. Clients sense it. Rushed emails, missed details, and distracted phone calls leave an impression. Especially early in your career, your reputation is built on the experiences you create for couples.

Time and energy deserve fierce protection. Boundaries allow for deep focus on the work at hand, rather than scattering yourself across commitments you can't fully honor. Declining an opportunity isn't failure—it's necessary. Saying no to one client preserves the ability to say a confident, enthusiastic yes to another, or even to yourself, granting space to rest and recharge.

Growth is less about volume and more about excellence. Weddings planned with care and passion lead to referrals, glowing testimonials, and loyal clients far more reliably than squeezing in another event at the cost of your health. Quality triumphs over quantity every time. Honoring your limits means honoring your craft—and your business will reward you in the long run.

For new planners, the glitter can be blinding. Big budgets, high-profile clients, and elaborate visions appear to be golden tickets destined to elevate portfolios and brands. Experience, however, teaches that not every dazzling opportunity is beneficial for you—or your business. Hidden behind the sparkle often lie red flags. A client might appear polite yet reveal themselves as dismissive or demanding. Some push for discounts or request unreasonable last-minute changes.

Your gut remains a powerful ally in these moments. Instincts draw from experience, perception, and subtle cues that logic might overlook. When something feels off, trust that feeling. Disregarding warning signs in hopes things will improve after a contract is signed rarely works out in your favor. Clients who trust your expertise and honor your boundaries create an environment where work flows smoothly—even when challenges arise. Those partnerships build confidence, business sustainability, and genuine fulfillment. Protecting your energy and honoring your limits will attract the clients who value your work and willingly pay for it.

Early in my career, I booked a wedding that looked like a dream: a large budget and a vision filled with chandeliers and a towering seven-tier cake. Yet, from our very first meeting, the bride questioned every vendor suggestion, demanded last-minute changes, and replied to emails with clipped tones. Despite my best efforts to manage the chaos, the wedding day felt as though it were unraveling. Vendors were confused, the timeline slipped away, and exhaustion hit hard. That paycheck wasn't worth the toll. The experience taught me that a big budget doesn't automatically mean a great client.

Another time, a couple who initially seemed warm and friendly gradually treated my time as limitless. Quick questions turned into daily messages, late-night calls, and requests for free extras. When I explained my fees and boundaries, they reacted as though I was unreasonable. That situation reinforced the necessity of clear expectations and firm boundaries from the start.

Mastering the art of saying no is a lesson that continues throughout a career. The best collaborations stem from mutual respect, shared enthusiasm, and open communication. Clients who value your expertise and process make the journey worthwhile. Those are the relationships that fuel confidence, elevate businesses, and bring genuine delight. Protect your energy, maintain your boundaries, and remember: the right clients will recognize your worth—and pay for it, without question.

THE WEEKEND THAT BROKE THE BINDER

I should have known better. When I agreed to coordinate three weddings in a single weekend, I convinced myself I could handle it. I even joked, "Just call me a wedding warrior!" My inbox was color-coded, my calendar wound tighter than a Swiss watch. The couples were all wonderful, their venues spaced just far enough apart to make the logistics technically possible. I kept telling myself I'd be fine. I'd handled back-to-back events before. How hard could one more be?

By Friday night, though, the cracks were already beginning to show.

The first wedding was a lakeside ceremony adorned with string lights and a jazz trio—a flawless plan on paper. Halfway through the vows, I realized I'd forgotten to double-confirm the cake delivery. It arrived late, slightly tilted, and missing the floral topper. The bride managed a graceful smile, but her mother shot me a look sharp enough to etch my name into my nightmares.

Saturday began at 9 AM, with the wedding set for 2 PM—a garden affair at a boutique winery. Expectations were high, and the timeline left no margin for error. My brain was still scrambled from the chaos of the day before, and during introductions, I blanked on the officiant's name. I called her "Father Thomas." She was, in fact, Reverend Claire—a woman wearing a bright floral stole. In that instant, I wished I could vanish beneath the linen-draped tables.

By Sunday, I was running on fumes, Gatorade, and under-eye concealer. Wedding three was the big one—a couple I'd been working with for a year, complete with an eight-piece band and 200 guests. My clipboard had disappeared. My notes were scattered across three tote bags.

I accidentally double-booked the florist and the DJ's load-in time. When the bride anxiously asked if I had her custom aisle runner, I just blinked. She started to tear up. I assured her I had it, then scoured my car until I found it stuffed behind a box of charger plates. The moment, though, had already been bruised.

I wasn't "on." I wasn't sharp. I was stretched so thin I barely recognized myself. That night, I sat alone in the parking lot, still in my black slacks and sneakers, staring at my hands. Pride was nowhere to be found; only exhaustion remained. I'd poured myself into three beautiful days, yet none of them had received the best version of me.

One lesson became painfully clear: just because I can do something doesn't mean I should. Now, I limit myself to one wedding per weekend—maybe two if the stars align and my instincts agree. These aren't merely parties; they're milestones. I owe it to my couples to show up as more than a clipboard with legs. I want to be present. I want to be whole. Because when someone trusts you to help shape one of the most significant days of their life, showing up halfway simply isn't enough.

WHY DO I DO THIS TO MYSELF?

It's fall. Peak wedding season. The air is crisp, my inbox is a raging inferno, and at 29 years old, I'm deep in what I like to call my planner prime. I feel unstoppable. Invincible, even. And somehow, I've landed… three weddings in one weekend.

Yes, three.

Triple wedding weekend.

Strap in.

Friday begins with a breathtaking setup—velvety autumn hues, the glow of candlelight flickering across tables, and florals so lush they practically make me weep. I adjust every arrangement, smooth every napkin fold, and finesse the sweetheart table until it looks like a centerfold in a bridal magazine.

Next stop: a ceremony rehearsal across town. My mind flips into a different gear mid-drive as I replay the processional order in my head and remind myself—for the twentieth time—that Aunt Janet refuses to sit on the aisle. Meanwhile, my assistant is holding down the fort at Wedding #2, sweet-talking vendors and putting out metaphorical fires. Bless that woman.

The logical choice after rehearsal would be to go home and rest. Naturally, I ignore logic and race back to the first venue because there's no way I'm missing the bride's walk down the aisle. That moment hits me every time. As the music swells and she steps forward, I find myself misty-eyed—even though I'm running purely on caffeine and raw adrenaline.

And that's just Friday.

Saturday and Sunday blur into twelve-hour marathons—a whirlwind of timelines, towering florals, vendor wrangling, champagne toasts, and a perpetual, photo-ready grin. Somewhere along the way, I inhale a granola bar crushed to dust at the bottom of my tote bag and pretend it's fine dining.

By Sunday night, my legs have the consistency of overcooked pasta. Collapsed on my bed, still half-dressed in my "planner chic" ensemble, one thought loops in my brain like a stuck record: *Why do I do this to myself?*

And then the answer surfaces.

It's the way candlelight dances off crystal glassware, the smell of fresh florals filling a room, the hush right before a bride walks down the aisle. It's witnessing a couple's vision materialize after months of planning. It's the gratitude, the laughter, the unfiltered joy on faces that remind me this work matters. Even when exhaustion sets in, I know I've helped create something unforgettable.

Next season, though? I'm spacing these things out.

(Probably.)

14
THE GOOD, THE BAD & THE UGLY

THE GOOD

There's something undeniably luminous about working with happy, gracious families during the wedding planning journey. When love, gratitude, and genuine delight underpin every interaction, the entire process transforms into something profoundly fulfilling. These are the families who say thank you not merely with words, but through their warmth, trust, and deep respect for the effort happening behind the scenes. Their kindness and spirit of collaboration make the work feel less like a job and more like a shared celebration of something extraordinary.

The delight of watching a mother's eyes brim with pride during a dress fitting, or hearing a couple burst into laughter during a cake tasting—those moments are the beating heart of this profession. It's not simply about timelines, budgets, or seating charts. It's about crafting an experience rich with meaning for people who are truly savoring every second. When a family expresses appreciation—whether through a heartfelt note, an emotional hug, or a simple, sincere "thank you"—it leaves an imprint that lingers. It's the sort of gratitude that makes late nights and long hours feel undeniably worthwhile.

Some weddings unfold like modern-day fairytales. They shimmer with possibility, steeped in a love so palpable it feels cinematic. Every detail—whether grand or small—becomes a brushstroke in an unfolding masterpiece. These events often come from working with remarkable souls: people who are kind, trusting, and genuinely thrilled about the beautiful experience blossoming around them. They're not fixated on perfection; they're embracing the wonder. And when that happens, the wedding seems to pulse with its own radiant energy.

Bringing someone's dream to life—to witness that electrifying first look, that tender first dance, or the tears of unfiltered happiness—is an honor and a privilege. It's a rare joy to help create a day destined to become a family's treasured memory for generations. Those are the weddings that stay etched in your mind long after the final sparkler has faded into darkness. They remind us that love, infused with gratitude and grace, possesses a kind of transformative brilliance all its own.

There's also something contagiously uplifting about graciousness. When guests arrive brimming with good spirits, and families trust the process and savor every milestone, that positive energy ripples through the entire celebration. Vendors feel it. Planners absorb it. Even photographers capture it in smiles and laughter suspended in time. These are the weddings where, despite exhaustion, you leave at the end of the night glowing with quiet satisfaction, knowing you helped create something not just beautiful—but profoundly meaningful.

YOU'RE FAMILY TO US NOW

Some weddings stick with you because of the chaos—the last-minute changes, the unexpected mishaps, or the glitter that somehow finds its way into your shoes for three weeks straight.

But others stay with you for a far deeper reason: the people.

This one—this one, like so many others, was special. The bride was an absolute dream to work with, radiating kindness, trust, and enthusiasm. The planning process felt like an inspired collaboration, filled with creativity and laughter. From the very start, there was an ease between us—a shared vision that made every decision, every detail, fall perfectly into place. The entire day pulsed with electric energy, like love on overdrive.

Everything clicked: the timeline flowed seamlessly, the vendor team operated like a well-rehearsed orchestra, and even the weather cooperated as though it was in on the plan. And when it was all over—when the final sparkler flickered out and the last rented chair was folded away—her mother found me.

She walked up with tears shimmering in her eyes, hugged me as if we'd known each other for years, and clasped both of my hands tightly in hers. Looking straight into my eyes, she said:

"Thank you for making my daughter's wedding day into pure magic. You did it all, really. We loved everything. Every idea you had—the details, the timing, the flow—it was more than we ever imagined. You're family to us now."

I could hardly find words. My throat tightened with emotion, and all I managed to whisper was,

"Thank you for trusting me with it."

Moments like that are why I do this work.

It's not just about centerpieces or color palettes or seating charts. It's about people. About building relationships strong enough that they feel like family. It's about creating a day so meaningful and memorable that it becomes woven into the story of who they are.

And sometimes, those connections don't end when the last song fades out. Families like this come back to me, year after year, for other celebrations—a milestone birthday, an anniversary, or when another child gets engaged and it's time to plan the next big day. Each new event feels like picking up right where we left off, adding another beautiful chapter to our shared history.

On that night, in that moment, I didn't feel like just a wedding planner. I felt like a part of their story. And that, more than any grand floral arch or flawless timeline, is the true essence of what I do.

FROM CLIENT TO KINDRED SPIRIT

Every once in a while, a bride comes along who isn't just a client — she's a total vibe.

And this one? From the moment we met, we were basically best friends. Enter the absolute delight that is Lucy — and her equally wonderful groom, Ernest.

We first crossed paths at an open house. Just a quick introduction, but it felt like professional love at first sight. Lucy's energy was magnetic. She lit up the room with her bright personality and pure enthusiasm, and I remember thinking, *Please let this girl book me.*

Spoiler alert: she did.

From that point on, wedding planning was an absolute breeze. Not because there weren't decisions to make or timelines to juggle — there were plenty — but because we were completely in sync. Every meeting felt like catching up with a dear friend.

Without fail, every time she saw me, it was: "Jen!! Oh, I am so glad to see you!!"

Cue the biggest hug and instant good vibes. When Lucy hugged me, it was like getting wrapped in genuine happiness. She radiated excitement, warmth, and trust. Even the trickiest vendor conversations became comedy routines instead of stress sessions.

And then there's Ernest. He's the more mellow half of the duo — cool, calm, and always wearing a relaxed grin that practically says, *Anything to make Lucy happy, I'm here for it.* I adored watching their dynamic. They're the perfect yin and yang: Lucy brings the sparkle and fire, and Ernest balances it with his easygoing steadiness. Their chemistry is the stuff that restores your faith in love stories — truly wonderful.

Soon enough, the wedding day was upon us.

Imagine: emerald green velvet linens draping tables like a royal cloak, black tapered candles flickering with moody elegance, and glimmers of gold catching the light in the most perfect way. Burgundy blooms intertwined with fall foliage created lush, dramatic floral arrangements that practically screamed romance. Against the backdrop of the Hill Country — sweeping views, golden-hour glow, crisp autumn air — it was downright swoon-worthy.

When Lucy stepped into the reception space for the first time, she gasped, covered her mouth, and hugged me so tight I nearly dropped my clipboard.

"Oh my gosh, it's perfect," she whispered. "It's exactly what I dreamed of. You did it."

Cue the tears of pure delight — hers and mine.

The entire evening was a whirlwind of laughter, warmth, and pure celebratory spirit. Ernest, true to form, was all smiles, looking at Lucy like she was his entire universe. Watching them dance under twinkling lights, surrounded by friends and family, felt like witnessing a scene from a romantic film.

And the best part? We're still friends to this day. Texts, birthday wishes, random life updates — Lucy's one of those rare brides who turned into a forever friend. Sometimes, the universe doesn't just send you a client. It gifts you a kindred spirit in a lace dress — and that's the best kind of bonus.

DOUBLE THE LOVE: TWO WEDDINGS, ONE WONDERFUL FAMILY

There are weddings you never forget—and then there are families you never forget. I'm blessed to have several like that in my career. But the Zammiello family is one that truly sparkles in my memory. They were the epitome of delight, warmth, and radiant happiness. It was an honor to bring not only Lisa and Tucker's vision to life but also Caroline and Joey's.

When all the planning wrapped up, I felt genuinely a little sad. I'd grown so accustomed to texting with their mom, laughing through planning calls with their dad, and feeling woven into the fabric of their family life.

It all began with their daughter's fall wedding. She arrived at our first meeting organized, glowing with excitement, and armed with a clear vision: warm tones, flickering candlelight, earthy florals, and heartfelt details. Her parents were involved every step of the way—in the best possible way.

And then—surprise! A few months later, I got a call from Mom: "Our son's getting married in the spring… and we'd love for you to be part of that journey, too."

Cue my heart melting into a puddle.

They were supportive, present, and so thoughtful that, even amid planning chaos, they'd pause to ask how I was doing.

Lisa and Tucker's wedding unfolded like a scene from a secret garden: lush greenery everywhere, pops of purple woven through florals and linens, and the soft rustle of leaves in the breeze. The energy flowed through the gardens, laughter rose like music, and gratitude poured out in countless small gestures and warm smiles.

When it came time to plan the second wedding just six months later, the whole experience carried a different kind of ease. Both weddings were joyful and relaxed in spirit, but the second one felt even breezier—like slipping into a familiar rhythm. I already knew the family, knew how deeply they trusted me, and that made everything flow effortlessly. Caroline and Joey's spring celebration was pure modern elegance—a hill country venue dressed in layers of beige, crisp white accents, and candlelight flickering like tiny stars.

Both weddings were absolute dance parties, each featuring live bands that kept the floor packed and the energy soaring. The music pulsed through the room like a heartbeat, vibrating in the soles of our feet. Guests twirled beneath swaying chandeliers and strings of twinkling lights, skirts flaring, suits slightly rumpled, laughter echoing above the rhythm.

At Lisa and Tucker's garden wedding, the band played against warm, wood-accented walls, with glass doors folded back to welcome the crisp fall breeze. Notes drifted into the night air, carrying the fragrance of fresh blooms and cool earth. Couples swayed across the dance floor, the soft glow of candlelight catching the shimmer of sequined dresses and the gleam of polished shoes.

Caroline and Joey's hill country celebration had a different spark. Inside the modern venue, candlelight flickered off stone walls while the band tore through classics and modern hits, each beat urging people to let loose. The dance floor pulsed with movement, friends and family spinning in joyful circles.

By the time that second celebration came to an end, I didn't feel like just "the wedding planner." I felt like family. The hugs were longer, the smiles carried deeper stories, and the parents whispered to me that they couldn't have imagined either wedding without me. Truthfully, the feeling was entirely mutual. I'd show up for them again in a heartbeat, anywhere, anytime.

Weddings come and go, but the relationships you build can last a lifetime. Being trusted not once but twice to help shape a family's most blissful days—that's the kind of privilege that leaves an imprint on your heart forever.

TRUSTED WITH THE DREAM

Some couples arrive with binders and vision boards, knowing precisely what they want—down to the exact variety of flowers for their bouquets. And then… there are the rare gems who hand over their vision with complete trust—a dream, a vibe, a feeling—and say:

"We trust you. You're the designer."

This was one of those couples. From the very beginning, they were calm, clear, and wonderfully collaborative. They shared their likes and dislikes, the style they envisioned, and the emotions they longed to evoke—timeless, romantic, elevated, and utterly unforgettable.

Then came the six words every planner dreams of hearing: "We want you to do your thing."

And I did.

From curating a five-star catering menu to selecting sleek black-and-white floor-length linens, crafting a floral story blooming with delicate textures and scents, and handpicking a seven-piece jazz band whose music would float through the room like silk—I was in full creative flow. Crystal chandeliers? Check. Gold flatware and floating candles? Absolutely. A towering six-tier wedding cake dripping with intricate sugar flowers? You know it.

Wedding day arrived.

I was placing final touches—fluffing florals, adjusting napkin folds to perfect precision—when I heard the door open behind me. The couple walked in. They froze. Gasped. A hush fell. The bride covered her mouth, eyes wide, while the groom let out a soft, awed whisper: "Wow."

They took it all in—the glossy black-and-white dance floor gleaming underfoot, the warm glow of a hundred flickering candles casting dancing shadows, the dramatic chandelier installation glittering like stars overhead. The band began to warm up with a soulful trumpet riff, and suddenly, it wasn't just a wedding anymore—it was an experience. Their experience.

The bride turned to me, tears shining in her eyes, and said:

"This is more than we ever imagined. You nailed it. Every single detail."

Those words… they stay with you. Because as a planner, you give so much—your time, your talent, your energy, your heart. But when a couple gifts you the creative freedom to build something extraordinary, the results are pure magic. Total trust becomes total transformation.

When a couple hands you their vision and lets you run with it, you don't just plan a wedding—you create a once-in-a-lifetime memory.

THE BAD

As much as we cherish the good days, there are others when absolutely nothing seems to go right—when even our best efforts feel like they're sinking faster than a bouquet tossed into the ocean. These are the days when every phone call is a five-alarm fire, every email delivers fresh chaos, and no amount of meticulous planning seems capable of taming the madness. It can feel as though the universe has picked that particular day to test your limits, leaving you juggling fragile emotions, tight deadlines, and sky-high expectations—sometimes all before your second cup of coffee.

Hard days on the job aren't merely stressful—they're personal. When a client is upset, or a vendor drops the ball, or a miscommunication snowballs into a monumental misunderstanding, it can rattle your confidence. The weight of a disappointed bride, an anxious parent, or a frazzled couple can feel crushing, especially when you care as deeply as most planners do. And in today's world, bad days sometimes morph into bad reviews—public echoes of private pain that can follow you long after the last guest has gone home.

Then there are heartbreaks no one sees coming. Sometimes, a couple decides not to go through with the wedding. Whether it's a mutual decision or a painful, one-sided choice, these moments are never easy. You've poured time, energy, and a hefty slice of your heart into planning their big day—and suddenly, it all screeches to a halt. There's real grief there, even for us as planners.

We've imagined their celebration, walked beside them through their excitement, and now find ourselves helping them unravel it piece by piece. It's a stark reminder that love isn't always linear, and weddings—no matter how exquisitely designed—exist within the messy, unpredictable realm of human life.

These difficult experiences may leave emotional bruises, but they also forge resilience. They teach us to listen more closely, to communicate more clearly, and to safeguard our own well-being while navigating the intricate terrain of someone else's story. The bad days sting—but they also shape us. And sometimes, they make for one hell of a story.

THE WIND, THE LADDER, AND THE DESSERT TABLE DRAMA

It was 2015. Business was good. I'd finally reached a point in my career where I needed help, but I hadn't quite built a formal team. My "assistants" were often a rotating cast of supportive friends, fellow coordinators, or John—depending on the weekend and the size of the wedding.

This particular summer Saturday was for a teacher bride (which, if you know, means summer wedding season was in full swing). It was a 300-guest affair—big crowd, big opinions, and a big opportunity for things to go sideways. And sideways, they went.

The First Red Flag

The mother of the bride called me at 9:00 AM sharp, demanding to know when my "team" would be arriving on-site. I glanced at my phone, confused. The timeline had us arriving at 11:00 AM. Apparently, she was expecting a crew to descend upon the venue like a wedding SWAT team. Newsflash: my "team" that day was three people—including me.

When we arrived, right on schedule, we dove straight into setup. And let me tell you—it was a DIY circus. Folding chairs, faux flower arrangements, chalkboard signs dripping with whimsy, and plastic gemstones scattered across the tables (a trend I'll never understand).

It felt more like we were decorating a Pinterest-themed garage sale than an actual wedding.

Then Came the Wind

As if the decor wasn't already unstable, the wind decided to RSVP "yes" to this wedding too.

First, the bride's portrait blew off its easel and shattered the glass front. Then there was *The Ladder.* Yes, a literal white ladder—propped up like an altar to Hobby Lobby—covered in photos and trinkets, all waiting to be sacrificed to the wind gods.

Unsurprisingly, the wind knocked it over, sending frames and mementos clattering to the ground. At this point, I was bouncing between the church ceremony and the reception site like a ping-pong ball in heels, trying desperately to keep everything intact.

Back at the reception, the bride's aunt had volunteered to handle the dessert table. Cute in theory—except when it was gone, it was gone. No refills. No backup. Just empty trays and a scattering of crumbs.

Enter: Mom's friend from New York. She floated around the venue like some self-important, spiritual planner-guru hybrid, dispensing "wedding wisdom" with the solemnity of a Vatican priest. This woman decided it was her sacred duty to verbally annihilate me in the kitchen. Loudly. In front of staff.

She cornered me, scowled at the half-empty dessert table: "You're a horrible wedding planner. A disgrace. Useless. Lower than dirt."

All this… because I didn't personally bake backup cookies? Let me rewind. The wedding was big, DIY-heavy, chaotic, and packed with 300 guests. The bride had asked her aunt to manage the dessert table. Once guests made their rounds, the trays were wiped clean, and there were no extra sweets to replenish.

It hit me like a slap. I felt so small. My stomach twisted, my face flushed, and tears burned behind my eyes. But I wasn't going to give her the satisfaction. Instead, I took a slow breath, looked her directly in the eyes, and said, firmly and professionally, "I'm truly sorry you're upset. The dessert table was provided and managed by a family member, not by my team. I understand this is disappointing, but it's outside the scope of what I was hired to handle today. My priority now is ensuring the remainder of this wedding goes as smoothly as possible."

Then I walked—no, marched—straight to the father of the bride and said, "I understand this is your wife's friend, but you need to keep this disrespectful woman away from me. At this point, it feels like harassment." He was understanding, kind, and visibly embarrassed.

But before I could even catch my breath, she came back. Not ten minutes later, still fuming, still ranting about cookies—**cookies!**—and berating me in the middle of the venue like this was some kind of wedding warfare.

Here's the thing: I've dealt with high-stress situations. I've navigated emotional moms, drunk guests, and unpredictable weather. But never had I been spoken to like that over something so entirely out of my control.

THE TAKEAWAY: People will project. They'll look for someone to blame. And in emotionally charged moments, the easiest target is the one holding the clipboard. But I know my worth. I know what I bring to the table. And no one—not even a cookie-crazed wedding guest with delusions of grandeur—gets to take that away from me.

DIY is not always your friend. Wind, time, and poorly glued photo frames don't mix. Dessert tables are lovely in theory—but if it's DIY, clarify who's responsible for replenishing. And maybe… keep a secret stash of cookies just in case.

THE TIMELINE TAKEDOWN

She was in her early fifties, polished and elegant, entering marriage round two with grace and style. We clicked right away—she had great taste, impeccable manners, and I genuinely looked forward to her wedding. She wasn't high-maintenance; she was classy. Or… so I thought.

Planning went smoothly. She agreed with my ideas, we shared thoughtful conversations, and I felt confident that wedding day would be a breeze. And since it was a dry wedding, I figured we'd dodge the kind of unpredictable behavior that sometimes erupts after one too many cocktails. (Spoiler alert: turns out, booze is not required for drama.)

Now, if you've ever managed a wedding, you know the timeline is our holy grail. But even the best-laid timelines are polite suggestions. Real weddings are living, breathing beasts, and you've got to read the room and adjust accordingly. That's what professionals do—and why it's crucial to review expectations during the final planning meeting with your couple.

Dinner service was dragging on. Guests were shifting in their chairs, water glasses sat half full, forks were down, and conversations had faded to that awkward low hum that screams, "Please… give us something else to do." It felt like the perfect time to kick off the cake cutting—to give people a little show, revive the energy, and cue the dance floor. Logistically, it made perfect sense to me.

To the bride? I might as well have suggested canceling the entire wedding and eloping to Vegas. She glanced at her watch, dramatically, as if we were live on TV and I'd just gone wildly off script.

"It's not time yet," she hissed through a tight smile. "We're supposed to cut the cake in thirty minutes."

I tried to gently explain why I'd made the call—to keep the momentum going, to avoid guests chewing on the tablecloths—but she wasn't having it. Scolded. Publicly. Soberly.

I apologized. Profusely. I swallowed my pride, kept my tone as smooth as fondant, and carried on with the rest of the night like a wedding planner who'd just been sentenced to time-out. And I did my job. The rest of the event ran smoothly. She got her picture-perfect send-off, and her wedding wrapped up precisely on schedule.

But let me tell you—there's nothing quite like getting dressed down at a dry wedding, in front of sixty people, all because you made a professional call based on real-time variables. I wasn't winging it. I was working it. Some clients want a coordinator. Others want a clock-watcher. Know the difference early— and always have a backup plan (and maybe an escape route).

BURNING QUESTIONS, NO BURNING FLAMES

Ah, rustic weddings—charming, intimate, and often hosted in places that could burst into flames with a single rogue spark. This one took place at a gorgeous old wooden barn, built sometime in the 1800s. The kind of place where you half-expect a cow to photobomb your first look photos. It had history. Character. And apparently, a very strict no-open-flame policy.

Here's the thing: I didn't know that. Neither did the bride. To be fair, I was hired as a day-of coordinator, which basically means: **Step in and work miracles with whatever has—or hasn't—already been planned.** Tessa (the bride) had DIY'd nearly everything: centerpieces, signage, even a bouquet recipe list she created for her florist.

She brought in pretty dusty blue napkins and chargers, and for ambiance, a hundred real wax candles in dreamy shades of blue. Very Pinterest. Very pretty. Very flammable. While I was setting the tables and preparing to light the candles, a woman materialized beside me—practically out of thin air—like the ghost of contracts past.

"Hi, I'm the venue manager. You can't light those candles."

Wait... what?

Where had she been for the past six hours while I set up an entire tablescape with an open-flame theme? She pointed up, around, and down—just in case I'd somehow missed the obvious.

"This is a barn. Built in the 1800s. One spark, and poof—it's a historic pile of ash."

I nodded. I understood.

No fire. No candles. Understood.

Left them unlit, but still pretty—as if frozen mid-performance in a *we're-supposed-to-be-glowing* kind of way. Meanwhile, I was sprinting between setup and the church, determined to get Tessa married. A last-minute LED swap wasn't happening. It wasn't a cathedral gala dinner—they were eating at literal picnic tables. Dinner would last maybe an hour before everyone headed to the other side of the barn for dancing. The moody glow of candles simply wasn't going to make or break the night.

Tessa? Cool as a cucumber. When I told her what happened, she simply shrugged and said, "Ah well. I'm not going to cry over unscented wax."

Then came *That Friend*. Every bride has one. She stormed up to me, eyes blazing, whisper-growling, "What are you going to do about this?"

Me: "About what?"

Her: "The candles. The fact that they're not lit. You need to go to the store and get LED ones."

Me (already mentally juggling a thousand other tasks): "Actually, no, I don't. But you're welcome to if it's that important to you."

Cue: Offended gasp. Dramatic exit.

Seventy-five minutes later, she returned, triumphantly brandishing bags from the nearest big-box store—which, I should mention, was nowhere close by. She stormed over, slapped a few LED tealights onto the tables, and glared at me as if she'd single-handedly rescued the entire wedding from imminent doom. Did they help? Absolutely not.

The lights were dim, uneven, and looked like tiny, forgotten hotel nightlights scattered across otherwise lovely tablescapes. But hey—she tried. Sort of.

LESSON: Always read the contract, even if you're day-of coordinating. Never underestimate how emotional people can get over wax. And remember: if your venue was built before indoor plumbing, they probably don't want you playing with fire.

THE UGLY

While the wedding industry is full of love stories, beauty, and celebration, there's also an undeniable undercurrent of moments we wish we could forget. These are the times when joy gets overshadowed—when grace gives way to entitlement, kindness is met with hostility, and the dream day begins to unravel not because of logistics, but because of people.

Rude families can be one of the most heartbreaking parts of wedding planning. Sometimes it's not the couple, but their inner circle—parents, siblings, extended relatives—who turn the process into a battleground. Power struggles, passive-aggressive remarks, or outright disrespect can suck the happiness straight out of the room. Instead of collaborating, you're suddenly mediating. You walk into meetings bracing yourself, unsure whether you'll be welcomed or criticized, thanked or interrogated. No planner should have to absorb that kind of emotional strain—but it happens. And it's ugly.

Then there are the guests who treat a wedding like an all-access pass to an open bar and a personal playground. They snap fingers at staff, ignore seating charts, and wander into private moments like the bride's quiet touch-up before her entrance. Their entitlement sticks out like a neon sign, and more often than not, it's the planner who bears the brunt. By the end of the night, you're not just putting out fires—you're singed around the edges from dealing with everyone else's sparks.

Alcohol can be entertaining. It loosens nerves and packs the dance floor. But when it goes too far, it transforms celebration into damage control. No one likes to see parents—who should be beaming with pride—slurring their words, stumbling around, or creating scenes better suited for a reality show reunion. The slurred speeches, toppled centerpieces, wildly inappropriate jokes, and occasional brawls are never the stuff of wedding albums. It's cringey. It's exhausting. Navigating such chaos with quiet finesse and steady nerves often becomes the planner's task, all while steering the evening safely forward.

What many don't realize is that a big part of the job is keeping a watchful eye on the bar. You're subtly checking in with bartenders to make sure they're not over-pouring, cutting people off when necessary, and trying to avoid turning the reception into an impromptu episode of *Cops*.

These moments don't define the job, but they are undeniably part of it. They remind us that weddings, for all their beauty, also reveal raw, real human behavior—and sometimes, that behavior is downright ugly. But even amid the mess, we learn. We build thicker skin. We sharpen our instincts. Lessons like these toughen us up, so that next time, we're wiser, quicker on our feet, and prepared to keep the day beautiful—even when chaos has other plans.

TIPSY TALES

THE ONE WHERE EVERYONE WAS WASTED

It's 11:00 PM on a cool winter's night. The music's thumping, lights are low, and your shoes are starting to stick to the floor—the classic wedding wrap-up vibe. Everything should be winding down smoothly.

Except… this wedding was anything but smooth.

It all started hours earlier, around 10:00 AM, with mimosas. By noon, shot glasses were clinking in the bridal suite, and beer cans were being crushed out back by the groomsmen. I knew it was going to be that kind of crowd—but even I couldn't have predicted the full spiral.

Fast forward to the reception: the bar never got a moment's rest. Guests were pounding drinks like they were in Cancun on spring break. And when I say pounding, I mean full-blown frat-party levels. The groom's cousin had Fireball on him at all times. The bride's aunt? Mixing tequila into her wine like she was inventing a new cocktail trend. I wish I were joking.

By 9:00 PM, people were slurring, stumbling, and turning shades of red I didn't know human skin could produce. By 10:00 PM, someone had passed out behind the venue—flat on the gravel, arms splayed out like they were making snow angels.

But the peak moment arrived at 11:00 PM: send-off time. We lit the sparklers. Everyone was outside, buzzing with excitement. The bride and groom did the magical walk, kissed in the middle—very cute—and hopped into the car as though they were off to live happily ever after.

Thirty seconds later… they came back inside.

The bride walked up to the bar, barefoot, makeup smudged, veil slightly crooked, and declared, "We want another drink!"

Umm… what? Your wedding is over. You literally just did the grand exit. The DJ has packed up. The bartender is wiping down the bar. It's time to go home. I grinned and said, "Alright, you guys nailed your grand exit. Let's not mess with perfection—it's time to call it a night."

They both blinked at me like I'd just canceled Christmas.

Outside, the driveway resembled a scene from a disaster movie. One guest was vomiting into a bush, while another lay sprawled in the middle of the gravel driveway like it was a Tempur-Pedic mattress on clearance. It was Coachella meets cautionary tale—and guess who had to gently guide people out, hunt down lost cell phones, and make sure no one attempted to drive home? You guessed it: me. Call an Uber.

REAL TALK: If you're going to start drinking early, pace yourself. Your coordinator did not sign up to be your babysitter by midnight. Also: the send-off means the event is done. When the car pulls away—stay in the car.

THE DRUNK GROOM AND HIS LONE STAR STRIP-DOWN

Alright, picture this: it's a sweltering summer day in the Texas Hill Country. The sun is blazing overhead like a spotlight on full blast, not a cloud in the sky, and the heat radiates off the ground in shimmering waves.

The wedding party is decked out in Ariat jeans (yes, that's a thing), crisp white shirts, bolo ties, and cowboy hats—looking every bit like they're about to ride into a Western movie. Everyone's prepped and primed, sweating bullets but still looking sharper than a cactus needle.

I stroll over to the groom's suite, ready to wrangle the guys into position for the ceremony. I knock on the door, half-expecting a quiet moment of nerves, maybe a group prayer, or at the very least someone popping a breath mint. Instead?

The door swings open—and brace yourself—the groom is standing there completely shirtless, looking like he just lost a wrestling match with a tumbleweed. Not a stitch of wedding gear in sight.

"Uh… sir," I manage, trying not to choke on my own spit, "where's your shirt?"

He shrugs, utterly unfazed, and says: "It's too hot, and the whiskey said I should take it off."

Because apparently, whiskey's a hell of a wardrobe consultant.

Meanwhile, the groomsmen are all frozen in place, glancing at each other like, *Should we intervene? Should we just let this happen?* The awkward silence is thicker than the Texas humidity. But time's ticking, and we've got a wedding to run.

I clap my hands and say, "Gentlemen, we're starting in five minutes. Shirts on. Hats straight. Let's look like we're here for a wedding, not the afterparty."

MORAL OF THE STORY? If you're a groom in Texas, remember that heat and whiskey can team up to sabotage your wardrobe choices. But for the love of all things sacred—save the strip show for the honeymoon, not the aisle. And please, keep that bolo tie on.

OH, AND A PRO TIP FOR COORDINATORS: always knock twice. You never know if you're about to walk in on a Lone Star State streaker. Honestly, I've seen the shirtless groom situation more times than I can count. It's like once enough drinks hit, some guys decide the ultimate sign of celebration is ditching the shirt altogether. It's practically become a rite of passage—like losing your shirt means you've officially declared, *This is my party now!*

THE SHY GROOM'S ALMOST-ROCKSTAR MOMENT

At first, this groom was reserved to the point of blending into the wallpaper—quiet, calm, and almost painfully polite. The evening began in a sleek, modern venue, where metal chandeliers cast a moody glow over the room. Hundreds of candles flickered across tables draped in deep charcoal linens, surrounded by lush arrangements of pure white florals. It all felt sophisticated, elegant… utterly classy.

As the night wore on and the drinks kept coming, things shifted—and classy quickly gave way to downright sassy. There I was, weaving through the dance floor, taking in the scene. The candles flickered like tiny spotlights, reflections bouncing off the polished metal fixtures overhead. It was peak modern romance—until suddenly, I heard a chant swelling from the crowd:

"Jump! Jump! Jump!"

I spun around—and there he was. The groom, shirtless, sweat glistening under the chandeliers, fist pumping like he was about to headline a concert. His eyes were locked on his friends, as if contemplating a death-defying stage dive into the crowd below.

My inner planner was in full panic mode. *No, no, no—please don't jump!* I was praying harder than a preacher at a revival. And then… he didn't jump. Praise the wedding gods.

Instead, he turned back to the crowd, gave a subtle nod and bow like a rock star deciding to save his big move for the encore, and kept the party going—no hospital visit required.

That night, I learned two valuable lessons: shy grooms sometimes harbor the wildest energy, and there's nothing quite like good timing—and maybe a healthy fear of broken bones—to keep a wedding from turning into a full-blown emergency room episode.

THE BOURBON WATCHLIST

The wedding was set in a gorgeous, newly renovated hotel—polished marble floors, velvet chairs, modern chandeliers dripping with elegance. A perfect place for love, laughter, and… potential bourbon-fueled chaos.

During our final planning meeting, the mother of the bride leaned in like she was about to tell me a murder plot and whispered: "There are some men you need to watch out for on wedding day."

She proceeded to produce photos from her purse like she was flipping through FBI's Most Wanted. "These guys," she said, tapping each photo for emphasis. "They *love* bourbon. Sometimes a little *too* much."

Cut to wedding day. Everything was perfect. The bride and groom were grinning like they'd won the lottery, floating through the day in a haze of wedded bliss.

Meanwhile, the Four Amigos (my new nickname for the bourbon enthusiasts) were behaving—for now. No slurred speeches. No interpretive dancing to "Shout." Not even a single necktie tied around anyone's forehead. But I wasn't about to let my guard down.

I'd gone full Mission Impossible. I gave every bartender and the catering captain printed photos of the "Most Wanted." One bartender even stuck the pics under the bar like secret cue cards.

"If these guys come asking for bourbon," I instructed, "make it light. Maybe suspiciously watery. Think *bourbon adjacent.*"

The bartenders were artists. They served dribbles disguised as drinks. A splash of bourbon, a gallon of soda water. Enough to keep the bourbon boys feeling festive—but not enough for them to attempt a stage dive off the sweetheart table.

Because in the wedding business, it's not just about the flowers or the timeline. It's about making sure the Four Amigos leave the night with dignity intact—and not starring in tomorrow's viral TikTok under the hashtag #WhiskeyWipeout.

THE CHAMPAGNE BRIDE WHO FIZZLED OUT

Let's talk about my absolute *least* favorite kind of intoxicated wedding guest: the bride.

Yes—the bride. The star of the show. The whole reason we've all gathered in fancy clothes on a Saturday. And on this particular day? She was glowing—but not with "bridal radiance." More like the glow you get when the bubbles hit and you've forgotten to eat breakfast.

The groom? Looking sharp in a tux, straight off the pages of GQ. Cool, composed, ready to say "I do." The bride? Well, she'd been getting cozy with the champagne bottle since the makeup chair. Barely a single bite of food crossed her lips all morning—just gloss, giggles, and endless prosecco refills.

Then—*and I wish I were making this up*—she takes a shot of tequila with her bridesmaids right before walking down the aisle. Like we're pregaming a bachelorette bar crawl, not heading into a lifelong commitment.

My inner planner voice is screaming: "*Why* are we doing this right now?! You're in a $5,000 dress, not in line for dollar shots on Sixth Street!"

The ceremony happens. She makes it down the aisle. But during photos, I notice she's starting to sway. Like a wind chime in a breeze. Her eyes have that glazed, vacant look—like someone who's physically present but mentally floating above the reception.

The sparkle is fading. Quickly.

We get through the main events—the cake cutting, speeches, first dance—but with each moment, she's slipping further into the cocktail abyss. Then, about an hour before the sparkler send-off, I get *the message*: "The bride is in the bathroom. She's throwing up. It's bad."

Fantastic. (Insert sarcastic jazz hands.)

She's in there for nearly an hour. Maid of honor holding her hair, guests starting to murmur, me debating whether we call it early or try to salvage the night. I knock gently on the door and ask if she wants to skip the send-off or attempt a rally.

She rallies. *Kind of.*

She emerges pale, a bit wobbly, still gorgeous—but now radiating the energy of someone who just lost a ten-round fight with a bottle of Brut. She powers through the send-off. We get them out the door. Meanwhile, I'm standing there thinking: "For the love of all that's holy, someone please get this woman a mint and a cool compress."

REALITY CHECK: Brides—by all means, enjoy a drink if you'd like. But please, don't black out at your own wedding. You're only supposed to do this once (hopefully), and trust me—the party is a lot more fun when you're upright, hydrated, and able to remember it the next day. Also, maybe eat a bagel next time.

PLANNER INSIGHT: In those final moments before the ceremony, emotions run high—nerves, excitement, happy tears. It's a beautiful build-up to a once-in-a-lifetime moment. But sometimes… someone in the wedding party suggests a bit of "liquid courage." Just one drink. A toast. A quick something to "take the edge off."

Here's the truth: as tempting as it may be, alcohol before the ceremony is almost always a bad idea. As the planner, I've seen it all—groomsmen sweating during vows, bridesmaids struggling to stay upright in stilettos, slurred toasts during the processional lineup (yes, really). It's not just about etiquette—it's about preserving the moment, the dignity, and the emotion of the ceremony itself.

When a bridesmaid or groomsman casually asks, "Can I grab a quick drink?" just minutes before showtime, I smile and say:

"Let's hold off until after the 'I dos.' You'll have a full glass soon enough—and the couple deserves everyone sober enough to remember this part."

If I need to soften the blow, I'll throw in: "I'll request that for you."

...and then promptly get *conveniently busy* with one of the other hundred fires I'm putting out.

Because protecting the couple's moment—even from their well-meaning, thirsty friends—is part of the gig. And honestly, champagne tastes way better when you're not slurring your way through the first dance.

FULL CIRCLE

Through all the highs and lows, the magical moments and the messy ones, one truth remains: this journey has meaning. Wedding planning isn't just about pretty details or picture-perfect timelines. It's about navigating the entire spectrum of human emotion—from total bliss to deep disappointment—and still showing up with heart, humor, and purpose.

There are days when everything flows effortlessly, when smiles are abundant and gratitude fills the air. Other days test our patience, challenge our professionalism, and make us question why we ever signed up for this circus. Even in the chaos—even in the downright ugly moments—there's something sacred about being trusted with a couple's most important day.

We keep showing up, not merely for the beautiful weddings, but for the beautiful people behind them. We do it for the love stories, the laughter, the grateful tears, and the incredible privilege of helping someone step into a memory they'll carry forever.

In the end, the good outweighs the bad. Even the messy moments earn their place in the story. Every scene—flawless or flawed—is part of the narrative we're honored to help create. That's what makes it all worth it. Amid the wild stories, these are the moments that shimmer a little brighter—a collection of soaring happiness that reminds me exactly why I keep saying "yes" to this wild, wonderful ride.

MORE THAN JUST WEDDINGS

In this industry, we see everything—the chaos, the nerves, the wine-fueled relatives, the curveballs thrown by unexpected weather. Yet woven through all of it are families and couples who remind me why I do this work. Over the years, I've been lucky to meet countless brides and grooms who radiate warmth and gratitude.

People who, in the middle of final planning calls, vendor meetings, or quick check-ins, take a moment to say: "Jen, thank you so, so much. We're so grateful for you." Not just words for politeness's sake, but genuine appreciation that rings with truth. It's as if they truly understand the hours poured into details, the endless juggling, the quiet emotional labor pulsing beneath every seamless wedding day.

At rehearsals, they've hugged me with the kind of fierce squeeze that feels like a burst of sunlight after a storm—an embrace that says, *"We see you. We feel your effort."*

On wedding days, I've watched brides, eyes shimmering with emotion, lean close to whisper words that stop me in my tracks: "I don't know what we would've done without you. You've meant everything." Cue me blinking rapidly, desperate to keep my eyeliner intact.

These moments remind me that, yes, I'm hired to plan weddings, but it's never just a job. It's personal. You invest your heart. You lie awake replaying timelines in your head, rehearse ceremony cues in the shower, pray for clear skies, and silently cheer when the groom shows up on time.

When couples and families recognize that devotion—and return it with genuine gratitude—it fills parts of me I didn't even know were running low. Gratitude travels far. When it's real, it shines a light back on why I keep saying "yes" to this unpredictable, beautiful journey.

15
WHEN DIY GOES WTF

If you're a wedding planner reading this, I know you're already chuckling to yourself. Because you, too, have lived through the trauma that is… DIY (do-it-yourself) décor. **"The question I've learned to ask is: if it's DIY, who's doing the Y?"**

These days, we categorize those items clearly under 'client items for placement'—to keep things fair and functional. You've met the bin moms. You've wrestled tangled garlands from the depths of Amazon boxes. You've seen the "vision" unfold… and then unravel.

THE U-HAUL ERA

Why on earth does your wedding require a U-Haul? Do you think this is going to save money? Save time? Be easier? Spoiler alert: it's not.

Now, in my early years, I didn't know better. I was green. Eager. I pulled up to a venue, excited to execute my beautifully curated timeline… only to see a U-Haul in the parking lot.

"Oh good, you're here!" the parents said, cheerfully. "Here's everything that needs to be set up."

Excuse me? Everything?

There were dozens of boxes. Faux greenery. Lanterns. Photos. Personalized signage. Twinkle lights. An arch. Custom guestbook table. Three ring lights. And a bubble machine (for reasons still unknown). And me, standing there thinking: This was not on my list…

I politely asked, "Do you have helpers coming for setup?"

They smiled sweetly and said, "We thought that was your job!"

Cue me calling friends in a panic to come help. That was the day I learned my very first and very important lesson: we ask the right questions now. Forms. Checklists. Protocols. Boundaries. Systems. Praise be.

THE BIN THAT BROKE ME

Fast forward to a few years later, and my team is well-oiled. There are five of us onsite. We're dialed in. We've prepped. We're ready.

Enter: The Mom with the Bins.

She rolls in with her SUV packed to the roof.

Bin after bin after bin.

Everything still in original Amazon packaging. No labeling. No mercy.

"Oh, sorry! I forgot to add some of this to the list!"

(Yeah… right.)

DIY linens. DIY flatware. DIY balloon arches. DIY signage. DIY place cards. There were literally three hot glue guns on standby.

Let me be clear: we now have a 3-bin MAX policy. Three. Count them.

But this family? They were sweet. Repeat clients. Hard to say no to. You know the ones.

So we did it. We opened the boxes. We sorted. We styled. We hustled.

And when we were finally done setting it all up… guess what?

She brought out more.

Like Mary Poppins' carpetbag, except full of unfinished craft projects.

THE SEQUEL WE DIDN'T ASK FOR

About a year later, that same sweet family hired us again for their final child's wedding.

This time, it was Mikaela's turn.

And bless her.

She texted me: "It's like they just kept everything from the last wedding in their garage and brought it all back."

Balloons. Lanterns. Leftover signage. It looked like Party City exploded in the reception hall.

No labels. No instructions. Just vibes. And anxiety.

Everyone was running around, frantically asking, "Where does this go?" "What do we do with these?" "Can someone iron this?"

It was a DIY do-over in the most chaotic way.

IF YOU'RE A BRIDE READING THIS:

Just rent. Please. It will save your sanity — and ours. DIY might seem like a good idea, but unless you're hosting a Pinterest convention in your sleep, it's often more work, more stress, and more… U-Hauls than anyone bargained for. We love a creative bride. We love a hands-on family. But we also love peace, order, and a timeline that doesn't include assembling 120 chair sashes at 9AM on wedding day. So here's to the lessons we learned the hard way — and the checklists we'll never ignore again.

THE GREAT CANDLE CRISIS

You know what brides love? Candlelight.

You know what DIY brides love? Buying all the candles themselves… on clearance… in bulk.

The couple had decided they wanted an ultra-romantic, candlelit reception — think twinkle, glow, magic. But instead of renting prepped, polished votives from a rental company, they hit up every clearance aisle from Hobby Lobby to HomeGoods like it was a Black Friday scavenger hunt.

When I arrived, I was greeted by bins (plural) of mismatched candle holders. Some still had price tags. Some still had wax from someone else's party. Some looked like they might explode if lit too enthusiastically.

And the candles? Tapers. Tea lights. Pillars. Battery-operated ones with dead batteries. A few of them were those cheap paraffin candles that melt at the speed of light and smell like crayons.

"We're DIY-ing the candlelight," they said with proud smiles.

I smiled back — planner panic hidden beneath a layer of waterproof mascara.

I asked gently, "Did you test any of these ahead of time?" Blank stares.

"Did you bring lighters?" More blank stares.

At this point, I'm Googling "how to remove sticker residue from votives" while my assistant is running to the nearest store for lighters and AA batteries. Meanwhile, Aunt Carol is unwrapping bubble wrap like we're launching a candle pop-up shop.

We started placing them. Some were cracked. Some wouldn't stand straight. A few refused to light. One immediately started leaning like the Tower of Pisa the second it was lit.

And as I stood there, hands covered in wax and sticker gunk, I thought: This is why people rent things. Eventually — after much cleaning, sorting, battery-replacing, and wick-trimming — the room actually looked beautiful. Romantic, even. The glow was real. The bride was thrilled.

BUCKETS, BOUQUETS & BLESS MY HEART

The bride had decided to DIY her florals to "save money." She'd watched some YouTube videos, pinned a few centerpieces, and decided it couldn't be that hard.

I arrive at the venue, timeline in hand, feeling good — until I see it. Buckets. Everywhere.

Big plastic ones. Little ones. Grocery store labels still attached. Sunflowers, baby's breath, a few wilted roses — all chilling in water with no purpose, no plan, and no hydration packets in sight. I blinked.

"Oh! We're doing the flowers ourselves," someone said proudly.

"We're just getting started!"

Mind you, this is just hours before guests are supposed to arrive. They had one floral foam block, three dull shears, and zero sense of urgency. I watched someone spend 15 minutes rearranging one mason jar. I did the math — we were never going to make it.

Now, I could've walked away. I could've stuck to my job description. But instead, the kind soul (and control freak) in me took over. I rolled up my sleeves, pulled out my emergency toolkit, and said: "Okay. Let's make this happen."

We formed a make-shift flower station. I grouped helpers. Assigned roles. Took over the boutonnieres. Reinforced the arches. Eyeballed bouquet symmetry like my life depended on it.

By some floral miracle, everything got finished — not just finished, but actually pretty cute! The tables had centerpieces, the bridal bouquet was full and fresh, and the ceremony arch looked intentionally wild.

The bride? Overjoyed. The photos? Gorgeous.

And me? Add "emergency florist" to the resume.

But let this be a public service announcement: If you're going to DIY your flowers, please, for the love of lilies — have a plan, a team, and more than 3 hours to get it done.

Or… better yet? Hire a florist, and give your planner one less trauma to tuck into her bouquet of memories.

THE BED SHEET BANQUET

Let me take you back to the moment I realized my rates were way too low. I walk into the venue, clipboard in hand, feeling calm, collected, and cautiously optimistic. Until I look over at the guest tables and notice something's… off.

The linens aren't quite hitting the floor. In fact, they're not even hitting the chairs. I walk a little closer. The groom, sweet as can be, waves me down.

"Hey! Just a heads-up — we couldn't find enough of that linen size you told us to get."

I blink. Okay… He grins — proud, even. "So we subbed in some bed sheets!"

I stared.

Bed. Sheets.

Black cotton fitted sheets. Flat sheets. Some with patterns. One with pillows still in the bag it came with. I wish I was kidding. It looked like a sleepover had been invited to the reception.

That was the moment — right then, surrounded by queen-size disaster draped over six-foot rounds — that I looked into the distance like I was in a dramatic documentary and whispered to myself: "Never. Again."

We did our best. We straightened, tucked, layered where we could, prayed the centerpieces would distract from the very obvious seams of a twin XL. But deep down, I knew something had to change. And that something was my pricing.

Because when you're not charging enough, you're not just undervaluing your work — you're leaving the door wide open for a pile of DIY linens and Bed Bath & Beyond to become part of your setup. I walked out of that wedding with a new policy, a new price sheet, and a burning desire to never steam a duvet cover on a banquet table again.

SPRAY PAINT, GLITTER, AND TEARS

Let me tell you about the time a bride proudly told me she had "taken care of all the centerpieces herself." Cue the internal red flag waving wildly.

She showed up on wedding day with bins (of course), each filled with what I can only describe as a Pinterest craft night gone rogue. Inside: mason jars — about 50 of them — all spray-painted in gold... but not just any gold.

Chunky glitter gold. Unevenly coated. Still a little sticky. Some stuck together. Some shedding like a golden retriever in summer.

She handed me a pack of LED tealights and said, "Just pop one in each and set them on the tables!"

Sure. No problem. Except...

Half the jars were still damp. Glitter was everywhere — on my hands, my assistant, the guest chairs, inside the salt shakers… it looked like the Tooth Fairy had been murdered. A few of the jars were sealed shut with paint and couldn't be opened. One shattered in my hand. So *cute*!

We improvised. We made it work. We placed the glitter jars strategically so no one would lose an eye or a cocktail napkin. Guests walked in, saw all the sparkle, and thought it was "so whimsical."

Meanwhile, we're in the back scraping gold dust off our palms and vowing to add "no wet crafts allowed" to our policies. And you better believe we did.

DIY can be meaningful and maybe budget-friendly, no doubt. But when your "just a few finishing touches" involve acrylic paint, twine, and a prayer—it might be time to reconsider what's worth the stress.

THE GREAT DONUT WALL COLLAPSE

The bride had this adorable vision — a DIY donut wall. Pinterest-perfect. Rows of fresh, colorful donuts hanging from pegs, acting as both dessert and décor.

Sounds great, right?

I asked in advance: "Who's providing the wall? Is it being delivered assembled?"

"Oh, my uncle made it!" she said.

Flag #1: Anytime a sentence starts with "my uncle made it," we brace ourselves.

I arrive at the venue and there it is: the donut wall. It's… charming. Rustic. Wobbly. Definitely made in someone's garage with love and maybe some leftover fence wood.

The pegs are installed.

The donuts are ready.

We begin hanging them gently, carefully — until we hear it.

CRACK.

One side of the wall shifts. A peg gives way. Then another. And before I can shout "DON'T TOUCH ANYTHING!", the entire thing tilts forward like a buttery avalanche of doom.

Donuts. Everywhere.

Bouncing. Rolling. Hitting the floor in slow motion. Powdered sugar in the air. One even landed in the coffee. It was tragic. And kind of beautiful.

I stood there, frozen, holding a lone survivor donut in my hand like Simba in The Lion King.

The bride walked in just after the crash. Her face fell. "The wall…"

I nodded, solemnly. "The wall has… fallen."

We pivoted. We pivoted hard. We took the remaining donuts, laid them out artfully on a table with florals, signage, and emergency flair. Someone called it a "Donut Grazing Board," and honestly? It slapped. The bride recovered. The guests ate. And the wall? It retired to the dumpster behind the venue, never to be seen again.

16

IN THE TRENCHES

Trust me on this one – I wish someone had told me when I started out as a wedding planner, it's this: **your feet will betray you.** Back in the day, I thought I had to look like a runway model to be taken seriously. I'd start wedding days in fabulous heels, strutting around feeling unstoppable. A few hours—and several miles—later, I'd swap into what I optimistically called my "more comfortable" pair of heels. Cute, sure, but only marginally less torturous.

Eventually, I'd surrender and slip into ballet flats, convinced I'd cracked the comfort code. Spoiler alert: I had not. By the end of those twelve-hour days, my feet looked like they'd been used as pincushions. Blisters. Throbbing arches. Toes begging for mercy. These days? I proudly rock cute sneakers. Stylish, practical, and perfect for sprinting across ballrooms without sacrificing my dignity— or my arches.

Okay, fine—on rare occasions, you might catch me in sleek pumps if I'm managing a super-upscale affair. But the moment the lights dim for dancing, my sneakers are back on. Because nobody coordinates a wedding gracefully while hobbling.

FOOTWEAR ASIDE, HERE'S ADVICE #2: Cover the ladies. Seriously. No one wants a front-row view of your cleavage while you're wrangling bouquets or pinning boutonnieres. Be professional. If you wouldn't wear it to church, don't wear it to work. Color-wise, black is the industry's trusty standby—sleek, chic, and safely neutral. But personally, I prefer blending in with the event's color palette. If it's a dusty blue and sage wedding, you'll see me in a sage green dress, white sneakers, statement earrings, and a pop of pink lipstick. Because a planner can be practical *and* fabulous.

ADVICE #3: Get off your phone. And stand up. You're the person everyone—vendors, family members, random uncles—turns to for answers and direction. Don't be the planner buried in Instagram while the florist's asking where to put the centerpieces. The only reason your screen should be in your face is if you're texting a vendor or confirming a detail with the maid of honor. Social posts can wait until the dance floor is packed and Aunt Patty is busting out the worm.

ADVICE #4: Eat something. Please. I spent years forgetting to eat on wedding days, then wondering why I was about to faint during cake cutting. A protein bar tucked in your bag is a lifesaver. Hydrate, too—preferably with water, not leftover champagne from cocktail hour.

ADVICE #5: Pack your kit like your life depends on it. Because one day it just might. Scissors, safety pins, stain remover, double-sided tape, a mini sewing kit, Advil, breath mints—you'll thank yourself when the zipper breaks or the mother of the bride discovers a stain five minutes before family photos.

ADVICE #6: Smile through chaos. Guests, vendors, and families feed off your energy. If you stay calm and positive—even when the cake topples or it starts raining during the outdoor ceremony—everyone else will feel reassured.

ADVICE #7: Follow up with your couple after the wedding. Reach out, congratulate them, and check in to make sure they were thrilled with everything. This business is built on relationships. A kind follow-up reminds them you care long after the last candle's blown out—and might just earn you referrals for life.

Planning weddings is not for the faint of heart—or anyone afraid of a 12-hour day of hustling. Wear the sneakers. Cover the girls. Put down the phone. Pack snacks. And remember: you're not just coordinating a day—you're creating memories that last a lifetime.

SMALL TOWN WEDDINGS

It was summertime in South Texas, back in the pre-Jameson days, when John and I packed up for a wedding weekend in Carrizo Springs—a small town boasting a single dance hall, one DJ, and a surprisingly decent hotel (thank you, oil boom).

After a nostalgic bite at Pizza Hut, we checked in and began prepping for the following day's festivities. The ceremony was scheduled in a quaint little church whose air conditioning barely put up a fight against the relentless Texas heat. I can still recall sweat trickling down my back as I stood at the altar during rehearsal, directing the wedding party while attempting not to melt into the carpet.

Fortunately, the bride showed wisdom in her wardrobe choices. The men wore short-sleeve collared shirts instead of full suits—thank goodness. The groom stood out in white, while the groomsmen sported light blue, each accented by pink and sage floral print bow ties.

The bridesmaids wore dusty pink chiffon dresses, styled with a single cross-shoulder strap and gentle gathering at the waist, each carrying bouquets of pink roses, baby's breath, and silver dollar eucalyptus, wrapped in burlap for that rustic touch.

The bride looked timeless in an A-line lace gown, cinched with a pearl satin belt, and carried a bouquet of white roses bound in delicate white lace. Simple. Elegant. And admittedly, a bit sweaty—but still elegant.

Once the vows were sealed with a kiss, we had a short window before guests made their way to the reception. I dashed off to the dance hall to welcome vendors and finsih turning an ordinary space into a celebration. That's when things got... interesting.

First: The Cake.
The baker arrived—a sweet older woman—carrying a towering seven-tier cake that she had already assembled. (Who does that?! Most bakers assemble onsite if it's that large.) The entire confection must have weighed at least eighty pounds. She asked for help getting it inside, and John, ever the gentleman, offered to assist.

"That cake was perched on quarter-inch plywood, sagging like a hammock. Scariest thing I've ever carried," John quipped afterward.

From the moment he lifted it, he gave me a look of pure panic. The cake was practically a skyscraper, and John couldn't see past it. I turned into his personal GPS: "Careful—cord ahead... shift right... easy... wait, let me fix the linen so it doesn't bunch up!"

By some miracle, he delivered it safely to the table. Though to this day, John has officially retired from cake-carrying duty.

Second: The Décor.
This was a DIY wedding, and the bride was enthusiastic but not exactly organized. Half an hour before guests arrived, we were still stringing twinkle lights and rigging a photo backdrop. John balanced on a ladder, while I scurried below, directing foot traffic and catching falling zip ties like a contestant on a game show.

Third: The DJ.
A kind individual—but clearly new to the profession and apparently didn't believe in background music. I glanced at John, mouthed "Music?" and tapped my watch. Since we didn't have radios back then, I dashed across the hall to intervene. Meanwhile, John approached him and said: "Hey man, the music needs to start—like, now."

Even so, it took several reminders to coax out a basic playlist before guests wandered into a room filled with that awkward, echoing silence—the kind where your ears start to ring.

Despite the rocky start, the reception itself went smoothly. Guests enjoyed the evening, the food was a hit, and the cake survived unscathed. Yet the DJ's silent interludes still haunt me.

Supporting small-town weddings can be incredibly rewarding, but Carrizo Springs taught me this crucial truth: When the vendor list is DIY and support is thin, the responsibility inevitably falls on the coordinator. We managed to roll with it—and did—but I now ask very different questions when booking events in rural areas.

IT GOT WEIRD

It was September 2020—peak COVID era. Business was scarce, weddings were rare, and you took whatever came your way. So, when a wedding inquiry popped up for West Texas, John and I said, "Why not, road trip?"

The ceremony was Catholic (bless the air conditioning), the church coordinators were lovely, the family was punctual, and I even wrapped rehearsal with a pop quiz for the wedding party—everyone aced it. I thought, *Okay, this is going to be smooth.*

Then... 2:00 AM.

Pitch black. Peaceful. Until the fire alarm shrieked like an air raid siren. John and I leapt out of bed, grabbing wallets, phones, and shoes. We peered over the balcony to see a fire truck rolling up and a crowd of bewildered hotel guests. False alarm. Someone a little too friendly with the bar had pulled the handle. Welcome to Midland.

Wedding Day.

9:00 AM. Makeup time. I was crouched on the floor curling my hair when John—bless him—showed up with hotel breakfast and strong coffee. I perched on the bed, sending out confirmation texts because, in unfamiliar territory, you triple-check everything.

- Church? ✔ Doors opening at 1:00 PM.
- Photography? ✔ Following the couple all day.
- DJ, Catering, Venue? ✔ All set.

Except... the florist. She was still working on the flowers that morning. No bouquets had made it to the hotel rooms. I offered to help. She politely declined and promised everything would arrive "on time."

Technically, she was right. When we arrived at the convention center around noon, the flowers were there—but let's just say they were underwhelming. Sparse eucalyptus, baby's breath, a few long-stem roses, and visible floral foam—a personal pet peeve. I took a deep breath. *This is what she ordered. I am not the florist.*

I kissed John goodbye—he was handling reception vendor logistics—while I headed back to the church to get our couple married.

Reception: Where It Gets Interesting

The couple wanted to party until midnight. No "Catholic gap," so guests started arriving at 3:30 PM. It turned into a ten-hour marathon. In hindsight, I should have charged double, but during COVID, I was just grateful to be working—especially alongside my best friend.

And then there was the DJ. He was a middle-aged gentleman, likely very kind—but a local guy. At one point, he untied his tie and began swinging it over his head like a lasso. Later, he started a conga line—entirely by himself. I kept blinking, wondering, *Is this really happening?*

As dinner wrapped up, I slipped away to prep for the cake cutting. Checked the kitchen. No plates. Looked under the cake table. Nothing. Asked catering—they had forks but no plates.

I did what any coordinator would do: asked the mother of the bride if she'd packed any extras. Nope. No hidden aunt stash, either.

Plan B: John dashed to the Dollar Store and returned a hero. Crisis averted.

Then, later in the night, John emerged from the restroom chuckling.

"What's so funny?" I asked.

He leaned closer and said, "I think a few guests have discovered the express lane to party mode."

My eyes widened.

"Well… that explains the DJ."

Honestly, it tracked. Oil field crowd. Ten-hour reception. Looking back, we should have anticipated a few extracurricular activities.

By midnight, the crowd was still going strong. Fortunately, the reception venue opened onto a side patio, making the send-off easy. No sparklers allowed—a blessing, given the crowd's state. I distributed ribbon wands instead—safe and photogenic. As I gave my usual send-off coaching— "pause in the middle for a kiss"—the bride just grinned and said, "Thank you so much. Everything was wonderful."

BOWS, BROS, AND UNEXPECTED SHOW

I was barely 24, running wedding coordination solo, armed with a clipboard, a color-coded timeline, and enough blind optimism to power the entire venue's chandeliers. This was one of my first big weddings—picture a grand estate with sweeping staircases, crystal chandeliers, and manicured lawns, the kind of place where fairytales unfold… or, in this case, where a live reenactment of *Magic Mike* collides spectacularly with wedding formalwear.

The day started off deceptively smooth. The groomsmen—all ten of them, because naturally there were ten—had been drinking since noon. Standard. I popped in with my best cheerfully authoritative voice: "Alright, gentlemen! Pictures kick off at 4:00. I'll be back around 3:45 to handle boutonnières!"

Meanwhile, the ladies were the definition of composed—bubbly in hand, laughing softly, and working the camera like they'd been cast in a bridal fashion spread.

DJ? Locked and loaded.

Catering? On point.

Officiant? Calm and sufficiently caffeinated.

Time to cue the ceremony. I lined up the groom and his band of merry men and ushered them outside like a slightly rowdy bachelor parade—mercifully still wearing their ties. Then I returned to bring the bride and her father down the staircase. She was glowing; he was fighting back tears.

A soft breeze rustled her veil, and a few puffy clouds rolled in just in time to save everyone from melting or squinting through the photos. We made it to "I do" without a single hiccup.

Fast forward through dinner, heartfelt toasts, and a flawless cake cutting. Everything was textbook perfect. I was already mentally drafting my glowing post-wedding report.

And then… it happened.

Cue "Pony" by Ginuwine.

Wait—what? Suddenly, the groom and his ten groomsmen appeared at the top of the grand staircase, strutting out like they'd just missed their call time at a Vegas revue. Bow ties? Check. Shirts? Nowhere to be found.

They began descending the stairs in perfect rhythm, like they'd been secretly rehearsing for weeks. There was coordinated thrusting. Synchronized clapping. One of them hurled a garter into the crowd like it was a $1 bill at a gentleman's club.

I stood frozen, somewhere between horrified and hysterical, my brain screaming: "Why… why on your wedding day?! Save it for the honeymoon. Or, I don't know… your fantasy football league."

The crowd? Lost their minds. Grandma? Shocked but giving a standing ovation. The bride? Laughing so hard she was crying. Me? Wondering how on earth I'd summarize *that* in my post-event recap.

From that day forward, seasoned-me always asks this critical question during planning meetings:

"Are there any surprises or 'performances' I should know about?"

Because no one—and I mean no one—wants to be blindsided by a staircase strip tease.

HEELS IN THE SAND, HUSTLING AT SUNSET

The ceremony was set on the sand in Port Aransas—a dreamy beach wedding bathed in golden light, with the Gulf breeze whispering promises of perfection. We arrived while the tide was still low, anchoring chairs deeper than we thought we'd need to. Guests kicked off their shoes, laughing as heels sank and the sand tried to claim them. A wooden arch stood at the water's edge, draped in flowing ivory fabric and adorned with soft peach blooms, swaying gently in the breeze.

The bride wore an elegant A-line silk gown, no veil—just a delicate beaded comb nestled into her side-braided bun, accented with a small cluster of fresh flowers. The groom was relaxed yet handsome in lightweight khaki pants and a crisp white Guayabera button-down. Both stood barefoot in the sand, grinning as the wind played with the bride's hair.

As I readied the bride for her sandy aisle debut, I tucked runaway strands behind her ears and straightened her sparkling hair comb. With the surf thundering beside us, I leaned in and grinned, *"The wind's no match for you. Now go knock him off his feet."*

The ceremony itself was sweet and intimate, lasting just fifteen minutes. After heartfelt vows and a kiss under the arch, family gathered for photos before heading off to a cozy indoor reception. That left John and me alone on the beach, ready to tackle clean-up duty.

But then… sunset arrived.

As the sky melted into breathtaking shades of lavender and peach, the tide began to surge—fast. What had been a wide stretch of sand only an hour earlier was rapidly swallowed by dark, rolling waves.

We hustled like crazy, arms loaded with chairs, scooping up candles, and packing décor as the water crept closer. Sand clung to everything—hair, clothes, equipment. Literally tossing everything into the truck frantically.

The light faded, and John and I moved in perfect rhythm, half-laughing, half-panicking:

"Let's move before we're floating out of here!"

By the time the last box was in the truck, darkness had settled over the beach, waves crashing where the aisle used to be. We'd hustled, underestimated how fast the tide could rise, and let out a huge sigh of relief as we finally drove off. But the couple was blissfully happy. They got their beach ceremony—and that's what truly mattered.

SCORPIONS, CENTIPEDES, AND OH MY!

Listen — I'm from Texas. I know the deal. You live here long enough and you learn to accept the occasional creepy crawler. It's part of the charm, right?

However, when you're coordinating a wedding, feeling cute in your black dress, clipboard in hand, everything running smooth… and then a scorpion drops from the ceiling onto your head — that's where I draw the line.

I froze. The bridal party gasped. One bridesmaid screamed. I swatted at my hair like it was on fire and probably invented a brand-new dance move in the process. It was fine. I survived. The scorpion did not.

But that wasn't the first — or the last — uninvited guest we've had. We've had plenty of run-ins with scorpions. Once, I was in the ladies' room minding my own business. I swung the wooden stall door open — and a scorpion fell right in front of my face and hit the floor. I screamed bloody murder, skipped the handwashing entirely, and bolted out of the restroom like I'd seen a ghost.

And who was right outside the door? The groom. Calmly passing by, just in time to see his wedding coordinator looking like a freak show, hopping around and gasping for air. "Oh, hello, Cody. Happy wedding day!"

We've even found scorpions under the cake table, hanging out like they were waiting for their slice of red velvet. My assistant, Paige, politely invited that one to leave… with a broom and a shriek.

Then there's the fuzzy menace of Texas: the asp caterpillar. Let me tell you, those little furballs look cute — like tiny toupées — but touch one, and it feels like you've set your hand on fire with a sparkler.

Picture this: I am cheerfully watching the bride and groom pose for romantic photos by a babbling stream. Birds chirping, sun filtering through the trees — pure magic. I casually rested my hand on a wooden beam. Mistake.

"OW!"

I handed my clipboard to my assistant like it was a live grenade. "Take over. I need Benadryl, a prayer, and possibly a new hand."

A couple sting relief wipes and some ibuprofen later, I was back in action. But let me tell you, two weeks afterward, I still had little dots on my hand. It took three weeks for that sting to fully heal.

And let's not forget the time I was fluffing a bride's train in a charming little chapel with original wood walls, only to spot something long, slithery, and absolutely not welcome crawling along the baseboard. A centipede — not the cute cartoon kind, but the big, juicy, multi-leg nightmare variety.

I gently guided the bride away like, "Let's... um... take a photo over here instead!"

Then there was the reception where a cricket chorus joined the string quartet. Honestly, by then, I was just impressed they managed to keep rhythm. In Texas, you never know what's going to pop out of the woodwork — literally. But you learn to roll with it.

Pack extra hairspray, keep a flashlight in your kit, and never underestimate the power of a well-aimed sneaker. I may be a wedding planner, but I'm also an amateur exterminator, professional bug screecher, and somehow… still cool under pressure. Just don't ask me to act normal when a scorpion lands on my head.

TEXAS SIZED LOVE, CANADIAN ROOTS

Penny and Daren were my seasoned sweethearts—a true second-chance love story if ever there was one. Years ago, they'd shared a romantic chapter in San Antonio. Life, as it often does, pulled them in separate directions.

Decades rolled by. And then, as if the universe decided enough was enough, Penny and Daren found their way back to each other. Naturally, they wanted to celebrate this full-circle love right where it had begun—in San Antonio.

The wedding planning journey with Penny was wonderful! Like so many couples of this era, we planned the entire event via Zoom. Across video calls, we gathered ideas, fine-tuned vendor orders, and examined color samples, linens, and floral mock-ups with a meticulous eye.

By the end of it, it felt like we were old friends—even though we'd never actually met in person.

I couldn't wait to finally meet Penny, and rehearsal day made it happen. The second we hugged, it was like greeting someone I'd known forever.

The setting was a charming, quaint bed and breakfast nestled along the San Antonio River. The B&B was the picture of historic Texas charm—wrought-iron balconies, shady oak trees, and ivy climbing brick walls like green lace. It was perfect... except for one tiny issue: it couldn't hold 100 guests.

You know what we did? We rolled up our sleeves and transformed the side grassy area into a spectacular tented reception. The color palette was pure romance: Tiffany Blue meets Texan Chic, accented with black, yellow, and shimmering silver. White decorated the tables inside the tent, casting a soft glow over tables adorned with crisp linens and sparkling glassware.

Yellow roses of Texas burst cheerfully from lush centerpieces, mingling with delicate greenery and elegant touches of black satin ribbon. Horseshoes, tucked discreetly into the floral designs, served as tokens of good luck—a sweet nod to Texas tradition and perfect for my bride who wanted meaningful details.

Every place setting held a customized favor box in iconic Tiffany Blue, tied with a sleek black satin bow. Inside were little treasures representing the best of San Antonio: Alamo-shaped chocolate, fiery local hot sauces, fragrant spices, and other local delights. It was like opening a tiny love letter to the city itself.

Now, it was the first Saturday in May—typically a lovely spring day in Texas. But Mother Nature apparently had other plans because that afternoon, the mercury soared to a sizzling 110 degrees. Those poor Canadians in Penny and Daren's entourage were sweating through their linen suits and pastel dresses, fanning themselves with ceremony programs and blinking at me in disbelief.

"It sure is warm out here, eh?" they kept saying. I smiled through the sweat dripping down my back, thinking, **Warm, alright. Bless y'all's hearts.**

Despite the heat, Penny and Daren said "I do" along the tranquil riverbank, framed by gently swaying cypress trees. Sunlight shimmered off the water, and dragonflies zipped around as if celebrating right along with us.

Joe, my trusty father-in-law, officiated the ceremony. He delivered heartfelt words that had everyone misty-eyed—even me, and I've seen hundreds of weddings. As the couple recessed back up the aisle, "Signed, Sealed, Delivered" burst from the speakers, and the crowd clapped and danced in the sun-dappled grass.

Anne Marie's Catering absolutely knocked it out of the park. Plates came loaded with Texas favorites and elegant bites, the kind of food that makes you loosen your belt and grab another plate "just to try a little more." Signature cocktails flowed like a river of their own, icy and refreshing under that blistering Texas sun. Thankfully, our culinary team kept us all hydrated and fed—crucial survival tactics for planners and guests alike.

Then the live band kicked in, sealing the party with electric energy. The dance floor filled up with twirls, cowboy boots shuffling, and even a few brave Canadians trying out line dancing under the glowing lanterns.

Wedding day was spectacular. Everyone was happy. And Penny and Daren were blown away by how it all turned out—the colors, the flowers, the music, and the love that wrapped the entire day like

Texas sunshine. Yes, it was hot enough to melt mascara and make your hair stick to your neck.

But Penny and Daren's day was nothing short of magical—a day that proved love, second chances, and a bit of Texas grit can shine even under a scorching sun. And as I finally took a breath at the end of the night, looking out at the shimmering lights reflecting on the river, I thought: *This is why I do what I do.*

THE LAST-MINUTE BOUQUET PLOT TWIST

Three days before the wedding, I get the call. "I've been thinking... I want to change my bouquet."

Now, to be clear — this was not a minor tweak. The bride wanted to swap out nearly everything for a new vision involving tulips. In September. In Texas. I paused, smiled through the phone, and thought to myself: Unless I'm growing a tulip farm in my backyard, this is not happening. So I did what any good planner/floral magician does — I problem-solved with grace.

"Okay," I told her, "Here's what we can do. While tulips aren't available right now, I can redesign the bouquet with gorgeous pink ranunculus. They'll give you that soft, romantic look, and I'll keep the shape cascading and modern, just like you envisioned. It's going to be stunning — promise."

She agreed — a little hesitantly — but trusted me. Fast forward to the wedding day.

I walk in with the bouquet, layered with lush ranunculus, delicate accents, and just the right amount of movement. I hand it to her, hold my breath... she starts crying. Not the something's wrong kind of cry. The I feel seen, heard, and absolutely beautiful kind of cry.

"It's more perfect than I imagined," she said through tears. Suddenly, all the last-minute juggling, the substitutions, the stress — all of it faded into a moment of pure magic. Because sometimes, it's not about getting exactly what you asked for. It's about getting something even better.

SUNSHINE, STORMS, AND A LOVE THAT WON THE DAY

It was a May wedding day in Texas—a month that's supposed to promise warm breezes and blooming wildflowers. Spring, they say. But Texans know better. May is also the season of thunderstorms and unpredictable skies, and that day Mother Nature was in one of her moods.

Karina and Sam had envisioned saying "I do" outside, surrounded by Hill Country views at Kendall Point—a venue that's practically a fairy tale brought to life. The color palette they chose was pure joy: soft pastels, shades of pink and dusty blue, delicate touches of buttercream yellow and leafy greens.

Inside, gold and glass candlesticks were scattered across tables, flames flickering gently as though whispering secrets to one another. Candlelight shimmered on tabletops, reflecting off glassware like tiny constellations scattered across a velvet sky. The florals were dreamy clusters of roses, ranunculus, and blue delphinium, each stem a brushstroke on the canvas of the day.

But by mid-morning, reality decided to crash the party.

Kristin, the venue owner—a true gem who always goes above and beyond—called me. Her voice was calm, but I could hear the tension hiding behind her words. "It doesn't look good, Jen. There are tornado and weather warnings."

Cue my stomach dropping to my knees. I hate these calls. But in Texas, you learn to pivot faster than a cowboy changing horses mid-gallop.

Our team arrived at the venue bright-eyed and hopeful, determined to make magic no matter what. We began setting up the inside space, but my stubborn wedding-planner brain refused to give up on the outdoors. A few quick showers rolled through, leaving silver droplets clinging to petals and leaves. Then the rain would stop, and the skies would tease us with glimmers of sun.

Thirty minutes before the ceremony, I glanced over and spotted Mr. Joseph Flores, one of my favorite officiants, standing at the doorway. He mouthed, **"It's hailing,"** and held up his hand to show me the size of the ice balls pelting down outside. They were not small.

My first thought was painfully honest: "Ahhhh—my pretty car!" But a second later, I snapped back into planner mode.

Guests were arriving, and there was no way I was letting them stand outside in a hailstorm. Outside, cocktail tables were tipping over like dominoes. Linen cloths whipped in the wind. Everyone leapt into action—catering staff, bartenders, Kristin and Paige. It was an all-hands-on-deck situation, with people grabbing tablecloths, catching centerpieces, and saving toppling chairs.

Meanwhile, I was hauling chairs from VIP tables, creating an impromptu ceremony layout and preparing myself for the dreaded conversation with Karina and Sam.

"Friends… we may have to get married indoors."

To their credit, they were visibly disappointed but handled it with poise, if slightly glassy-eyed resignation. As the last guests trickled in, soaked umbrellas in hand, most found seats at their dinner tables, convinced that indoors it would be.

And then...

The clouds split open. A brilliant beam of sunlight poured through as though heaven itself was giving us the green light. I practically shouted: "We're getting married outside!"

It was a beautiful, chaotic scramble. The Kendall Point team dried chairs and sopped up puddles on the turf. The DJ, bless him, rallied and moved his entire system back outside at warp speed. I raced to tell the wedding party the good news, practically skipping like a kid on Christmas morning.

And so, beneath the timeless white gazebo draped in flowing white fabric and clusters of dusty blue flowers, Karina and Sam said yes to forever. Sunlight glinted off the water, casting ripples of gold and silver, and a light breeze rustled the draping like a soft sigh.

After formal photos, the sky rumbled like a giant clearing its throat. Thunder cracked overhead, and we all scooted back inside just in time to stay dry.

Inside, fairy lights sparkled above a custom white vinyl dance floor. The aroma of delicious food mingled with the scent of fresh flowers and candle wax. Laughter rose in waves over the music, mingling with the clink of glasses and the shuffle of dancing feet.

When fireworks burst into the night sky, their colors shimmering across the pond, it felt like the perfect exclamation point to a day that had tried its best to go off-script—but we prevailed.

It's days like this that remind me why I love this job. When a rockstar vendor team pulls together, pivots on a dime, and makes magic happen for our number one priority: the couple.

Karina and Sam's wedding wasn't flawless by the letter of the timeline. But it was perfect in all the ways that matter. And that's the kind of story I'll tell forever.

THE MOUNTAINS MADE ME DO IT

It all started with a road trip. Because when you're planning a destination wedding **and** designing the flowers, it only makes sense to load your truck with brass candlesticks, terra-cotta pots, bud vases, and a forest's worth of succulents—and drive yourself across state lines, right?

This was our first (and so far, only) Colorado wedding: a rustic-meets-elegant mountain soirée that was equal parts breathtaking and backbreaking. The bride had a vision, and we were determined to bring it to life… even if it meant scaling literal mountains.

We arrived at the rental house—an adorable cottage nestled right in town—and like any good family-run operation, I brought backup. The dream team included my in-laws, Jameson, John, my coordinating bestie Mikaela, and her crew. Gail was our designated child wrangler slash snack distributor. Joe was the muscle. Everyone had a job. No one escaped the flower room.

Speaking of which—our flowers arrived two days before the wedding. Great timing. Except for one tiny hiccup: the yellow jackets. One innocent step near the stairs and I unknowingly stirred up an underground nest. They retaliated with a vengeance. I took a sting to the leg. Then the ankle. And then, poor Jameson—my sweet sidekick—got stung too. He handled it like a champ. I, however, discovered I'm allergic. Swelling, redness, and a full "why me?" moment. But there was no time to wallow. Bouquets don't build themselves.

At 5:00 AM the next morning, I got to work like a floral gladiator—bandaged leg and all. By lunchtime, we paused for a breath of Colorado magic. The air was crisp, the mountains majestic, and for a brief moment, it almost felt like vacation.

Then came rehearsal. The venue was only 14 miles away, but somehow took nearly an hour to reach. The drive felt like a deleted scene from *True Grit*—narrow switchbacks, gravel trails, and speed limits that clearly weren't made with cargo vans in mind. But the payoff? Pure cinematic perfection. Lush green pastures, a panoramic bowl of mountains, grazing cows, and the most picturesque barn tucked into the hillside. The kind of place that whispers, "Slow down, stay awhile."

Wedding day arrived, and by 9:00 AM sharp, we were on site and ready to transform the space. The ceremony altar? A towering 16-foot wooden arch. The terrain? Rocky, sun-soaked, and uneven. Every arrangement had to be done there, from scratch. And the wedding was early—ceremony at 3:30 PM sharp—so every minute mattered.

I lost count of how many trips we made hauling décor: antlers, candles, florals, succulents, dinnerware. My legs were screaming. My scalp? Sunburned. My side braid? Doing its own thing.

But I was in the zone. We styled every table, fluffed every napkin, placed each charger with military-level precision. We hustled right up until guests began to arrive. And you know what? It was fabulous.

The couple was glowing. The guests were enchanted. The golden hour light bathed the whole valley in a warm glow that felt like a reward for every ounce of effort. I may have looked like I'd just descended Everest, but I was beyond proud of what we pulled off.

Would I do it again? Maybe. But next time, I'm just the planner. Floral design at elevation? That's an Olympic sport. I'll never forget that weekend. The laughter. The teamwork. The adrenaline. The pure joy of watching two people say "I do" in a place that felt carved by nature just for them. Sore legs, wild roads, yellow jacket drama and all—it was one of my favorite adventures to date.

THE SECRET PIANO SURPRISE

Some weddings remind you exactly why you love this work. This one? It's a forever favorite.

It all unfolded at Park 31—a venue that strikes the perfect balance between masculine strength and feminine elegance. Think soaring industrial beams softened by glamorous chandeliers, raw stone walls paired with leather lounges. It's the kind of place where you feel both the grandeur of architecture and the intimacy of romance the moment you walk in.

That June afternoon, the space practically glowed. Tables brimmed with vibrant blooms—rich magentas, fiery oranges, pretty peaches—nestled into rustic terra cotta vases. Above it all, papel picado in white danced from the chandeliers, casting playful shadows that shifted like lace in the breeze. Candlelight flickered across gold and glass candlesticks, spilling a warm, inviting glow that felt almost like a heartbeat pulsing through the room.

Mike and Anahi had brought me on board about three months earlier, after bumping into me a handful of times at various open house events. They'd secured the venue and had a fuzzy vision of what they wanted—but the details were wide open. With my trusty timelines, color swatches, and a few "firm but friendly" nudges, we locked in every vendor within weeks. Everything was running as smooth as satin ribbons.

Then I got *the call*. It was Mike.

"Hey Jennifer," he said, voice charged with both nerves and hope. "I'm planning a surprise for Anahi… and I'm hoping—with your help—we can actually pull this off."

Cue my planner senses going full throttle.

Over a few coaching calls, Mike revealed his secret mission: he wanted to surprise Anahi with a musical performance. But not just a simple serenade. No, Mike was dreaming big. Picture this—a gleaming black baby grand piano, him playing and singing, and (wait for it) a full mariachi band bursting in toward the end of the second song.

My first thought? *Okay, let's do this.*

My second thought? *This man is brave.*

Mike was as sweet as he was determined—but his nerves were very real. Therefore, I became part-planner, part-pep talker:

"You've got this."

"She's going to love it."

Behind the scenes, I was orchestrating a logistical ballet. I secured early venue access so the piano could be delivered and tuned in secret. At 9:00 AM sharp, the glossy black piano arrived. By 10:15, it was tuned and ready to sing.

John, my ever-resourceful right hand, just happened to have a tarp in his car (because of course he did). Together, we camouflaged the piano right there in the middle of the ballroom. We covered it with floral arrangements, scattered clipboards, and enough "planner chaos" to pass it off as a florist's work station.

Then Anahi arrived.

She floated into the room, eyes sparkling, clutching a few DIY pieces she wanted to show me. She barely glanced at the "workstation," completely enthralled by how gorgeous everything looked—the jewel-toned flowers, the terra cotta accents, the flickering candles, and those custom papel picado banners overhead. She never even noticed the piano, hidden in plain sight. To this day, it makes me giggle. Rose-colored glasses, indeed.

Finally, the moment came.

Mike was pacing, palms sweaty, mouthing lyrics like a man rehearsing for the biggest performance of his life. He'd only practiced with the mariachi band once before that day.

And then—he sat at the piano.

He played.

He sang.

Halfway through his second song, the doors flew open and the mariachi band poured in—trumpets blaring, guitars strumming, velvet-clad musicians filling Park 31's towering space with jubilant music.

Anahi gasped, one hand flying to her mouth, tears welling up until they spilled over her cheeks. A standing ovation followed. Thunderous applause. Not a single dry eye in that room filled with flowers, candlelight, and color.

It was one of the most magical moments I've ever witnessed. And to know I played a part in bringing it to life—that's why I love this job. Because wedding planning isn't always about timelines and décor—it's about building spaces where love can do something unforgettable. On that day, Mike didn't just surprise his bride—he reminded all of us what love sounds like when it's brave.

MAY THE FORCE BE WITH YOU

In a galaxy not so far away—specifically, a charming Texas wedding venue decked out like a Star Wars film set—Jamie and Jon decided that Friday the 13th was the perfect day to get married.

And in classic Jamie fashion, she proclaimed: "I don't give a hell what people think about me. This is my wedding day!"

And honestly? That's the energy we should all aspire to bring to life.

From the moment guests arrived, they were swept into a world where fantasy ruled. Twinkling lights mimicked starlight overhead. Tables sparkled with sequin linens, dotted with flickering candles and scattered tiny figurines of stormtroopers and droids.

Jon, ever the cool and steady counterpart to Jamie's vibrant spirit, grinned from ear to ear in a perfectly tailored suit with a subtle nod to the theme—a custom lining printed with miniature Millennium Falcons.

Jamie, on the other hand, made her entrance like an interstellar queen. Her dress, classic in silhouette, was anything but traditional once you noticed the custom cape train flowing behind her—a black gown adorned with tiny red crystals and black sequins, shimmering like the galaxy itself. A delicate tiara nestled in her vibrant hair sparkled with tiny lights, like stars winking in the night sky.

And because this was Jamie's wedding, there was, of course, a twist. Just as the ceremony began and the music swelled (the Imperial March, naturally), a hulking figure emerged from the side aisle—hockey mask glinting under the venue lights. Jason Voorhees, machete in hand, lurked forward, only to stop beside Jon and nod solemnly, stepping into the groomsman lineup like he belonged there.

Guests gasped, then burst into laughter, smartphones snapping photos as Jason calmly folded his hands and waited for the officiant to continue. Because why wouldn't Jason show up at a wedding on Friday the 13th?

Once the crowd settled, Jamie and Jon exchanged a knowing look—a tender, quiet moment where Jon's eyes brimmed with tears and Jamie whispered: "Ready to rule the galaxy with me?"

Jon just smiled and said, "Always."

The ceremony continued beneath an arch formed by towering oak trees. As Jamie and Jon exchanged heartfelt vows, the glow of autumn cast soft, golden hues across their faces. Even Jason looked a little emotional behind his mask.

After the pronouncement of marriage—and an enthusiastic "May the Force Be with You!" from the officiant (Joe, my father-in-law), who was dressed as Obi-Wan Kenobi—the real party began.

Inside the reception, the Star Wars theme continued in spectacular fashion. Centerpieces featured sculpted black-and-white helmets adorned with red flowers and black dried elements. Black candles flickered atop sequin-covered tables, casting a cosmic glow.

The bar served Galaxy Drinks with names like "Sith Punch," "Jedi Juice," and "The Padawan," each topped with Death Star-inspired boba berries. There was a galactic-themed cake, perfectly on-theme in red, black, and silver, decorated with tiny robots and miniature spaceships.

Guests danced under iron chandeliers and laser projections that transformed the entire dance floor into hyperspace. At one point, a spontaneous lightsaber duel broke out between two guests, complete with dramatic choreography and roaring cheers from the crowd.

Through it all, Jamie and Jon beamed, moving from table to table, sharing laughs and hugs, completely in their element. They were the perfect balance—Jamie, fearless and fiery; Jon, steady and sweet.

As the night came to a close, cold sparklers erupted outside as the newlyweds bid farewell. Guests poured onto the lawn, lightsabers still glowing, laughter echoing into the warm Texas evening. Jamie and Jon's wedding was more than just a celebration. It was a universe all its own—a cosmic collision of love, humor, and unforgettable memories. And as they left the venue hand in hand, lightsabers held high, one thing was certain: The Force—and an incredible love story—was definitely with them.

THE THREE-WEEK WONDER

A few years ago, smack in the middle of fall wedding season, I faced a wedding planner's bittersweet reality: one of my couples parted ways and canceled their wedding on a wildly popular October date.

I was genuinely heartbroken for them—but the business owner in me was screaming inside:

"I've got to fill this date!"

Someone up there must've been listening, because just a few days later, my phone rang. On the other end was a couple sounding equal parts panicked and hopeful. They'd just secured that very same October date at the same venue—but had precisely four weeks to plan an entire wedding.

Three. Weeks.

I felt a surge of adrenaline and immediately slipped into mission mode. We booked every vendor practically simultaneously.

Florals? Check.

Photographer? Check.

Hair and makeup, cake, officiant? Check, check, and check.

The venue made things infinitely smoother since they handled the food, bar, and rentals all under one roof. And I made it easier because, lucky for them, I'm both a planner *and* a florist. Two hats, one woman, zero time to spare.

Truth be told, it wasn't nearly as crazy as you might think. In fact, there's a certain magic that happens when you have less time to overthink every single decision. No hours-long debates about napkin folds or shades of ivory. No weeks of Pinterest spirals.

Instead, my couple simply looked at me and said: *"We trust you. Just make it beautiful."*

Music to any planner's ears. We landed on a stunning color palette: rich burgundy paired with fall tones—deep russets, soft golds, and warm burnt orange. It was the kind of palette that practically *glows* against the backdrop of autumn leaves.

On wedding day, the sun poured golden light over the venue grounds. Guests arrived to tables draped in elegant linens, accented with shimmering gold chargers and glimmering glassware. Centerpieces spilled over with lush blooms—burgundy dahlias, caramel roses, bronze mums, and sprays of eucalyptus cascading like a gentle autumn breeze.

Candles flickered everywhere—tall gold candlesticks casting soft shadows across the tables, while votives added an intimate glow. The entire room felt like stepping into an autumn fairytale.

The bride, radiant in a sleek lace gown, carried a bouquet brimming with burgundy and rust blooms tied off with silk ribbons. The groom looked dapper in a classic charcoal suit with a burgundy boutonniere tucked neatly into his lapel.

And you'd never guess this wedding had been pulled together in less than a month.

As they stood hand in hand exchanging vows, I felt that familiar lump in my throat. Because despite the time crunch, the stress, the dozens of emails, and the lightning-speed decisions—it all came together.

By the time guests were laughing on the dance floor, sipping signature cocktails, and raving about how "this wedding was *so* them,"

I found myself grinning. It was proof that sometimes the best weddings aren't those planned over a year and a half.

Sometimes, the magic lies in the urgency, in leaning on your experts, and in focusing on what matters most: Two people, deeply in love, ready to start forever. And to this day, that remains the quickest—and one of the loveliest—weddings I've ever planned.

TINY HUMANS, BIG PERSONALITIES

One of my favorite parts of wedding day? The pint-sized members of the wedding party. Because let's be honest: while grown-ups are busy worrying about photo angles and boutonnières, flower girls and ring bearers are living their best lives, unbothered—and often absolutely hilarious.

Take, for instance, THE FLOWER GIRL WHO WENT LONG.
She was about four years old. Cute as a button. Sassy as can be. I had the entire wedding party lined up, ready for showtime. Her mom stood nearby, whispering encouraging words. The music swelled. The doors opened. And our little flower girl stepped forward, basket in hand, eyes sparkling.

For one glorious second, she looked like she was going to nail it. Then—out of nowhere—she pulled a move worthy of a football highlight reel. Instead of heading straight down the aisle, she hooked a sharp left and bolted. Basket on the ground, flower petals flying everywhere, tiny legs pumping like she was gunning for a touchdown. Apparently, wedding aisles were *not* her thing that day. And honestly? I respect it.

Then there was the trio I'll never forget:

THE OVERACHIEVERS AND THE BANSHEE.

Two flower girls, ages eight and ten, and one ring bearer, age seven. The girls? Serious professionals. They'd been rehearsing their flower scattering technique with the dedication. They made sure I placed their baskets carefully on the table and insisted I hand them over *at the exact right moment*. No premature petal tossing on their watch.

Meanwhile, the ring bearer was tearing around the venue like… well, a wild banshee. He was zipping between cocktail tables, hiding under chairs, and at one point, I'm pretty sure he was considering scaling a decorative pillar.

When it came time for my official pep talk, I gathered the three of them aside. "Okay, team. When you get to the front, ring bearer, you're going to hand this little box to this gentleman right here. This is Mr. Best Man."

The ring bearer blinked at me, eyes glazed over, clearly still imagining himself as Spider-Man.

The flower girls exchanged a look, then turned back to me and, with solemn faces, said:

"We don't think he's ready for this job."

And right there, in the middle of an elegant wedding day, I nearly lost it laughing. We went through it a few more times, and everyone did their part beautifully.

Of course, no modern wedding tale is complete without THE FLOWER PUPS AND RING PUPS.

Listen—I adore animals. Truly. But can we keep it to the photo session, please?

Yes, I've seen it go perfectly well. The dog prances down the aisle, tail wagging, crowd swooning. But... I've also seen it go sideways. Which, let's be honest, is most of the time. Dogs are animals. And when they see their humans? They lose their little doggy minds. They get jumpy, spin in circles, or—like the shy flower girl—they decide, "Yeah... today's not my day to be center stage."

PRO TIP: DO NOT TIE THE ACTUAL RINGS TO THE DOG'S COLLAR.

One time, a bride would not take no for an answer and insisted on tying the real wedding bands to her dog's adorable bow tie. The rings made it down the aisle just fine... until the ribbon came loose, and they plopped into the grass.

Cue bridesmaids searching the ground, fluffing skirts and scanning for tiny flashes of gold. In my head, I'm thinking, *"I told you so."*

Another piece of advice: if you're going to have your fur baby onsite, **hire a dog sitter.** Make sure your pup is cared for, not just locked in a crate for hours while you're knocking back bubbly and living your best wedding day.

These tiny humans and furry friends keep wedding days real. Because no matter how perfectly planned the timeline or how meticulously fluffed the drapes, there's nothing quite like a flower girl bolting, a ring bearer getting a professional performance review from his peers, or a dog deciding to freestyle the ceremony. And you know what? I wouldn't have it any other way.

17
REFLECTION

As the ocean breeze drifts through my long red hair, I lean against the railing of a cruise ship somewhere between Florida and Jamaica. The air is warm, the sea is endless, and in this moment, I am equal parts sparkle and substance – young enough to dream, old enough to know better.

Looking out over the water, I feel small in the best way—like the world is still full of possibility. I've lived a beautiful life so far. There have been wins and missteps, unexpected turns and second chances. I've learned so much—how to nurture relationships, raise a child, be a partner, a good listener (still a work in progress), a businesswoman, and a creator. I've learned how to stretch a dollar and also how to spend one with joy.

From inside our cabin, I hear Jameson and John laughing—debating the high-stakes politics of the ship's arcade claw machine. Jameson proudly won about thirty rubber ducks during our spring break cruise—red ones, blue ones, some dressed like tigers and baseball players. He carried them around like trophies. As for me, I hit the jackpot in the casino—that turned into a guilt-free Louis

Vuitton purchase. I earned it fair and square, and John, as always, cheered me on.

Moments like these are grounding. Simple. Happy. And when I'm still, when I let myself breathe deeply and reflect, I start to wonder: *What's next?*

Here I am—36 years old. Married to my soul mate. Mother to a wonderful little boy. Running a business I built with grit, grace, and a few good spreadsheets. And still… I want more. Not more things—*more purpose*. More growth. More impact. A deeper reach into the lives I'm meant to touch.

It's funny, when people ask me, *"When did you know you wanted to be a wedding planner?"* I always say, *"I just knew."*

Even back in middle school, I was designing seasonal wedding vision boards, pasting magazine clippings into binders, writing "Prince Charming" on the groom line. Long before I understood what entrepreneurship meant, I knew I wanted to build something that mattered.

But the road to that dream was anything but direct. There were college classes and internships, side gigs and second jobs. I worked full-time corporate roles while hustling weddings on the weekend. I scraped by. I stretched every penny. And in 2015, I finally landed a feature in *San Antonio Weddings Magazine*—a few real weddings, a headshot, and validation that I was doing something right.

Then came Jameson in 2016, and everything changed again. I took a step back while John held us steady. Returning to work while nursing a newborn was one of the hardest seasons of my life—and if I could go back, I'd give myself more time. But as fate would have it, the wedding world didn't wait, and neither did opportunity.

I connected with a husband-wife team who needed a coordinator. I needed the income. It was a perfect match—and eventually, a beautiful friendship. Eventually, I had to part ways professionally, but so happy we became trusted friends.

In 2018, I rebranded. *Events by Jennifer Craft* became JC Events—short, sweet, and full of heart. John became more than my behind-the-scenes cheerleader; he became my right-hand man. When I couldn't find a weekend assistant, guess who packed his bag and hit the road with me? From Carrizo Springs to Colorado, we turned every wedding weekend into a mini road trip—equal parts hustle and adventure.

Of course, everything changed in 2022 when John officially joined me full time, trading in his corporate hat for one that now reads husband, partner, and co-visionary. These days, he's my carpenter, inventory manager, financial tracker, and all-around right-hand. Between the two of us, we wear at least ten hats each—and somehow, we still make it work with love and laughter along the way.

Watching people stand up and choose each other in front of everyone they love—it still moves me. It's not just about seating charts or centerpieces. It's about creating space for something sacred.

Every time a bride steps onto the dance floor with tears in her eyes, every time a groom squeezes my hand and whispers, *"Thank you for today,"* I feel the purpose in my work. Every celebration is deeply personal. Every detail carries weight. And every time, I'm reminded why I fell in love with this industry in the first place.

This business has never been just about weddings. It's been about people—about stories, about transformation, about building a life of meaning one event at a time. I've seen so many kinds of love take center stage—quiet, bold, complicated, imperfect.

But the one love story I return to, over and over again, is my own. John is still the one I want to ride shotgun with, whether it's to a wedding in Corpus Christi or just down the street for tacos after a long week. Our love isn't flashy, but it's real. It's steady, and it reminds me why I fell in love *with love* in the first place.

I've always been the dreamer—the one with big visions, endless ideas, and a heart that beats to the rhythm of "what if." John, on the other hand, is the analyst. He's the numbers guy, the steady one, the voice of reason when I'm halfway to the moon with a new idea. He is the yin to my yang, the calm to my chaos, the grounding presence that keeps me centered. He brings me back down to earth—but never in a way that dims my light.

Instead, he helps shape my wildest dreams into something tangible, something real. Together, we're the perfect balance of heart and logic, passion and precision. And honestly? I wouldn't want it any other way.

And now, looking out over the ocean, I realize this isn't the end of the story. It's a pause. A breath. A reflection point before I dive deeper. I know the best is yet to come—because I'm not done dreaming. Not even close.

I began this journey with a binder and a dream—and now, alongside John and the team we've built, I get to turn love stories into memories that last a lifetime. That's the gift… one couple, one day, one celebration at a time.

BONUS CHAPTER

THE ZILLAS

The question I get asked at least 90% of the time—usually with wide eyes and a whisper—is: *"Have you ever had a bridezilla?"*

Well… yes. Of course. But let's not stop there.

The truth is, the term *zilla* gets tossed around too easily, and reality TV has warped everyone's expectations. What you see on-screen? It's entertaining, sure—but it's not the whole story. I've lived through the *real-life* zilla moments, and let me tell you: it's usually not the bride causing the chaos. It's her mother. Surprised? Didn't think so.

Weddings today are a far cry from the cake-and-punch gatherings of the '80s and '90s. Back then, a sweet ceremony followed by a modest reception was the norm. Fast forward to now? We're talking signature cocktails, choreographed dances, and floral installations that could rival a royal garden. With more moving parts (and Pinterest boards), comes more pressure—and more personalities.

So buckle up. We're diving into the wild world of wedding zillas: the brides, the grooms, the moms, and yes—even the dads. No one's safe. It's all in good fun, and if you've ever planned a wedding, you'll probably laugh (and wince) in recognition.

BRIDEZILLA

Ah yes. The icon. The legend. The bride who strikes fear into florists, photographers, and planners alike. While most brides are joyful, gracious, and just trying to keep their grandma from bringing Tupperware to the reception, every now and then... a *zilla* emerges.

You'll know her by the shriek heard 'round the venue: **"THE CAKE IS HIDEOUS!! This is salmon—not blush!!"**

Never mind that 120 guests are about to slice into it without a single thought about Pantone swatches.

Or the tears—*so many tears*—because her veil caught a gust of wind during the outdoor ceremony. "It ruined the moment!" she sobbed into her new husband's chest while the guests cheered and dabbed their own eyes. (From joy. Not wind trauma.)

Some classics from the Bridezilla Hall of Fame:

"My MOH wore her hair down. I *specifically* said 'soft updo.' Please fix it before photos."

"Can you Photoshop the candlelight to be a warmer tone in every image? It's giving LED."

"I know I approved the seating chart, but I had a dream last night that Table 9 causes drama. Move them. All of them."

"I want to *re-do* the first look. I wasn't giving enough whimsy."

"Is it possible to have more doves released? Like... dramatically?"

"I need to rehearse the kiss. With my fiancé. Right now. Everyone out."

"The peonies need to be OPENED. I don't care how. Breathe on them. Sing to them. I want them in full bloom by photos."

"If you see any kids, kick them out. This is an *elegant* affair. Not a Chuck E. Cheese."

"The aisle runner has a wrinkle. *I can't walk on that.* My entrance deserves respect."

"Tell the DJ to change the walking-down-the-aisle song. I'm not feeling 'Canon in D' anymore. Maybe something from *Twilight*?"

"The flower girl isn't throwing petals correctly. Do you want me to show her? Because I *will*."

"I don't want to see my cousin's boyfriend in any of the pictures. Can you crop him out of the entire day?"

"It's *way too sunny*. Should we delay the ceremony until the light gets moodier?"

"Can the birds chirp quieter? It's ruining my audio."

"I'm sorry, but these chairs are *too chair-y*. I asked for *romantic seating*, not folding funeral furniture."

"Does the champagne come in a prettier bottle? It's not giving *aesthetic*."

"I asked for romantic lighting—not 'we're all going to prom in a barn' lighting."

"That groomsman smiled in a goofy way during the recessional. Can we re-do the whole walk back?"

"I shouldn't have to *see* the servers. Can they crouch or something?"

"I love that my fiancé is emotional, but can someone hand him a tissue that matches our color palette?"

It's not that she's *mean*—she's just... emotionally heightened. And maybe a little addicted to TikTok wedding reels and unrealistic expectations. The pressure to have *the perfect day* can turn even the sweetest bride into a walking stress cloud wearing stilettos.

But here's the truth under all the tulle: even Bridezillas are just brides, deep down, who care a whole lot. Sometimes too much. Sometimes... in gold foil font.

GROOMZILLA

You'd think it's the bride who's going to have a meltdown over linens, right? Wrong. Sometimes, it's the groom—cool, collected, and silent for six months—who *suddenly* has a lot of opinions two weeks out. And I mean *a lot*.

He's the one with a Pinterest board titled "Elegant But Masculine Vibes." He sends you a text at midnight: "Hey, quick question… are the chairs *mahogany* or *espresso*? Because espresso would really throw off the ambiance."

Or this gem: "I've just redone the seating chart. Again. Aunt Sue has been demoted. New layout incoming. Check your email."

He insists on taste-testing *every* cocktail personally—twice. The caterer now refers to him as "the Gordon Ramsay of grooms." He's memorized the lighting cues for the DJ and wants to rehearse his entrance three different ways—"just in case the mood shifts." He wants to arrive at the ceremony via vintage motorcycle, and insists his groomsmen wear pocket squares that *match his energy,* whatever that means.

Oh, and don't even *think* about calling it "her day."

"This is *our* wedding. Why is everyone asking what she wants? What about my needs? I'm emotionally invested in the charger plates!"

Groomzilla with the Garnish. Let me paint the scene.

The ballroom was glowing. Candlelight flickered, guests sipped champagne, and the servers were gracefully gliding around with plated entrées. All seemed well—until I felt a tap on my shoulder.

A strong tap. A *furious* tap. I turned to see the groom, face flushed, jaw clenched, eyes locked on me like I had just stolen his dog and driven it off a cliff.

He leaned in and hissed, *"That. Is. Not. The garnish."*

At first, I thought he was joking. Maybe a little pre-toast nerves. But no—he was trembling with rage. Apparently, the menu had *very clearly* stated "micro basil," and the chef had the audacity, the gall, the absolute disrespect... to use a seasonal edible flower instead.

"I told you," he seethed, "that garnish was important to me. It ties the whole dish together. It was on our tasting menu. It's the *visual anchor* of the entrée!"

Visual. Anchor.

Y'all. I've seen brides sob over wilted peonies. I've seen a MOB throw a fit because her corsage was too tight. But I have *never* seen a grown man that emotionally devastated by a sprig of something green.

Turns out, the chef—bless his calm, steady heart—had made a last-minute decision to swap it for something seasonal, fresh, and equally beautiful. But the groom? He saw betrayal. Dishonor. Culinary chaos.

He insisted on a public apology. From the chef. About the garnish. I offered him a drink instead. Two, actually. In the grand scheme of life, the garnish likely didn't matter. But in that moment? It was his hill to die on. His micro basil mountain.

Groomzillas are rare... but unforgettable, yet unexpected diva. They want mood lighting, midnight fireworks, *and* a custom signature cocktail named after their dog. (Which must be served at precisely 8:07 PM because "that's when she first said I love you.")

And honestly? You've got to admire the passion. Terrifying? Occasionally. But passionate nonetheless.

MOMZILLA

You think bridezillas are intense? Groomzillas dramatic? Let me introduce you to the Momzilla — a rare breed of couture-clad chaos wrapped in Chanel No. 5 and generational expectations. She doesn't walk into a venue — she *arrives*. She doesn't *ask* questions — she delivers ultimatums with a smile and a monogrammed clutch. Let me tell you about a few I'll never forget.

The "It's *My* Day Too"
She looked stunning, I'll give her that — gown rivaling the bride's, heels higher than her standards. But from the moment she entered the bridal suite, it was clear: this woman had not emotionally let go of *her* wedding in 1989. She pulled me aside and whispered, "Can you ask the bride to change her hairstyle? That updo doesn't photograph well — I know from experience."

I gently suggested we trust the hair and makeup team. She blinked. Then pulled out a photo of *herself* from the 80s as "reference."

The Floral Saboteur
We had carefully designed soft blush garden roses with trailing greenery. Momzilla wanted red carnations and baby's breath — *why?* "Because they're classic. And they're cheaper."

Next thing I know, she's on the phone with *her own florist*, trying to "surprise" us with *her version* of the bouquet. I intercepted that delivery like a linebacker protecting the end zone.

Bride never knew. Floral crisis averted. I still have PTSD when I pass a grocery store flower bin.

The Secret RSVP-er

We had 150 guests. Or so we thought. Day of, I get a call from my assistant: *"There are thirty extra people not on the seating chart, all claiming to be part of mom's family."*

I confront her. She smiles sweetly and goes, "Oh! I might've added a few people from my tennis league. It's fine. We're *family*." Family does not feed thirty unaccounted-for guests filet mignon on a plated menu.

She was stunned when we did not have a place setting for them. I was not.

The Champagne Dictator

This mom brought her *own* case of champagne because the venue's brand wasn't "celebratory enough." She told the bartender: "Only serve *my* bottle to the guests at table one through four — the *important* people." She *labelled the bottles herself* with gold stickers: *M.O.B. Reserve*. I wish I was joking.

The Venue Re-Decorator

I arrived on wedding day to find the layout completely changed. Turns out, the bride's mom arrived early and decided *she* didn't like the reception setup — so she moved *everything*.

Welcome Table? Outside in the sun

Sweetheart table? Now in front of the *kitchen door*.

When I asked why, she said, "It flows better this way."

It did not, and we flipped it back in 30 minutes. She flipped out for days.

Momzillas come in all forms — glittery, passive-aggressive, well-meaning but wildly misinformed. They're a force of nature. And while some just need a little guidance and a few hugs (and maybe a mimosa), others are fully in their *Broadway villain* era. And honestly? Weddings wouldn't be nearly as entertaining without them.

DADZILLA

Silent in the planning process… until suddenly they're *not*. These are the men who claim "whatever she wants, I'm just the wallet," but turn into **Tommy Lee Jones in Men in Black** – gruff, no-nonsense, secretly running the show. Let's meet a few of the legends.

The Timeline Enforcer

He showed up to the rehearsal *thirty minutes early* with a clipboard he printed himself.

Not the one we gave him. *His own.* Color-coded. Laminated.

"Let's get this thing moving," he barked, like we were preparing for launch at NASA.

The bride hadn't arrived. The groom was still at the bar. The officiant was in traffic. Didn't matter. We started on "his time." Sir, we legit can't begin with the bride and the groom.

The Open Bar Overseer

This dad wasn't concerned about the décor or the seating chart. But when he learned there was a signature cocktail called *The Blushing Bride* and no whiskey flight? He staged a small revolt.

"*What do you mean no bourbon?!*"

Sir, we have prosecco, mocktails, and minty things in etched glass.

"I didn't mortgage my house for minty things."

Spoiler: the bar staff added a bottle of Buffalo Trace behind the scenes labeled *For Dad Only*.

The Weather Worrier

The forecast showed 5% chance of rain. He sent *hourly* updates to the bride, me, and 14 members of the wedding party.

"I downloaded four radar apps," he told me.

I said, "We're good to go."

He said, "Better safe than soggy," while dragging two pop-up tents across the venue lawn—one of which had a Dallas Cowboys logo. It did not rain. But it *would have* ruined the aesthetic...if I hadn't hidden them before guests arrived.

Dadzilla vs. The Great Candle Conflagration

The bride's vision was pure romance—hundreds of flickering candles lining the aisle, dozens of votives clustered on every table, and towering candelabras dripping with wax. In her mind, it was the stuff of fairy tales. In Dad's mind... it was an open invitation to spontaneous combustion.

I'll never forget the moment he cornered me in the venue walk through eyes wide, voice dropping to a panicked whisper: "You're telling me we're lighting *all* those candles? You want *what*—a medieval banquet in there?"

He gestured wildly at the tables, which already gleamed under the glow of battery-powered candles (his carefully negotiated compromise). "We'll be up in flames before the first toast!"

Turns out, Dad had done his research: code violations, fire marshals, tragic wedding inferno horror stories—he had them all bookmarked on his phone. He even printed out diagrams of the venue's sprinkler system to prove the point.

"If one of those tapers tips over—poof! Wedding gone, family heirlooms ashes, happy couple... toast."

The bride, bless her heart, was circling the room like it was a cathedral of light. Candlelit tables, candlelit bar, even candlelit *bathrooms*. "Dad, it's my dream," she said softly, brushing his arm. "Candles everywhere."

He swallowed hard. I could see his survival instinct kicking in. Over the next ten minutes, we negotiated:

- Battery-operated "flame effect" candles along the aisle
- Real tapers *only* in hurricane glass on reception tables
- Strict "no flipping or dancing near them" rule announced in the program
- A dedicated "Candle Safety Czar" (aka Aunt Marlene) armed with a fire extinguisher

On wedding day, the place looked like an enchanted forest—soft pools of light dancing across linen and lace. Dad hovered nearby, with a hawk's eye on every flame.

As the candles were lit and the music swelled, he exhaled… and allowed himself a small, relieved smile. Because sometimes, making Dad happy means finding a way to have your dream *and* keep the venue standing. And that, my friends, is how you survive a candle crisis—one safety compromise at a time.

Dadzillas don't roar like Bridezillas. They lurk in the shadows. With coolers full of beer, suspicious tools in the back of their SUV, and a firm handshake that says: *This is my moment, too.* And you know what? Maybe it is. Just… with fewer laminated schedules would be great.

AUNTZILLA

Not the bride. Not the groom. Not the parents. But somehow… the main character in their own minds. These women arrive with matching lipstick and unsolicited opinions, ready to direct, decorate, and *dominate*—armed with a crossbody purse, 47 years of family gossip, and a "Don't worry, sweetheart, I've got it" energy that's both endearing and *terrifying*.

Let's unpack a few unforgettable Auntzilla moments.

The Dessert Table Tyrant

She was "just in charge of placing a few cookies." That's it. A charming little nod to the family's Italian heritage. But when I walked into the reception room pre-guest arrival, the dessert table had turned into a *Vegas buffet*.

There were tiered trays stacked to heaven, three crockpots of *some kind of sauce*, and signage that said "Homemade with Auntie's Love" in Comic Sans.

The bride had asked for "a clean, modern look." What she got was *Aunt Gina's Bake-Off & Balsamic Bar*. And don't even get me started on the glitter sprinkles. Everywhere.

The Flash Photographer

She had one job: sit in row two and smile. Instead, Auntzilla brought her *own* Canon camera with a shoulder strap and neck lanyard combo like she was press at the Met Gala.

During the vows? Flash.
First kiss? Flash.
First dance? FLASH. FLASH. FLASH.

She even *stood* in front of the paid photographer during the ceremony, waving him out of the way like a crossing guard. "Let me just get one for the family album," she said. Ma'am, please. Sit down.

The Gift-Giving Guerrilla

The bride and groom had politely asked for no gifts. They were saving for a house. Auntzilla?

She brought *seven*. Wrapped in glitter tulle. Each with a speech.

She forced the couple to open them—*one by one*—at the rehearsal dinner, in front of everyone.

Three were hand towels. Two were religious books. One was a crystal swan. The last was a framed photo of herself with the words *"Never forget who loves you most."*

The Outfit Scene-Stealer

The couple asked guests to wear muted tones. Neutrals. Think soft sage and champagne.

Enter Aunt Rhonda. In head-to-toe *fire engine red sequins*, with a matching fascinator and elbow-length gloves.

I said, "Oh! You look… festive."

She said, "It's couture, sweetie."

But between the unsolicited tasks, rogue decisions, and dramatic entrances, they somehow manage to stir up more glitter, flashbulbs, and fondue fountains than anyone asked for.

And yet…Every time I hear, *"Oh, don't worry—my aunt's handling that,"*

…I *worry*.

(And pack extra Advil.)

MAID OF HONOR ZILLA

AKA MOHzilla. Supposed to be the bride's ride-or-die, hype woman, human tissue box, and keeper of the emergency bobby pins. But every now and then... she transforms.

One day she's organizing the bachelorette with military precision, the next she's sobbing because her spray tan turned out "too orange to be in the photos." I've seen it. I've lived it. And I've got the group chat receipts to prove it.

Take one wedding where the MOH had created an actual itinerary—*for herself.* It was color-coded, and included things like "3:42 PM: Dab bride's forehead (T-zone only)." She took her duties *very* seriously.

At the rehearsal, she pulled me aside and asked, "When should I make my grand entrance down the aisle?" I blinked. "You mean... when you walk like everyone else?"

She frowned. "No, I was thinking a slow solo walk. Something elegant. Maybe a rose toss?"

MOHzilla, engaged.

Then there was the bridesmaid who vetoed every dress option. The bride gave her five choices, all lovely. She responded with, "None of these are *me*." Sweetheart, it's not *your* wedding. We just need you to wear the blue satin and stand still for 20 minutes.

Oh, and don't forget the MOH who hijacked the mic during toasts. Her speech began with, "Well, I'm surprised they lasted this long..." and just snowballed into a ten-minute stand-up set that made Grandma clutch her pearls. The groom was less amused.

Let's not forget the emotional meltdowns over hair appointments, seating arrangements, and why they weren't in more Instagram photos. One bridesmaid even demanded to walk down the aisle *alone* because her assigned groomsman "gave off weird vibes." (He was the bride's brother.)

But in the end, even the most extra MOHzilla usually comes through. She fluffs the train, wrangles the guests, and ugly cries with the bride as she walks down the aisle. She just might do it with a megaphone, a sequin robe, and a full face of contour. At the end of the day, a MOHzilla is still showing up out of love… just maybe a little louder than necessary.

GUESTZILLA: TABLE 7 HAS NOTES

Ah yes, the GuestZilla. The wild card. The person who wasn't involved in the months of planning, the budgeting, or the 17 versions of the seating chart—but arrives with *opinions*. Big ones.

You know the type. Their place card may say "Mrs. Smith," but their energy says "self-appointed wedding critic." These are the guests who summon staff like they're at a Michelin-starred restaurant instead of a ranch venue with folding chairs and a brisket buffet.

"I think the AC is a bit aggressive."

It's August. In Texas. We *want* it aggressive.

"This rosé is a little *dry*, don't you think?"

It was $12.99 and poured with love. Please hydrate.

"I just tried to use the bathroom near the dance floor and the handle is loose."

Duly noted, Carl. Thank you for the Yelp review mid-reception.

GuestZillas are the ones waving down the planner (hi, me) midtoast because their water glass hasn't been refilled. "Could I get a lemon wedge?"

Ma'am, the groom is crying and I'm prepping for cake cutting. Priorities.

Then there's the GuestZilla who asks if the music could be turned down "just a tad"... while on the dance floor. At a wedding. During "Yeah!" by Usher.

Or the classic: "Do you think the couple would mind if I took home a few of these centerpieces?"

Sweetie, those are rentals. If you leave with that candelabra, we're charging your card.

And let's not forget the ones who treat the dessert table like a Black Friday sale. I've seen a woman smuggle six cake pops into her purse and then look *me* in the eye and say, "I'm helping clean up." Sure you are, Susan.

But the crown jewel? The guest who asked if we could *pause* the ceremony so she could take a phone call. "It's just my realtor. This could be *the* house."

GuestZillas. They're part of the ecosystem. Uninvited chaos with a clutch bag and opinions about the mashed potatoes. But hey—at least they give us stories to tell.

ACKNOWLEDGEMENTS

I'm not sure where to begin, but I know exactly who to thank.

To my husband—thank you for being my steady foundation, my calm in the chaos, and the one who always reminds me it's okay to dream big. Your unwavering support grounds me.

To my son—thank you for your patience, for understanding when Mom works late or misses a weekend. This is all for you. One day, you'll see the why—and I hope it inspires you to chase your own dreams with just as much heart.

To my family and friends—thank you for cheering me on, encouraging me through every chapter, and reminding me I'm never alone. Your belief in me gives me strength to keep going.

To my incredible clients, brides, and families—thank you for trusting me with your most meaningful moments. Your joy has become my joy, and your stories will stay with me always.

www.ingramcontent.com/pod-product-compliance
Lightning Source LLC
Chambersburg PA
CBHW030056301025
34736CB00002B/127